THE
SINGLE
MOTHER'S
BOOK

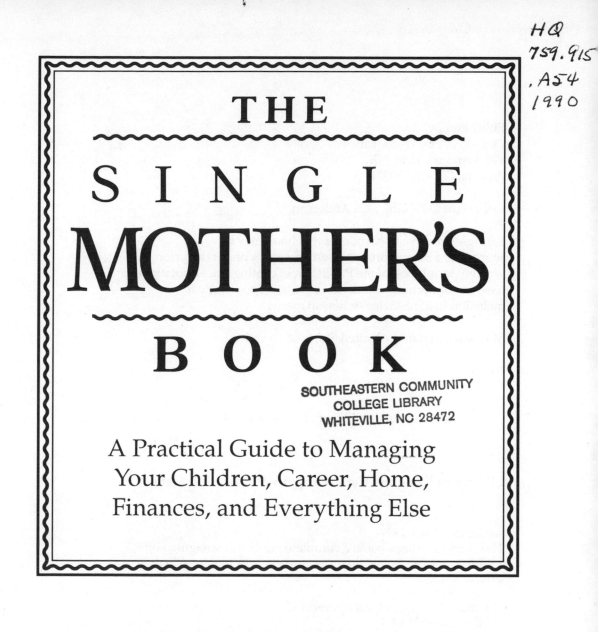

THE
SINGLE
MOTHER'S
BOOK

A Practical Guide to Managing Your Children, Career, Home, Finances, and Everything Else

JOAN ANDERSON

PEACHTREE PUBLISHERS
Atlanta

Published by
PEACHTREE PUBLISHERS, LTD.
494 Armour Circle, NE
Atlanta, Georgia 30324

Manufactured in the United States of America

10 9 8 7

Design by Candace J. Magee
Cover design by Jennifer Ellison, Lytton Design

Library of Congress Cataloging–in–Publication Data

Anderson, Joan, 1947-
The single mother's book: a complete guide to managing your
 children, career, home, finances, and everything else / Joan
Anderson.
     p.   cm.
 Includes bibliographical references.
  ISBN 0-934601-84-4
  1. Single mothers—United States—Life skills guides. I. Title.
HQ759.915.A54 1990
306.85′6′0973—dc20   89-28640
                                                            CIP

All verses used in the text are the original work of Joan Anderson
unless otherwise cited.

To Laura, Jonathan, Andrea and Michael with the hope that you will always say *yes* to life, reaching outside yourselves to embrace others because, in the end, we are all one family

CONTENTS

Acknowledgments

Writing a book can bolster your faith in people. Perfect strangers—individuals and representatives of organizations and agencies—will go out of their way to help you find information and offer their ideas for the project. And like ingredients for a good stew, each person's offering makes the finished product a little better.

As I reflect on writing this book, I would like to offer personal thanks to the following generous contributors: the women who participated in the original Vanderbilt University Single Mothers Group, especially Diane Sword and Ellen Jewel; my parents, Maxine and Ralph Anderson; the Margaret Cuninggim Women's Center staff, especially Nancy Ransom, Kathy Thornton, Susan Seay, and Judy Helfer; consultants Marguerite Anderson, Moses Dillard, Glenda Lingo, Margaret Meggs, Carol Wedekind, Jim Cheek, Jean Strecker, Mary Frances Lyle, Pam Bergman, John H. Cobbs, Nancy Evins, Penny TeSelle, Joe Driscoll, Melanie Allen Cail, Eddie Settles, Joyce Beisswenger, Margaret Behm, Annell St. Charles, and James Cooper; writer John Egerton, who generously offered to make *the* phone call to Peachtree Publishers; my editor, Susan Thurman, who pulled and pushed when I needed it; Melinda Boyer, and all the other Peachtree folks; my friend and neighbor Frank Ritter, who says the first rule of good writing is "keep your ass in the chair"; Hogan Yancey, who has been a steady source of faith for this and all my endeavors; and my two resident children, Laura and Jonathan, who chose to make some sacrifices so that their mom could write the book.

Introduction

One night in October 1986, four women, strangers to each other, gathered in the Vanderbilt University Child Care Center for the first meeting of the Single Mothers Group. Organized by the Margaret Cuninggim Women's Center of Vanderbilt, the group was the first of its kind in Nashville. None of that was important to the women, for they had come as single mothers to talk about their lives with others who, they hoped, would understand. All four women soon learned they shared the same problems: difficulties with an ex-partner, overwhelming responsibilities, too little money, uncertain futures.

The Vanderbilt group grew in numbers and in a sense of community. In coming together, the mostly middle class women aired problems of practical life skills and human relations, and they found solutions to those problems. Members of the group discovered effective ways to reduce their feelings of isolation, frustration, anger, desperation, low self-esteem and, on occasion, hopelessness, and they replaced them with a sense of empowerment.

Ellen Jewell and I co-facilitated group meetings. For four years, I, too, had been a single mother, and I identified strongly with those group concerns which had been or still were my own as well. Because other women in the Nashville area wanted to attend meetings but were unable to do so, it soon became apparent that one way to share the information generated by the group would be to write a book. The tremendous work of the Single Mothers Group members in identifying their problems and finding solutions became the foundation blocks. With the help of many people, the idea has become real.

For the purposes of this book, the term "single mother" identifies:

♦ Unmarried mothers who were married to the fathers of their children, i.e., divorced women who have not remarried

♦ Unmarried mothers who have never been married

♦ Mothers who are married but who live apart from their husbands

♦ Mothers who are married to or living with stepparents to their children, i.e., who have remarried or who live with a partner

♦ Anyone else who considers herself a single mother, including widows who have children and may or may not have remarried.

Since all single mothers have children, but not all single mothers have been married to the fathers of their children, the term "ex-partner" is used whenever possible. While there are circumstances when the term "ex-husband" is more appropriate, you might consider these two terms as interchangeable, except in sections where "ex-husband" implies specific legal rights.

On a personal level, this book offers a game plan. It points out choices, presents new information and contains advice that has worked for other mothers. Research and contemporary thought on single motherhood is mentioned throughout. You will find a resource section at the end of the book for further information.

The stories of single mothers who have met their own challenges and prevailed are meant to be instructional and inspirational. It is as if the women you will read about are on the other side of an invisible ravine holding out their hands to single women coming along behind. That is the nature of the book. It shows paths that others going before have taken. It includes a collection of personal challenges, strategies, triumphs and wisdom.

In looking at single motherhood, we see that it can have certain advantages: *Control of the use of your time and resources. Doing things your way. Not having to be accountable or subservient to a partner.* Still, single motherhood is never an easy road, especially in the early stages, when economic and emotional crises often overwhelm a woman's life. But crisis does not mean doom. The Chinese character for crisis is a combination of the symbols for "danger" and "opportunity." To the extent that you can overcome your fear, maneuver through the danger and take advantage of the opportunities for positive change which inevitably do come with the crisis of single motherhood, you will grow stronger.

When a woman first becomes a single mother, her problems sometimes seem unsurmountable. Some women collapse emotionally under the weight of their responsibilities. For many, their very real problems are due, in part, to a faulty societal structure which pays women too little for their work, does not legally provide for working mothers to stay home with their newborn children, undervalues the importance of good quality, affordable child care and too readily excuses fathers from their caretaking responsibilities.

If you are a single mother, it is up to you as an individual to carve out your own success. While the possibility of disappointment is real, so is the possibility of success. With careful planning and the passage of time, your life can and probably will settle down in a secure and comfortable pattern, and you will see that you have done a fine job for your children—and for yourself.

I hope this book serves as a useful tool in that process.

CHAPTER 1:   Redefining the Family

An overview

The Wall of History

"Who am I now?"

An overview

Some time after you have become a single mother you may wake up in bed one morning and ask yourself, "What happened? The kids are tucked in their beds, and I'm in mine. Only there's supposed to be a man in this bed, too." Maybe your hand glides slowly over the empty sheets next to you. You remember well a man, the father of your children. Gone.

If you were married to him, you had what is sometimes called the biological family—Mom, Dad and the kids. That traditional family pattern no longer represents an overwhelming majority family pattern. In the 1980s, of families with dependent children in the United States, 61 percent had a father and mother living together; 24 percent were headed by single parents with custody of the children; 12 percent were blended, that is, there was a stepparent living with the family; and 3 percent were made up of other combinations (U.S. Department of Commerce, Bureau of Census, Marital Status Poll, No. 433, 1988, p. 20).

It is important to know the great numbers of families that now fall outside of the traditional pattern. In fact, since World War II, the family has changed dramatically. Television is one media indication of change, and the series "One Day at a Time," which premiered in 1975, was the first to feature a divorced mother and her children. By now, people are well aware of the single mother with children as an alternate family pattern in society. What most people do not realize is that in our society in terms of dominance, alternate family patterns are now almost equal with the traditional family pattern.

In the biological family, when Dad moves out, what becomes of the biological family unit? It no longer exists in the same way. Though its structure changes, it lives on, redefining itself by the members who die, are born, marry or divorce within it. The essence of family remains regardless of whether there are two parents or only one parent in residence.

With or without Dad, the family nurtures, protects, promotes, worries about, nudges, celebrates with and otherwise interacts with its members. When there is a commitment to living and loving together, there is family. And because of this, non-relatives may be accepted as part of the family. Children are quick to pick up on this. They seem to think operatively, so that their Dad's new live-in partner, for example, may soon be part of their family. "Parents," then, would mean biological Mom in one house and biological Dad and Dad's live-in partner in another house, when a child says, for example, "I wish the parents would take us to see that new movie."

When the biological family breaks apart, the family is not shattered like glass but rather knocked horizontal for a while, like fallen building blocks. Usually, by the time the judge pronounces a husband and wife divorced, the family has already been rebuilt in a different form. Later, the single mother may add other people, like building blocks, to alter its form again. If a man leaves his wife, people may comment, "He broke up the family." And they could be right. But the wife needs to remember that she has the power to redefine her family and rebuild it into a structure which suits her as much or more than the original family. It will not be an intact biological family, but it need not be inferior, either.

A lot of guilt can come with single motherhood, whether the wife leaves her husband, or vice versa. Because society has placed so much emphasis on the importance of the biological family, the breaking up of that family carries with it strong feelings. Even to say that the family has "broken up" connotes failure. How refreshing to read Owen Edwards's article for *Working Woman* magazine (September 1981, pp. 53-57) entitled "There Are No Failed Marriages." He writes, *"Even when a marriage doesn't last, it often can be viewed as a success rich with the rewards—children, knowledge, growth— that do last . . . a lifetime."* He talks not about his own "divorce," but about his "completed marriage." While that concept, standing alone, may sugar-coat the wrenching feelings and the complicated and sometimes expensive process which surrounds getting a divorce, the idea has merit. When you think about your marriage as "completed," you allow for the good times, for the meaningful intimacies, the rituals, the explorations and the struggles together—

the closeness which was also a part of your life with the partner who is the father of your children.

Seeing and accepting your marriage or relationship as part of a continuum of your life's history is useful. If your partner had died, you would not burn all the evidence of your lives together just because the leaving was painful. Nor do you have to deny the value of your completed marriage—the good part *and* the bad—just because it is over. To deny it would be to bury part of yourself. The more open you can be about your completed relationship, the easier it will be for you to learn from it and accept your involvement in it with assurance.

Your openness will also allow your children to talk with you about what happened rather than dwell privately on their muddled thoughts for years. One 12-year-old boy, for example, overheard his mother complain that the children did not keep their rooms clean; then she left the family without an explanation. The boy went to his bedroom, cleaned it up and announced, "She didn't leave because of my room." But it was clear that he did think that. Throughout his teenage years his room was always oddly immaculate, and since his mother never explained why she went away, the son was left with a sense of guilt and a groundless, self-imposed penance. Talking openly with your children about your completed marriage will absolve their perceived guilt, should they have such feelings, and help them through a difficult period, allowing them to feel good about their family history and claim it for their own.

From the time you and your children's father no longer choose to live together, your "family" and the children's "family" are different. Your family is you and your children. Your children's family, on the other hand, includes you, their biological father, and any stepparents and relatives who may come along later on either side of their family. It is as if the original biological family has become two overlapping circles, with the children in the middle, so that when you talk about "our" family, your children think, "Mom's side of my family." And it is natural for you to speak to your children about "your other family," or "your other house."

The Wall of History

In my home, when I remarried and moved in with my new husband, there were pictures all over the house of his female friends and his former wife—all of which caused a slow burn somewhere in the seat of my insecurities. I wanted those pictures removed, especially those of his ex-wife. He would have none of it. "That's my history," he would say. "Do you think I was a virgin when I met you? And what about my kids? They need to be reminded of their mother. She's part of their life." He had a point, but I had a lousy feeling I had to get rid of. First, I retrieved a photo of my own ex-family (my children, my ex-husband and me) from my ex-husband's attic. I went through photo albums and got several photos framed. Then I gathered up all my new husband's photos from around the house and nailed most of them up on what I called "The Wall of History," along with my photos—his on the left, mine on the right. Fortunately, everyone loved the wall. It localized his history, maximizing it as a statement about the important people in his life, but minimizing its negative impact for me as I walked through the house. Through the years, we have added to the Wall of History, so that it now represents "Yours, Mine, and Ours" in a kind of chronological family review. I look often at the photo of my "first-husband family." In it the children are young. I am young. We were a unit, and we had good times, and my ex-husband was a part of that. In a way, the photo represents the best of our lives together. Putting the picture up on the wall has enabled me to claim that part of my life with some pride. It has been six years since my divorce, and my ex-husband can still push the buttons that make me furious or depressed, though he does so much less frequently. But the photo tells the better part of our relationship; it is the gift of allowing myself to think and feel good things about my ex-partner family. Somehow, that reflects positively on my own self-image. And it makes a positive statement to the children about their biological family. It makes them feel more secure.

"Who am I now?"

When a woman first becomes a single mother, she is apt to be confused about her identity. Previously she was defined, in part, by her husband, as in, "This is Sarah, John's wife." The more independent Sarah's life was from John's, the more she has to lean on while rebuilding her family structure and personal identity. Even so, she was John's wife. Now she is not. It takes time to separate herself emotionally from her ex-partner. Saturday night when she might have been at home with her ex-partner thinking, "We never go out on Saturday night anymore," she is now at home by herself, not being able to think "we" thoughts but feeling a void. "Who am I now?" is a question which even the most independent woman asks at some point.

The answer is, first of all, that you are a provider and protector for yourself and your children, since food and shelter come first in the natural order of life. Secondly, you are a nurturer in the traditional sense of mothering. The traditional roles of provider and nurturer are no longer split between two partners, the man and the woman, but reside within the same person—you. Even in a joint custody agreement, during the time the children reside with you, you are responsible for fulfilling these dual roles. And in your role as provider, typically your salary will be from one-third to two-thirds less than your ex-partner's, making you less well able to support yourself and your children.

Only a few women receive enough child support and alimony to allow them to stay at home and care for their children. Even then, that money often comes after a bitter court battle which is destructive to the adults and the children. And while men often complain that child support payments drain them unfairly of a large part of their income, the average man's standard of living goes up after his divorce, while the average woman and children's standard of living goes down, often dramatically, the first year after the divorce. There is a discrepancy, then, between society's view of the man as the provider of his family, and the reality that 24 percent of families are headed by single parents—most of them women—with custody of their children and who are the major providers for their families.

The societal view of the ideal family remains Mom, Dad and the kids. But that biological family is having a hard time surviving intact, according to contemporary divorce statistics which predict that 50 percent of all marriages will end in divorce. Eighty-five percent of those couples who divorce will remarry to form new families, many of them blended families with children from previous marriages. But blended families fare even worse than biological families with 60 percent ending in divorce, according to census figures. The third family structure, single parents, has its own set of problems, which this book deals with in detail. To say, then, that any of these three family patterns is "ideal" is misleading.

In the best scenario, the biological family in which Mom and Dad live together and are best friends and nurturing parents is the least complicated family structure. The problem is, it just doesn't happen often. Partners lose touch with each other over time and forget to nurture each other. The stress of dual careers in a fast-paced society places pressure on the family. The temptation to wander from one lifelong partner to other partners in a society emphasizing the thrills of sex in new encounters destroys some families. So this best scenario of Mom, Dad and the kids living happily ever after fights heavy odds to prevail.

The other two family structures—the single parent family and the blended family—have their problems, as well. The first is that these families are immediately more complicated than the biological family. But the problems are solvable, the compensations bring their own rewards and these family structures, while also fighting heavy odds to prevail, can also be nurturing to each of the family members. And they can be an improvement for the individual members over the biological families which preceded them.

From my point of view, the three most important elements in the success of any family are economic stability, commitment to each family member and unconditional love. Each of these elements involves work. Commitment is active; you do it daily. Unconditional love is active; you do it daily. Through thick and thin, you stick together with your family, work out your problems and share the good times and the bad. That's it. And whether that happens for you best in the biological family, the single parent family or the blended family, it is possible in all three. And that combination of economic stability, commitment and unconditional love should be the definition of the ideal family.

The answer to the question, "Who am I?" for you as a single mother begins with the roles of provider, protector and nurturer for your children. Beyond that, how you choose to define yourself (your work, your community and social involvements) and to structure your family is in large part up to you.

There is a freedom that comes with single parenthood: Friday night relaxing with just the children, a video, and a bowl of popcorn; sleeping till noon one day a week (when the children are with Dad); doing things *your* way. With freedom comes responsibility. But you must understand and believe that as the years pass, you will become stronger emotionally and financially, and you will have more time for youself as the children grow. And watching those children flower into healthy, caring adults will be the joy you counted on before they were born.

The choices that you make through time will define you. The rhythm of the days will become a new, familiar hum in your life. Your children, needing to be fed, needing to be bathed, needing to be hugged, may keep you frazzled for a while, but will also keep you grounded in reality and will draw out of you a strength you did not know you had.

As a single mother, you may feel you are alone in your struggle to answer the question "Who am I?" and to build your new family structure. But you are not. Over 14 million single mothers in the United States are living out the same process. A few of them will probably become your friends, along with other new friends. As with much of the rest of your life, the choice is yours.

CHAPTER 2: Your Ex-partner and His Relatives

"Hello!" he said.
blindly into the receiver.
I heard the call
in the bell forest of colored wires
vibrating anticipation.

It could have been anyone,
a friend from work,
or someone who might become a friend, or
a lover.
It even could have been
a light bulb seller.

I said, "Hi," and heard
his flat response.
The wind of his voice,
even the jagged wind,
was gone.
It wasn't anyone.
It was a function calling.
Yes.
His ex-wife.

Till death do us part

Strange things happened to me when I went through my divorce. I remember sitting in the lawyer's office with my soon-to-be ex-husband and crying as we divided our assets. Doing business and crying. It was to become a pattern.

And I remember the judge pronouncing us divorced some months later, and my whole body pricked up and felt—nothing. I had expected to feel different and to feel differently about my suddenly ex-husband. Instead, I felt just the same. I certainly didn't feel divorced, whatever that was supposed to feel like.

I learned that with divorce or separation you do not erase your ex-partner like you can erase a pencil mark. All the time you spent together counts toward making a profound impact on your life. A few years of sharing meals and bills and seasons with a man melds the two of you together, even if you weren't having a good time. That togetherness does not go away with brief words spoken in a courtroom.

And while appearing before a judge can end your marriage, it simultaneously *begins* your divorce. Divorce is an active thing, a living thing. Just as you are married till death do you part, you are continually divorced until death do you part. Even when you remarry you remain divorced to your first husband forever.

"I'm gonna wash that man right out of my hair"

The good news is that time heals all wounds (yes, and wounds all heels). But it takes years to wean yourself emotionally from your ex-partner. You think about him. You get angry at him. You spend emotional time with him even though he's not around. The longer he's gone, the less he will be an emotional factor in your life.

Second thoughts on divorce

If you left your partner, or if you and your partner agreed that divorce was the only way to settle things, you actively chose the divorce. Still, it is normal to ask the question, at some point, "Were we right to get a divorce?"

It may come up when you are financially stretched and you see the children doing without. It may come up when you see your ex-partner drive up in his car, which is nicer than yours, and get out wearing a suit—or jeans and a sweater—and looking good. It may come up on a Saturday night when you are without a man, even just a male friend to watch TV with.

There is no simple answer to that question. But a low point in your life is no time to be evaluating the worth of a relationship. When that question comes up, the best thing to do is to sleep on it. In the morning, when the sun is shining, usually the question will have vanished. If it has not, you should take a cool, unemotional look at the pluses and minuses of the relationship and weigh them. You can take out a piece of paper and make two lists: Good Things and Bad Things (about the marriage). Add up the totals. If you feel you or he were too hasty in running from the relationship, there may be time to give it another try.

Lark was a woman who was divorced when I met her. Lark's husband had withdrawn emotionally from their relationship, and Lark wanted him to go to counseling with her. He refused. She got the divorce and custody of their two boys. They sold the house, etc. About two years after the divorce, he asked her out to dinner. They went. That began the road back to a renewed life together. They remarried and had a third child, their first girl and the delight of the family. One day, Lark said to me, "You know, the bad times count, too." She meant that all the time they were quarreling and living apart was glue which bound them together. They had a common history of suffering through the divorce period, and they could share that with each other.

Such happy endings don't always happen. A woman named Belinda had a daughter with her live-in companion. They separated, and Belinda got custody of the child. Later, they began living together again and, finally, after a few cancellations, got married. Belinda got pregnant with their second child. Things soured again, and he moved out leaving Belinda pregnant, jobless and facing a couple of rough years ahead.

Other couples almost throw away their marriages. Rachael, for example, was happily married. Her husband came home one day and said, "I'm leaving you. I've fallen in love with Diane (a good friend of theirs), and we are going to live together and get married." They did. Rachael was very bitter. One day, several years later, Rachael's ex-husband—who was now helping to support his new wife's children plus pay child support to Rachael—said to Rachael, "You know, looking back on it, there was nothing wrong with our marriage. I just got carried away." Everyone knows about other marriages which have "survived" through years of domestic war and which are destructive for parents and children alike.

"Were we right to divorce?" poses an unanswerable question. The concept of right or wrong is not the issue. Commitment is the issue. And the more compatible you are with a man, the easier it is to keep your commitment. But he has to keep his commitment to you, too. If the two of you want to carry through, you will. If one of you does not, you probably won't. Like the decision to marry, the daily decision to *stay* married is a matter of choice.

I look at first-marriage couples who have been together for years. The pictures of their common children and grandchildren grace their homes. They have a settled quality, a certain ease with each other brought about by years of working through things. They often argue, but they defined and set acceptable boundaries for arguing long ago. They have a sharing of life with one another that cannot be bought. They were young together, middle-aged together and old together. That's a long road, and I remember Lark's words that the bad times count, too.

Sometimes people cut and run too soon. If there's a way back, I'd say explore that first. If there's no way back, then don't look back.

When your ex-partner gets married

When a woman and man split up, they almost always have negative feelings about each other: anger, resentment, repulsion, fear. But even if a woman says to herself, "I wish I never had to see that man again in my life! I can't stand to look at him. He turns my stomach," she may go through a difficult time when she learns "that man" is going to marry another woman.

The single mother may well feel a sense of loss. At one time, the man was her man. Even after they no longer lived together, they lived in the shadow of the relationship. But when he marries another woman, a sense of no turning back enters their non–relationship. There is a sense of "This is really the end. Now he's gone forever." It can be a big letdown.

You can doubt your femininity. After all, another woman is replacing you. She may be younger or prettier or smarter or wealthier. Whatever her qualities, she will best you at something, and that can make you feel less than adequate, less worthy as a woman.

The children may go through a tough time, too. Their feelings may be complicated by wanting Daddy to be happy, wanting the new stepmother to like them and wanting to be loyal to their mother at the same time. It's a kind of push-pull way of looking at their father's marriage.

If you know what lies ahead, you can prepare for it. You can recognize the symptoms of distress when they happen and see them as normal. You can realize that while the new woman in his life may be better than you at some things, you are better than her at others. It's probably a trade-off. In the end, he doesn't want a perfect woman—which neither of you is—but a friend to live with. You were OK. She is OK. He is out of your life, as far as commitment goes, so let him try for that golden ring of happiness. If he gets it, he will feel better about himself and have good vibrations left over for the children—and even for you.

Have a talk with the children. Ask them how they feel about their father marrying this new woman. Listen to what they have to say. You can tell them how you feel, too. Avoid all temptations to say negative things like, "I hope they rot in hell together," or "She's probably a sleaze bag," or, "Stepmothers can be hard on kids that aren't their own. If you have any trouble over there, you let me know." You can—and should—be absolutely honest with children, as in, "Frankly, I feel a little funny about your daddy marrying this woman. I hope they are happy together, and that they love you very much, but I want you to remember that I am your one-and-only mother. Don't forget me." They will respond with love, and probably be glad for the chance to clear the air on this issue.

Some women have a party on the day of their ex-partner's wedding. They invite friends who love them and are there to have a good time. Others go out for a quiet evening, perhaps dinner and a movie with a friend. An Atlanta woman flew to San Francisco for the weekend when her ex-husband remarried. Planning a special event can be a most supportive experience, a far better one than dwelling on your ex's wedding—at home alone. It's times like this that friends are solid gold.

Your children's ally

When you share children with a man, he may well be with you in many ways until your children are grown. Emotionally, you don't want him on the scene. But if he wants to be involved in the lives of his children, you have to relate to him in innumerable ways to make arrangements and even to help you out when you need it.

Each child comes into this world with two biological parents. In cultures which have standard extended families living in the same house or cluster of houses—grandparents, aunts, uncles and cousins—the loss of one parent can be better absorbed by the family. But in the United States, where the automobile, the airplane, the telephone and specialized occupations have busted up families geographically, often children do not know their extended families well. They live in other cities and are not much support on a daily basis to the children or their parents. So with divorce, the mother and father have to work hard to maintain that daily support for the children.

Your ex-partner, the father of your children, need not be the enemy. He can be your best ally in the care and promotion of your children. He can provide that male role model we are always hearing about. And numerous other things: Diane's ex-partner provides substantial child care money to Diane, though he lives in another state. Lynn's ex-partner provides a farm where her son can play with the cows and catch crawdads in the creek. That Jane's husband shares child custody allows time that Jane can count on to break up the strain of 24-hour child care; he also pays for music lessons. Carol's husband keeps the children when she travels on business—or for pleasure.

None of these ex-partners are especially revered by the mothers of their children, but they all provide something which adds to the quality of the lives of their children. It makes good sense to support your ex-husband's image in the children's eyes so that they will be proud of him, look up to him, feel more stable about who they are, have better self-images and be better able to cope with life as adults. And when you look ahead to such big-ticket expenses as a college education, it makes sense to promote a solid relationship between your children and their father so that he will be more willing to share his resources with them.

Maybe the children would be better off with him

A common fear of single women is that their children might be better off living with their father. Since a typical single woman's standard of living goes down, often dramatically, while that of her ex-partner goes up, she has practical reasons for that fear. Take Sheila, for example. She lived in a small house with her two children and a dog and not much discretionary money coming in each month for things like movies, eating out or new clothes. Bills were an ever-present concern. Her ex-husband and his second wife lived in "the big house on the hill," which had large, nicely decorated bedrooms for each of the children, a playroom with a computer for them, a whirlpool bath and more. They had lots of money to eat out, buy clothes and travel. One day when she was feeling down about finances, Sheila sat with her daughter on the front porch swing and asked if the daughter might like to live with her father instead. "Oh, no!" the daughter cried, "I want to live with you. I love my bedroom in the other house, but I would miss you, and Mindy [the dog], and the fires in winter. And here it's . . . it's more relaxed. We can mess things up, and it's OK. It's freer here. And you just understand me better than Daddy does." She went on for a while, and Sheila was surprised at how strong her daughter's reaction was.

Of course, every case stands on its own. Some children *would* be better off living primarily with their fathers. But financial status is not the only determining factor. If your children feel unconditional love coming from you, their time with you is gain. They need their mother as well as their father, and the price or amenities of her house or apartment have nothing to do with that feeling of love. If your children were to win a million-dollar lottery, they would become instantly rich, but they can't win love with money. Love is its own gift—and the best one.

Getting along with him

Pride and hurt, anger and revenge are big obstacles standing in the way of getting along with your ex-partner. When they lead the interaction between the two of you, look out.

Louise had just had her fourth child when she left her husband and moved west with the children. At the time of the divorce, the court awarded joint custody to the parents, but since then, living in different cities has made it difficult to shuttle them back and forth, so that now they live with Louise most of the time. Jim pays hefty child support for the four children. He resents not being able to participate in their lives more, he resents the heavy child support payments and he resents Louise's leaving him in the first place. He sometimes gives Louise only 24 hours notice when he wants to pick up the children for a trip to his house. He takes Louise to court regularly to try to reduce his child support. He sends her registered letters about the children which she must go to the post office to sign for and pick up (not a welcome errand when you are already working and caring for four children full time).

Louise fights him all the way. In court. Through the mail. With the children. She calls him immature and irresponsible and a rat. He calls her unreasonable, a neglectful mother and an ass. They talk to each other through the children on the phone. "Tell your mother. . ." "Tell your father. . ." One day as Jim was driving into town to claim the children for a visit which Louise had not approved, he happened to spot her van. The children were with her. The van was stopped at a red light, and Jim drove up beside Louise. She saw him, and when the light changed she took off like a bullet. They chased through the city streets until Louise saw a police officer. She screeched to a stop and told the officer that her ex-husband was trying to take the children illegally. The officer directed Jim to leave town, without the children, and to solve their problems in court. Can you imagine how the children reacted to all this?

All too often, certainly in the case of Louise and Jim, court solves nothing. If you have to work together for the sake of the children, building an unemotional relationship with your ex-partner can bring true peace and freedom to your lives. It's a business relationship. Some divorced couples are fortunate never to go through a nasty period in their post-divorce experience. But most do. Some never get over the nastiness. If you can, you are so much better off.

In that bruised period immediately following divorce, it's hard to be forgiving. But that's what is necessary in order to wipe clean the slate of miscommunication, imbalance, thoughtlessness and whatever else is there between two people who divorce. You need to give your ex-partner clemency, in the sense that all people are forgiven. We're all prone to error. And everyone needs to try to learn from their mistakes, and then to carry on.

So one of the toughest jobs of the single mother is to forgive her ex-partner for whatever he did during their relationship that caused her pain. If he was alcoholic or on drugs, she has to see that as an illness and carry on. If he wouldn't do his share of the housework, she has to let that go and carry on. If he was negative or abusive with her and the children, she has to let that go and carry on. Or it will eat at her in all her dealings with him. And that kind of emotional acid is too destructive to allow it to continue unchecked.

The more businesslike your relationship, the easier arrangements will be—vacations, babysitting, freedom from the fear that your ex-partner will kidnap the children and fuller lives for your children through contact with their father, whom they need.

If your ex-partner is sick or dangerous, it makes sense that you would have to structure and limit your children's contact with him accordingly. But if he is within the range of normal—chock full of strengths as well as weaknesses—then you can probably build a business relationship with him.

But you will have to compromise. If you want guitar lessons for your son and your ex-partner wants violin, you might go with violin. Your son will still learn music theory on a stringed instrument. Later he can make a fairly easy switch to guitar if he chooses. If you want the children to go to a camp three states away and your ex-partner wants them to go to a day camp in town, you might consider the day camp this year and the away camp next year. If he wants child care reduced by $50 per month, consider whether you can swing that, if you know that your ex-partner has a good reason for it and genuinely has your children's interest at heart.

This does not mean that you let him do what he will with his time and resources, demonstrating little responsibility to the children or regard for your wishes. But the two of you are very different people. That probably contributed to the divorce. So you are going to have different views on things. That works to a child's advantage when the parents live together, but when they live independently and each wants to be the sole director of his life, that can be a disadvantage. You need to prevail some of the time, and he needs to prevail some of the time. Even though you are divorced, your relationship should still be one of give and take. If it's all one way, the one who does all the giving and none of the taking is going to feel cheated.

One nice thing about you and your ex-partner being two very different people is that he can provide your children with a world view different from your own. This gives your children a fuller view, more to think about, a broader range of choices. But it can be frustrating in the area of values and lifestyle. Take, for example, Charese, who felt comfortable about letting her son roam for miles with his skateboard and friends around the city. He could go exploring, she told him, as long as he returned by twilight. Charese's ex-husband felt that Charese should know where their son was at all times, and that he should stay within limited boundaries in their neighborhood. He accused Charese of being dangerously loose with their son. She accused him of being unrealistically conservative. They also disagreed on religion. She had the two children on Sundays, and sometimes she took them to a "blue jeans church" and sometimes didn't take them at all. He felt that the children should have regular and rigorous religious instruction. They did not compromise on these issues, though they did on others. The two houses were very different, but the children operated well in each. There were aspects of both houses that they did not like and aspects that they did. Fortunately, in this case, both parents viewed the different lifestyle options as a plus in the lives of their children.

It's OK to be friends

One day you might be by yourself after your ex-partner has picked up the children. He came, he got the kids, he left. And you are thinking, "He's not such a bad guy." Is this heresy? You might even say to yourself, "But he's my ex-partner, and he's not supposed to be a good guy." The unspoken logic might conclude, if he's such a nice guy, why did you split up?

Two people split up because they want to. That's all. And they can *both* be decent people who simply chose not to live together.

No one will strike you dead because you start to have positive feelings about your ex-partner. The good feelings will help you support your ex-husband with your children. And they help you make it through the frustrations that are bound to continue in your relationship with each other. When the good feelings come, it means you have put some distance between yourself and your ex-partner. It means you are relaxing. It means that you have done some good work to cool off emotionally, maybe at first for the benefit of the children, then in your own behalf and, you now realize, for your ex's benefit, too. Some divorced couples even see each other socially, with the new spouses, especially on family occasions like Thanksgiving and birthdays, though this is the exception rather than the rule.

But to be able to feel good about your ex-partner—*and* his new wife—and to become friends again, is healing.

At first, however, other people outside the family are usually uncomfortable with that friendship. One woman was out registering voters at a grocery store as part of an organized effort for a presidential election. She asked the site director who would relieve her when her shift was over.

He read a woman's name.

"Oh, that's my ex-husband's new wife!" the woman said.

He looked disturbed.

"I know her well," the woman continued, "I checked her out when I found out she was going to be my children's stepmother. She's really a great person."

The site director looked at another man standing nearby and said, "I'm not even going to touch that comment."

What other people do not understand is not your problem. There are few rules when it comes to divorce. *Whatever works* is the main rule. Make yourself as comfortable as you can with your relationships—even with your ex-partner.

Communication breakdown

Nothing can push Camille's buttons like her ex-partner. He can send her out of control faster than Halley's comet. He can drive her up one wall and down another. If she's up, he can knock her down. If she's down, he can knock her out. A typical comment about her ex is, "He's such a jerk!" And the truth is, both Camille and her ex-husband try to get along because of the children. Sometimes they succeed.

Sometimes they don't. It usually happens on the telephone. A subject comes up, like paying the children money for good grades, and they will disagree. They both feel strongly about the issue, and they can't find a compromise. She raises her voice. He matches hers and raises the volume. She says he has never understood the value of . . . . He says she is just as blind as she always was. This can go on until one of them (usually Camille) hangs up the phone on the other one. They are both left with unresolved business and a ton of anger.

When a communication breakdown happens, there is always a way back. **There are always options.**

Cool off. Give yourself time to stop, deflate, cool down and think. Maybe that means a walk around the block (walking works off depression and anger in a physically beneficial way). Maybe it means trying to forget about it until tomorrow. Maybe it means screaming into a pillow and cussing out your ex's photo until you have spent your anger.

Ask yourself some questions when communication fails:
◇ *How can we resolve this for the benefit of the children, short-term? And long-term?*
◇ *How can I provide him with more information, so that he will understand what I am trying to say?*
◇ *What if we did what he wants to do? What is the worst-case scenario? Would the children suffer? Would I?*
◇ *What might the benefits of compromise be? Do they outweigh the liabilities?*

Keep on asking questions. Work it one way and then another until you think it through. Then . . .

Telephone him. Begin the second conversation with a safe remark like, "I would like for us to try to talk about grades again. Is this a good time for you to talk?" Words like "us" and "we" are non-confrontational and work to promote unity. Or you can

Write him. If you think you can't control yourself over the phone with him, write to him. This has the advantage of you doing all the "talking" without interruption. Make your case. It also lets him read your letter without feeling that you are looking for his weak spots, and it can be easier for him to "listen" to what you have to say. Try to keep your emotional reaction out of the letter. Keep cool.

Another way is to

Go through a third party. If you have a friend, relative, counselor or clergy member that your ex-partner respects, you can ask that person to help you talk with your ex. The third person can literally make a phone call for you, or you and your ex-partner can meet and talk in his or her presence.

Use the "I" statement. When you feel confused, upset, frustrated, etc., you can tell your ex-partner in a non-threatening and non-judging way. The pattern goes, "I feel _____ *(emotion)* whenever you _____ *(action)* because _____."

For example, "I feel *threatened* whenever you *mention paying the children for good grades* because *I am afraid they will grow up thinking that they don't have to do anything unless they get paid for it*."

With the "I" statement, you are not judging your ex-partner or his logic, you are just telling him how you feel. He may counter with, "Well, that's just not going to happen." You can repeat, "But I feel threatened because. . ." and that can encourage your ex-partner to join you in a fuller discussion of the issue, this time without emotional overcharge. A corollary to all of the foregoing is

Never use the children as intermediaries. To involve them as intermediaries puts them smack in the middle of a conflict between two people they love. It's not fair, and it's destructive to the children. They may feel anxious, insecure and helpless. It imposes too much responsibility on them, responsibility that would probably not be theirs in a two-parents-in-one-house family structure.

It is OK to tell the children that you and their father are having some communication difficulties. In fact, if they are around when it happens, it will probably help them to air that fact. You might add that all people have trouble communicating from time to time, and that you and their father intend to work through this problem to a satisfactory conclusion. That lets the children know that you respect and trust them by being willing to share your concerns with them, but that you are responsible for the solution to your problems, not them. It also tells them that you are confident there will be a resolution to the problem, and that undergirding the current communication problem, all is well. Or at least OK.

Parents' time out

When you are talking on the phone with your ex-partner, and things are obviously heading toward a major clash, you can say, "I feel frustrated/angry/embarrassed and I can't talk about this any-more right now. I need to go. I'll get back to you later." And hang up. *Do not pick up the phone if it rings.* If your children answer it and say, "Daddy wants to talk to you," tell them, "I can't talk on the phone." Don't allow your ex-partner to use the children to give you messages and don't respond to him with, "Tell Daddy to go to hell," or whatever. Repeat to the children, "I can't talk on the phone," and go to a room where you can shut the door. Put out a "Do not dis-turb" sign and cool off. Whenever you feel yourself out of control, cut off a telephone conversation with as much tact as possible and "I'll get back to you later."

Training your ex-partner

Try to get your ex-partner to stick to whatever commitments he makes with you. If he is *always* 30 to 90 minutes late, for example, take the children with you and do a small errand so that no one is home when he comes to pick them up, late again. Give him a pre-announced 15-minute grace period, then take off. When you return, if he is there, waiting, explain you thought he had been held up, so you decided to do a small errand. If he still has not arrived, well, at least you accomplished the errand. But if he does have to wait for your return, after a few times he may become more prompt.

Men often believe that their job is more important than yours, their time, their money, their involvements. To the extent you allow your ex-partner to inconvenience you because he is not carrying through with his commitments, you are reinforcing that mindset. And you will pay in lost time, frustration and even money. But if you hold your ex-partner to the agreements you two set, keep in mind that you need to abide by them, as well.

Negotiating

Negotiating deals with your ex-partner will, you hope, be an ongoing process. Because as long as you have to deal with him, that means he will continually be relating to your child in some way, even if only financially. And as long as he is relating to your child, your child will benefit (with a few exceptions mentioned below).

Since you and your ex-partner will often not see completely eye-to-eye on things, peaceful negotiation for solutions which are acceptable to both parties becomes a goal to work toward constantly.

There is an almost universal pattern of moving from raw nerves, unkind remarks, even teeth baring between you and your ex-partner, none of which are unusual at the moment of separation, to a more workable relationship as the years go by. Time does heal wounds. And time works out negotiating processes. A natural thought at the time of separation is, "At last I'll be able to do things *my* way." A second thought is, "And if he doesn't like it, he can go soak his head. I'm through with his trying to control what I do."

An ex-partner might think, "She got the kids, she got my money and I'll be damned if she's going to get anything else out of me."

So we have two people who are predisposed to face off against each other with armored tanks pointed straight ahead. In a situation like this, there is little trust, little give-and-take. It's a setup wired for difficult communication, one easily short-circuited by short tempers.

Let's say your ex-partner wants to have custody of the children for half of Christmas Day. He normally has them on weekends, but this year Christmas Day is on a Wednesday. You suggest he move his celebration with the children to Saturday to comply with the normal visitation pattern. He says you are being unfair, that as their father, he should have a right to see them on Christmas Day. You say you understand how he feels, but for the sake of the children, you feel that the stress of the holiday season will be less on them if they do not hop back and forth Christmas week more than usual. You refuse the request.

That is one option: to refuse a request. There is nothing wrong with refusing a request. What you risk is that your ex-partner will be angry with you and try to take it out on you directly (verbal battering or even back to court), by talking bad about you to the children ("I wanted to be with you on Christmas Day, but your mother wouldn't allow it; basically, she doesn't have your interests at

Tips on negotiation:

1. It's OK to have rules that you do not negotiate with your ex-partner, such as how much notice he has to give you before he takes the children out of town. These are your bottom lines.

2. It's OK for both you and your ex-partner to ask for special favors from the other person, such as "Will you take the kids for me this weekend? I'm swamped with work."

3. Keep enough flexibility to sometimes say yes and sometimes say no to special requests. If you always say no, you are setting up a power struggle, and the children lose.

4. When you say yes, be sure your ex-partner <u>knows</u> you have made a concession in good faith to him, even though you would have preferred to do otherwise with the children. (Not "You are getting your way this time, and don't you forget it," but "This plan is not my first choice, but I understand your point of view, and I'll do it your way this time.")

5. Give in to him whenever you can, in order to chalk up "good points" for when you have to stand your ground on an issue. Give so that you can take later when you really need to. Keep track of your own concessions and remind him of them, but only if you really need to.

6. Avoid seeing him as the enemy. You may feel like he is your enemy, but unless he is physically, emotionally or sexually abusive to or neglectful of your children, he is their friend.

7. Say thank you to your ex-partner when he agrees to a request from you; this allows him to make his concession without losing face. ("I know you want to do otherwise in this situation, but I really appreciate your helping me out in this way. Thanks.") Do this, and he may be a little more likely to say yes the next time.

8. If your bottom line on an issue and his bottom line do not match up, you can talk it out to a resolution, agree to disagree or avoid talking about the issue until it resolves itself in one way or another (for example, how long to leave children unattended).

heart"), or by pulling away from the children ("OK, the bitch can have the children. I'll have Christmas anyway, and we'll just do McDonalds on Saturday).

There is, however, something wrong with refusing *all* requests. If you are refusing all requests, you might take a look at whether your head or your bruised heart is making the decisions. Some of your ex-partner's suggestions are bound to be logical and productive for the children.

If one option is refusing a request, the other option is to grant the request, again, for the sake of the children. This is hard to do, because your ego may be tied up in a continuing power play between you and your ex-partner. It feels like having to "say Uncle." Like giving in, giving up, giving over, it feels weak.

But there is strength in granting concessions to your ex-partner as often as you can, and as gracefully. It's a pressure release in your relationship. To say, "Well, I really would like to have the children until Saturday, but I understand how you feel, and I will agree to your special request. Have it your way this time," tells your ex-partner that you are flexible, that you are willing to give a little, that you might even be a nice person. And building those fragile blocks of trust and good will are so important in building a solid working relationship with him for the benefit of the children.

Not all men become reasonable people in a separation situation, however. Like petulant toddlers screaming "No," some seem stuck in the Terrible Twos phase of behavior, wrapped in an adult body. Some men, often those who are insecure and with low self-esteem, are going to lash back at their ex-wives no matter what. They want power and control over their women. They are angry. If you are dealing with someone like this, you may have to do a majority of your communicating through a lawyer, a time-consuming and expensive practice.

When your ex-partner threatens you

Sharice finally left her husband, who had physically battered her for much of their 12-year marriage. It was worse near the end. Some time after she left him, he came over to her apartment and broke the front door, trying to get in. For safety, she took the three children to a battered women's shelter. He began calling her at work every ten minutes to harass her. He threatened to drag her out of church on Sunday and create a scene. Sharice tried getting help from the police, and that was a deterrent, but in the end, she moved to another town for safety.

If your ex-partner threatens you or the children, call the police immediately and ask what police help and aid from other sources is available to citizens in your community. Do not live in fear. Get information and seek out sources of help in order to protect yourself and your children from a harassing or potentially dangerous ex-partner.

Raising the children the "wrong" way

Diane got home from work one day to find a note on her door from a social worker from the Department of Human Services (DHS). Her ex-husband had called the department to ask them to investigate his ex-wife's care of their four children, accusing Diane of neglect. Diane had to go to DHS and defend herself. A home visit from the social worker followed. And on the day the note was left, all three of her school-aged children had been dragged out of class to be interviewed by the social worker. The children were frightened. Diane was enraged.

The ex-husband lived in another town. He and Diane could barely communicate civilly with each other. Talking on the telephone did not work. Writing letters at least conveyed information without the explosive emotions brewing between these two. Because they were unable to communicate, the ex-husband was unable to talk with Diane about his fears about how she cared for the children. The social worker fiasco was just one incident in a string of sad miscommunications and power plays.

The social worker found nothing wrong with the way Diane cared for her four children. Diane's responsibilities were heavy, but the children were well fed, adequately clothed and obviously loved. The ex-husband's fears were unfounded.

However, even when children are well cared for, how they are managed can cause great conflict between separated parents. Issues of values, safety, sex, friends, dress and any number of things are fertile ground for conflict.

Take movies, for example. You may feel it is all right for your 14-year-old to see R-rated movies; your ex-partner may feel that PG is the limit. Your partner may ride your child around town on the back of his motorcycle for fun; you abhor the idea. You may allow your child to cut and color his or her hair in any desired manner; your partner says the child looks like trash and tells you so.

You say, "So what? When the child is with me, I set the rules." Right. The flip side of that is that when the child is with the other parent, that parent sets the rules. This can be amusing. With the hair, for example, you let your son grow it long. He goes to your ex-partner's house where he has to get a haircut. He comes back to your house and shaves half of his hair to the nub and spikes the rest, very popular at school. He goes back to your ex-partner's house, and your ex-partner goes into cardiac arrest.

Some issues—freedom and control, widely varying value differences—never resolve themselves. However, it's a good idea to recognize that

---

- ♦ No two people (parents) will agree completely on how to raise any one child.
- ♦ A child, especially an older child, will side with one parent over the other when the parents disagree.
- ♦ It is not up to the child to decide how to be raised. A child needs and wants guidance.
- ♦ There is value in a child's experiencing two different lifestyles and parenting styles; the child will probably find some good in both.
- ♦ As long as you can trust your ex-partner's motives toward your child, allow him to guide your child as he sees fit, giving him the same freedom you demand for yourself.
- ♦ If your ex-partner is involved in drug abuse or behaves in ways which a court would determine are abusive or neglectful toward your child, take appropriate action.

When your ex-partner flounders

Financially, your ex-partner may go through hard times following the divorce at some point. This is not the normal pattern, but it can happen. While he is dealing with his reduced financial resources, it may well affect the children through irregular or reduced child support, or in other, more intangible ways. They may worry about their father and express that worry to you. You can support your children by explaining what you know of the situation (not "Your know-it-all father got fired," but "Things weren't working out for your father at his work, so he is out of a job right now. He's looking for another one"). Keep the image of their father as untarnished as possible. Children need a dad they can look up to. And, in fact, everyone makes mistakes, everyone goes through slumps. We need to support each other—even ex-partners—when that happens in order to keep the fiber of our families strong.

Emotionally, your ex-partner may experience depression, self-doubt, loneliness—heavy-duty negative feelings that he can't seem to shake for a while. This can affect his behavior toward your children. With the children, explain the altered behavior (not "Well, your father has finally gone wacko," but "Your father is going through hard times right now. This is when you need to be sensitive to his feelings and try to be helpful and cheerful.) The idea of family, after all, is that we support each other and stick together through thick and thin. Your children's family includes their father, and this can be a useful opportunity for them to take on some responsibility for caring for a temporarily weak link in their family chain.

At the same time, if the emotional problem is ongoing, if it is depression brought on by alcoholism, for example, or if the children are exposed to physical or emotional violence or you suspect that your ex-partner is an unfit parent, either temporarily or long-term, you must protect your children.

Some options are:

1. Confront your ex-partner with your concerns in as calm and objective a manner as possible. Express to him your fears of how his

behavior may adversely affect the children and then ask him how he feels about the situation. He won't tell you anything unless he trusts you, and even if he does, he still may tell you nothing, but he'll know you are aware of a problem. It's good for him to know you are monitoring the situation, and he may try a little harder to control himself around the children.

2. Call one of the following sources for advice on how to handle the situation:

> *alcoholism*—Alcoholics Anonymous, especially its Al-Anon liaison;
>
> *depression*—a social services counselor who can help advise you on what to do for the welfare of the children;
>
> *suspected emotional abuse of the children*—a counselor and, if possible temporary limitation of visitation seems advisable, your lawyer.

The following are illegal and can be grounds for denial of visitation rights or even imprisonment: physical abuse ◊ sexual abuse ◊ neglect

---

If you suspect that your ex-partner is mistreating the children in these ways, you may temporarily deny him visitation rights (see your lawyer). Do not let your children get into a situation that you feel is dangerous for them. Your first responsibility is to protect your children.

Every day we read stories in the newspapers about children who have been victims of child abuse. Some of those children are put in foster homes. Some are put through gut-wrenching trials where their divorced mother and father battle to prove guilt or innocence; the evidence, accusations and pain becoming public knowledge and the children feeling forever scarred with shame, scandal and guilt.

What to do when you suspect your ex-husband of abuse or neglect is cause for grave concern and caution. If you tell anyone about the suspected abuse, that person is legally bound to report the abuse to the authorities. Only lawyers, the clergy and certain mental health practitioners (psychiatrists are, counselors are not) are legally allowed and professionally bound to keep that kind of information confidential. Once the authorities—police, Human Services, etc.—know about the suspected abuse, their job is to investigate it and take action. If they find abuse or neglect, they may remove the children from that parent. If the abuse is severe enough, they may bring the parent to trial. Whenever the authorities become involved, you lose control over the situation.

If you tell a lawyer about the suspected abuse, the lawyer can act confidentially as an intermediary and outline to your ex-partner his options:

♦ Give up visitation, at least temporarily
♦ Get counseling
♦ Join a child abuse prevention program
♦ Face a trial on the charges

Your ex-partner will at least listen to a lawyer, and the lawyer will report back to you the results of the conversation. You can choose to proceed privately or publicly, depending on the outcome of the conversation.

Or you can contact the authorities yourself with your report of suspected abuse, and let them handle it.

Child abuse is such a tough, heartbreaking situation that there are always scars. Decisions surrounding child abuse are never easy. Think about these steps:

1. Get the children into a safe situation immediately.
2. Try to get more information about the nature of the abuse before going to the authorities; if you are going to make a formal complaint, going on the record in charging child abuse, you must be able to establish some validity in your accusation.
3. Confront your ex-partner about the abuse, either directly or through a lawyer.
4. Get information on child abuse and abusers from professional agencies like the National Association for the

Prevention of Child Abuse.

5. Decide on an action plan which you hope and pray will do the least damage to your children and still prevent the abuse from ever happening again.

For anything less than child abuse and neglect, it is best to try to encourage your ex-partner to seek help for his personal problems. You can do this either directly or through an intermediary, such as a friend or relative. If you can be supportive and work to maintain a healthy bond between your ex-partner and your children, then everyone concerned benefits. Your children need a father, even an imperfect one.

Ex-partner in prison

Robert Jr., was 18 months old when his father went to prison for armed robbery. The father was in prison for 13 years and then was released. For many of those years, his son cried every Christmas because his father was not with the family, not with him. When a man goes to prison for a sentence of ten years or longer, usually his wife will divorce him to "get on with her life." The prisoner often understands and harbors no bitterness, though he loses his interest in her as a life companion should she still be single when he gets out.

Fathers in prison want to get out of prison, want a female life companion and want a relationship with their children, in that order. Family members of the prisoners sometimes work to prevent the father from relating to his children by telephone, letter, and in person—through denying prison visits. When they are old enough to express themselves, the children say, "I want my daddy."

A prisoner can be a good and loving father, even though he made a mistake in society. Most stepfathers don't have the feelings for your child that the natural father has. There are often strong emotional bonds between prisoners and their children. If your ex-partner is an inmate and you feel he loves your child and would not emotionally, physically or sexually abuse the child, strongly consider fostering that emotional bond. Again, every child needs a father.

The weekly phone call

More than one divorced family gets together to talk regularly about the children. One formerly married couple gets together annually to have a Dutch treat lunch and talk about their visions for the children in the coming year.

Some ex-partners get together "every once in a while" to talk over business whenever it seems to stack up to the critical point.

And there are conference calls. In one case, where both parents have remarried, they, and one of the two new spouses, get together on the telephone every Wednesday night after the children's bedtime to talk over whatever business comes up. Each parent has a list of items to discuss, and anything goes: finances, school, friends, health and hygiene, growth and development. Often this is a time when the parents share stories about the children that the other parent would miss, such as the time the daughter had her first romantic conversation with a boy, or the time the son cried when his best friend left town. This weekly phone conversation fleshes out a better understanding of the children for all the parents. It is a useful time for problem solving as well as devising and scheduling action plans for the children's enrichment and growth—music lessons, summer camps. It is a way for all the parents to work together for a common purpose and for harmony in the family.

The weekly phone call came about out of counseling sessions designed to promote better communication between the two very different households. At first, the parents resisted the effort, but in time it proved to be so successful that they have continued it for more than two years at this writing. And the children know that they are the topic of discussion every Wednesday night. They feel their parents care about them in setting aside this time. They feel important, and they feel loved.

Your ex-partner's relatives

Jane's ex-partner had custody of the children during the summers and some holidays. He was a salesman and traveled part of the time. While he was away from town, his parents kept the children and provided them with walks to the park, cookie baking and round-the-clock care by loving grandparents.

Lisa's children's stepmother, Megan, was from New England. Her parents, brothers and sisters and their spouses lived there. Megan's close and happy family held twice-yearly reunions to which Lisa's children went eagerly. In addition, Megan took her stepmother role seriously and conveyed her love of nature, her interest in politics and her knowledge of health to the children.

Joyce's husband died of cancer leaving two young children for Joyce to raise. Her mother-in-law lived in the same city and continued to play an active, positive role in the lives of the children, including providing crucial help as an emergency child care source and cooking and hosting family holiday meals.

In so many ways your ex-partner's relatives, sometimes including those of his new wife, can contribute to your children's lives. They can provide child care, a broader perspective of the world and love for your children. Lucky are the children whose father's relatives care enough about them to want to participate in their lives.

Sometimes, of course, they can interfere in the same way that your ex-partner may: asking for too many special visiting privileges or trying to tell you, either through your ex-partner or directly, how you should be raising the children. If you have a good business relationship with your ex-partner, you can tell him how you feel about the problem and request his help. Otherwise, you have to negotiate directly with the relatives or try to ignore the problem.

Marlene was an unwed mother of a perky little toddler. The parents of the father found out about the little girl and wanted to visit her regularly. Marlene refused, saying that she wanted nothing to do with any of her child's father's relatives. The grandparents took Marlene to court; they presented their case. The judge asked Marlene what she thought about it. She said, "Your Honor, I'm trying the best I can to raise my daughter. Her father does not participate in her life, and I just want us to be left alone to start over. Give me a break." The judge looked at the grandparents and said, "Give her a break." And he denied all future visitation. They did not appeal. Marlene felt that her chances of finding a man who would want to marry her *and* adopt her daughter would be better if she and her daughter were solo. It did work out that way, but it was a risk, as is so much of single mothering.

Fearing your ex-partner's relatives

At first, Lisa, in one of the examples above, felt threatened by Megan's obvious gifts. But Lisa's daughter said clearly, "I like Megan, but you're my mom," which helped ease Lisa's fears. Later, she observed that Megan, while gifted, was somewhat inflexible with the children. Both Lisa and Megan conveyed their gifts and weaknesses to the children. In the end, Lisa believed that the children were in good hands with Megan, and Lisa knew her own place in their hearts was secure.

It is natural to fear the emotional tie between your children and your ex-partner and his relatives. If there were all positive interactions between them and your children, and all negative ones between you and your children, the children might decide they wanted to go live with Dad. It never happens that one house is all good and the other is all bad. But it does happen that children sometimes desire a change, especially teenagers who are looking for a closer relationship with their fathers or who are looking for a more perfect parent. Sometimes you just have to let go.

Penny's son had never lived with his father, a research scientist in Germany. When the son, Peter, was 14, he said he wanted to go live with his father. Everyone agreed to let him go. After a year, he returned to his mother's home, which he ended up preferring. But sometimes it works out the other way, and you need to be ready to let go.

If you fear your ex-partner's family because they offer more material things than you, that fear is unfounded. Children need love, not fancy things.

If you fear your ex-partner's family because they offer your children as much love and attention as you do, that fear is unfounded. Children can never get too much love, and they will not give up yours. The more people who love them, the better their support system is. Allowing your children to have contact with their father's loving relatives is good mothering.

If you fear your ex-partner's family because you feel they can offer more material things *and more love* to your children than you offer, take a good look at that fear. It may be unfounded; instead, you might have a problem with low self-esteem. But it may be a valid fear because you don't have a positive working relationship with your children. In either case, you might think about getting counseling.

As may be the case with your ex-partner, his relatives may be difficult for you to deal with. But since your children can almost always profit from contact with them, it is worth some expended energy on your part. It's best not to stand in the way of those relationships and even better to encourage them with confidence and appreciation.

CHAPTER 3:   Legal Concerns

The system of family law

Joint custody

Custody concerns

Alimony

What is reasonable child support?

Getting child support from a
reluctant partner

Renegotiation

Mediators

Going back to court

The cost of litigation

Finding a good lawyer

What to tell the children

Go with a partner

Plan time for healing your
court wounds

The system of family law

Family law is rapidly changing, and that affects the way divorces are structured. The first no-fault divorce law in California, for example, in 1969, changed the way divorces were structured financially. Palimony cases, joint custody and other newer divorce concepts have likewise had their impact as our society continues to redefine sex roles and the range of acceptable divorce relations.

Family law is growing in sophistication in the preparation of divorce cases. For the division of property, family assets—including real property, lifelong earning power, pension plans and more—require someone with expertise in finance, so that these days many family law lawyers consult with tax lawyers in drawing up the divorce plan with their clients. Child custody alternatives—custody with mother, custody with father, joint custody and visitation rights—increasingly involve a psychologist or psychiatrist who interviews the child and testifies in court. Sometimes, two such professionals interview and testify, one expert for each parent, each supporting opposite claims.

There never has been room for slipshod practice in putting together divorce and post-divorce litigation. Today, the growing complexity of family law demands that, in order to best serve their clients, lawyers keep pace with the changes as much as possible by having financial and human relations consultants on hand to provide accurate, well-tempered advice.

Joint custody

These days, many more fathers are asking for—and getting—custody of their children. In this country, while preference is still given to mothers, the more vocal demands of fathers have given joint custody more strength as a court option. Some states have proposed or passed laws presuming joint custody to be the preferred outcome of divorce.

A consistent theme in research is that for the best results, both parents need to approve of the joint custody arrangement and to pass on that approval to the children. Otherwise, the children may be adversely affected and they might be better off with one parent having custody and the other visitation.

Depending on their maturity, older children, starting at about age 12, can participate in the decision about custody structure. One couple in Florida had two daughters, ages 12 and 13. When the parents divorced, they remained in the same town, and the mother was awarded custody of both girls. The 12-year-old did not adjust well to the divorce and soon began making life horrible for her sister. With the children's approval, the parents agreed on a joint custody arrangement whereby the mother had one daughter for a week at a time while the father had the other one, switching each week. It worked out fine.

In another divorcing family, the children wanted to stay in their home, so the parents switched residences each week between the house and an apartment.

While many fathers genuinely want to raise or help raise their own children, sometimes a father chooses to ask for custody or joint custody as a way to control his wife. Or as a way to punish her. One father whose wife sued for divorce asked for and got joint custody of his children. Sometimes he would show up to get the children as scheduled, and sometimes not. He was not dependable and was outraged when the ex-wife complained. He made last-minute demands for changes in the custody schedule deciding (on his own) to keep the children for two weeks instead of one. And for the three months of summer vacation, he left the children in the care of his elderly mother and father in another town, seeing the children infrequently. He did not tell the ex-wife where the children would be during the time of his custody.

When joint custody works well, it can benefit everyone, for neither parent carries the crushing responsibility of 24-hour care, day after day. Both parents savor their time with the children, since it is not always part of a daily routine. The children grow up in two different households with different rules, different values, different economics and different opportunities. Such differences afford the children the view that life is a matter of choices. They learn to recognize that both homes have different benefits. More important, the children have an opportunity to live with both of their parents, not as guests, but as members of each household with both privileges and responsibilities. When problems occur, each parent and child can struggle through them together. Struggling together is part of the glue of family.

For satisfactory parenting and minimally complicated joint custody, certain guidelines apply:

◊ Both parents agree to and support the arrangement
◊ Each parent affirms the other as a good parent to the child
◊ Parents trust each other enough to provide a positive environment for the child
◊ Parents are able to forgive each other
◊ Parents carry through with what they say they will do (being on time, sharing supplies between the two houses)
◊ Parents plan ahead to schedule family vacations, camps and other events that require flexible custody agreements when "your time" overlaps into "my time"
◊ Parents talk to each other civilly about the children and are able to work out mutually agreeable arrangements
◊ Parents keep each other informed about the children's activities, telling the other parent about the dates of baseball games and music recitals, as well as passing along report cards, school notes, etc.
◊ Parents are patient with children who leave things by mistake at the other house, such as coats, medicine, tomorrow's homework, etc.
◊ Parents understand the importance of keeping the children together as they move between homes (there are beneficial exceptions to this, as in the previous example of the two Florida sisters)
◊ Parents live in the same community, so that children are not separated from their friends, especially important as the children approach their teens.

Joint custody arrangements which do not accommodate all the above suggestions may still be beneficial to the children. But it helps to remember that joint custody is probably the most complex custody arrangment, and the more frequently (and the farther) the children move between houses, the more complex it gets.

Custody concerns

Once the divorce decree is granted, custody cannot change without the mutual agreement of both parents through informal discussion, mediation or going back to court.

As children get older, they often have definite views about where they would like to live, views that may conflict with the divorce decree and which the parents may or may not honor. A familiar pattern is for a teenager who lives with one parent to want to live with the other parent, sometimes because the other parent has little visitation interaction with the child. Pamela's son Jim, for example, had a father who lived in another town and who saw Jim only on vacations. When Jim was 16, he decided he would like to go live with his father and new stepmother. His mother agreed to let him move. He and his father had never been close, and Jim wanted to make a last effort, during his senior year of high school, to form a stronger relationship with his dad. It was a difficult year for both of them and the new stepmother. But Jim learned much about family in that year and was glad that he had gone and glad he was able to move on to college.

Many mothers listen to their children's requests to move, and while they are reluctant to let their children go, they put aside their own desires and do just that. Sometimes the children come back after a period of time; sometimes they do not. But allowing teenagers a voice in where they live gives them a sense of control over their lives. It prevents them from resenting the custodial parent for refusing to let them go and from harboring unrealistic images of their non-custodial parent as the perfect parent who would solve all their problems, with whom life would be perfect. Living day in and day out over time with the (formerly) non-custodial parent allows both the child and the parent to get to know each other, so that when they say, "I love you," they know so much more who that person is whom they love.

Alimony

Alimony all but died in the 1970s, as courts began to divide property equally but neglected provisions for future earnings for women who had invested their lives in their homes in support of their husband's careers. The term "displaced homemaker" was coined from the many thousands of newly divorced women who had been homemakers in lieu of developing careers. At the time they were divorced, these women found themselves at ages from 30 to 60 with no career training and no job experience. Suddenly, they were faced with having to find some way to make their way in the world alone, with few resources or options.

It became commonplace in the 1980s for courts to award rehabilitative alimony to women who had no job skills or recent job experience. They would be awarded a lump sum or two to five years alimony in order to give them a means to live while they went to school or otherwise sought job training and worked to develop a career. For women younger than 40, this remains a standard procedure, although women have been successful in getting lifetime awards when they had earlier contributed significantly to the career development of their husbands, as in the case of the woman who had worked to put her husband through college and medical school, and then he divorced her. His future earnings were deemed by the court to be partly hers, since he would not have been able to go through his medical training in the same fashion without his wife's financial support.

A new trend in courts is toward greater consideration for long-term homemakers. Lifetime alimony awards are being given to older women who begin their job market participation at ages which limit their ability to build careers equal to their probable chances if they were in their 20s or 30s. Sometimes a limited alimony, say, 40 percent of expected financial needs, is awarded for life. This is a healthy trend, as it validates the contribution of homemaking skills in our society and provides compensation for women who have fulfilled a role in good faith sanctioned by that society.

What is reasonable child support?

The state now decides. As of October 1988, all 50 states have been mandated by the federal government to draw up a state advisory plan for child support. All courts in that state are obliged to follow those guidelines making the awarding of child support less problematic.

These fixed guidelines allow for uniformity throughout the state and from court to court. The aim is to ensure adequate aid for the children, to prevent gross injustice to either the paying or receiving parent, and to reduce the court's time and the parents' animosity in struggling with this emotional issue.

Getting child support from a reluctant partner

Another 1988 federal law, the Family Support Act, mandates a wage assignment directly from the employer to the court to the receiving spouse. That means that the court will go to the employer to garnishee the wages of the delinquent spouse. In effect, the court acts as bill collector for you through the employer. The very first time an ex-spouse is late with a child support payment, the receiving spouse should file an appropriate petition with the court. Too many women wait until their ex-partner has failed to send payments totaling $1,000 to $7,000 or more before they seek legal help. In doing this, they allow the paying parent to take the responsibility casually, to the detriment of the children. And when the financial liability becomes staggering, the court may forgive part of that liability, which means that the receiving parent has to cover finan-

In Tennessee, the **state guidelines for child support** coming out of the net income of the paying parent are:

21% for one child
32% for two children
40% for three children

cially for the failings of the paying parent. This means her resources for the children do not go as far. The children lose.

Another way to risk losing some of that back child support is to deny your ex-husband visitation privileges. A judge may penalize you by erasing some or all of the debt for the period of time you denied visitation. In reality, the judge is penalizing the children, but it happens. And on the other hand, if you deny visitation solely because your ex-partner has not paid his money, again, the children lose out on potentially valuable time with their father which has nothing to do with money. Whether the control weapon is money or visitation, both the parent and the children suffer.

To file a petition, you do not need a lawyer. The court clerk will help you go through the process. It pays you and your child to avoid huge arrears.

If your state's Department of Human Resources or similar body maintains an Office of Child Support Recovery (In Georgia, for example, there are regional offices throughout the state and ten suburban offices in the Atlanta area), by all means call for information. Such offices are staffed to answer general questions and will send you publications upon request.

Renegotiation

Divorce decrees are awarded to fit the circumstances of the year in which they are awarded. You try to anticipate future needs in drawing up your proposal, but life circumstances can change dramatically: parents move and remarry, people change or lose jobs, children grow older and express their own needs. Changed circumstances may cause one or both parents to want changes in the divorce structure.

You don't necessarily need to go to court to renegotiate. If you and your ex-partner can agree on how you want to alter the divorce agreement, you can simply implement that new plan. The new agreement is non-legal and non-binding. If your partner should default with the new agreement in some way, then you may want to see a mediator or a lawyer.

Mediators

Negotiation can take place between just two people. If those two people cannot work out a satisfactory deal, a third party (one or more persons) can work with the two people to arrive at a solution satisfactory to everyone.

Mediators can be anybody—mutual friends or professionals. While what follows refers to professional mediators, keep in mind that the same principles apply to non-professionals. In fact, some professionals who mediate do not call themselves mediators. In the property settlement of one divorcing couple, for example, two tax lawyers got together and worked out a satisfactory deal without the presence of either divorcing partner. Both tax lawyers were consultants for the clients' primary lawyers. This was a safe and painless option for the divorcing parties because their financial mediators were thoroughly familiar with financial benefits and financial law. In order for both parties to make informed choices and fair compromises, their legal experts need to be familiar with that kind of law. For divisions of property, a tax lawyer or a CPA would be appropriate, depending on the circumstances. Your primary lawyer should have a financial consultant.

People who call themselves mediators, however, are a relatively new development in the area of family law. They are not lawyers. They are most frequently psychologists, social workers and clergy. Their aim is to avoid destructive litigation in favor of mutually acceptable resolutions to conflict. There is no higher-education degree program for mediators, at this writing, but there are 40-hour courses and workshops designed to train people to mediate, largely in the area of child custody arrangements.

A potential benefit to the parties is that mediator fees are, on average, approximately 60 percent of a lawyer's fee, understanding that both lawyers' and mediators' fees vary.

But the greater advantage may be that the process of mediation is fundamentally different from litigation. In a court dispute, both parties face off against one another in an adversarial role as the structure of the courtroom system defines their relationship. The lawyers present facts and arguments, and the judge decides the dispensation of property, children, etc. There is a winner and a loser. Judges do have their biases, so you never know how the decision will go until the judge announces it. The process may make you feel debilitated, dehumanized and powerless. You have little control over the outcome except to select a lawyer who will present your case in the best way.

In mediation, however, the two parties do not face off against one another, but come together to discuss the issues. They design their own solution, and it is mutually acceptable. The result is not win/lose, but win/win. There is a feeling of power, in that both parties are in control of the outcome. Ideally, there is a spirit of cooperation and even mutual support. The children may be far less disturbed by a peaceful resolution than by a courtroom battle. According to F. M. Margolin, court resolutions to conflict between divorcing parties are six times more likely to be appealed than are mediated settlements ("An Approach to Resolution of Visitation Disputes Post Divorce: Short Term Counseling," dissertation, U.S. International University, San Diego, 1973).

One disadvantage of mediators is that there are no state licensing boards, at this writing, to set minimum standards of education, experience and specialized training. But licensing is coming, and it will probably come to California first.

The California court system was the first to mandate that divorcing families with children must go through mediators before going to court when there is a custody dispute. They work out a resolution with a mediator to avoid court conflicts and to avoid further litigation by dissatisfied parents. Delaware and Maine now have similar mandates which require mediators to work with the lawyers representing both parties. At several points in the process, the mediators meet with the lawyers to obtain information and present the custody plan for approval. The lawyers then present the plan to the judge in court. The judge simply approves the plan.

Lawyers may not approve of mediators, notwithstanding the threat of mediators taking away potential business, for some good reasons. Because mediators are a new and unregulated service

group, they are viewed as highly risky. Mediators may not understand legal concepts that lawyers spent three years in law school
learning. In matters of property, possessions and children, a simple
division of 50/50 just won't do. Issues of joint custody and unequal
parties—one controlling and one passive—may affect the mediated
resolution negatively. It is possible for two parties to go through
mediation and feel satisfied with their resolution only to learn, later,
that the real-life implications of their mutual decision are unwork-
able. Then it's back to mediation, back to court, or carry on with
disaster.

So the risk in court is the quality of your lawyer's skill and the
bias of the judge. The risk with mediation is the legal knowledge of
the mediator and his or her skill at human relations.

If you want to make some changes in your divorce decree and
want to investigate working with a professional mediator, call
counseling practitioners and mental health centers in your community and ask for the names of mediators. Interview mediators by
phone and ask if they have had workshop training in mediation.
Ask about their mediation experience, ask for client references and
talk with those clients about the mediation and their response to the
settlement before you decide.

Going back to court

"It takes two to make peace. It only takes one to make war,"
says lawyer Mary Frances Lyle. The court system was developed
with the ideal of providing justice to victims. When you need to
protect yourself or your children, the court is an option. Many
women do not go back to court for an appeal or for new litigation
because they fear losing. They do not want to take the risk. However, that means that they do not have the opportunity to benefit
from a decision in their favor, and that benefit can be considerable.
The choice may be costly, both emotionally and financially, but if
you decide to go back to court, get the best attorney you can afford.
If your ex-partner brings a case against you, of course you have no
choice.

The cost of litigation

There are up-front costs and costs if you lose. While most attorneys require a retainer, others may waive the retainer, especially if they think a case is either a sure thing or challenging in some way.

Courts can award "frivolous" fees to defendants. One woman, for example, had multiple sclerosis and could not work. Her ex-husband was an optometrist. Two years after the divorce, he filed to terminate her lifetime alimony. He won. She appealed to a higher court. She was sick. She had no money and no way of making any. She stood up for herself. She took a chance. And she won. The higher court awarded "frivolous" fees to the woman for her ex-husband's wasting the court's time with a frivolous case.

One way to save costs is to call a well-known, expensive woman lawyer and ask her to recommend a less expensive but competent lawyer, one whose courtroom record is very good but whose reputation does not yet price him or her out of your budget as a single mother.

Some lawyers will work with low-income people on a sliding-scale fee basis; if your income is low enough, they will give you a break. Your local YWCA and other women's centers may have resource files of lawyers who operate in this way. If they don't, you might ask them if they would work to create one as a service to you and other single mothers. In some cities, the local bar association may provide a free lawyer referral service to the community (look under "Attorneys" in the Yellow Pages).

When you have compiled a list of lawyers who offer financial breaks, ask about their courtroom reputations. The last thing you want to do is throw away your money or your rights. Other lawyers will know about reputations. Call up a good woman lawyer (family law) in your town; if you explain your situation, she will probably be glad to give you good advice about the lawyers on your list.

Legal Services is also available to women who meet their financial requirements. If you have a low income, call Legal Services to find out if you qualify. If not, ask them for suggestions. If they say they do not give advice on lawyers, ask them who does.

Federal, state, county, city governments, and even small municipalities, provide community services and public information offices which can refer you to local agency sources or legal aid societies in your area.

Finding a good lawyer

If you need a new lawyer, word of mouth beats all. Ask relatives and friends, especially women friends and those who have been through divorce. Call up your local newspaper office and ask to speak with the reader advocate, ombudsman or legal expert. Call a law professor at your local university. Call a clergy member. Ask for a lawyer who is honest with good courtroom skills and an excellent record of "wins." Ask for several recommendations, because prices vary (there are both flat and hourly fees), and you need to shop around for someone you can trust and afford, who will listen to you and whose language and reasoning makes sense to you.

You can ask a lawyer for a preliminary conference, at which you can ask questions about how the lawyer operates and get a feel for whether this would be a good lawyer/client relationship. Before you make an appointment, ask if he or she charges for this; some do, some don't.

Don't feel obliged to accept a lawyer's services after a phone call or a preliminary conference. You don't have to say yes. If you have any doubts or negative feelings about the lawyer, and he or she asks if you are ready to commit, say that you always take time to think over a decision before you make a commitment. You will call in a day or so with your answer.

What to tell the children

Be honest, as always. If you know they are aware you are going to court, or if they suspect "something is up" but they don't know what and are afraid to ask, tell them you are going to court and what the general issue is. Try not to go into details. Let them know it is OK for them to love their dad just as much as ever, if you can. You can tell them that you are upset with their father, if you are, but that this problem is between you and him and that they should not feel they are the cause. Seeing their parents argue upsets children, so if you need to talk with your ex-husband and you know it is going to be an emotional conversation, do it while the children are not at your house or his. If he calls you when the children are at home, tell him you need to talk with him when the children are out, and make a phone appointment. If he keeps calling, unplug the phone. Letting the children know that the court is responsible for making a decision will help remove them from a situation emotionally charged with the anguish of "What shall I do about Mom and Dad's problem?"

Go with a partner

Dee sat all alone in court with only her lawyer to share her experience. Across the way sat her ex-husband with his new wife, who stroked his arm and looked concerned. Together, they looked like a loving, supportive couple. Dee looked friendless and forlorn. And she was forlorn in that lonely courtroom, but she was not friendless. She could have asked a friend to be her court partner, a move which might have impressed the judge and which would have supported Dee emotionally.

If you go back to court, think about taking a court partner with you.

Plan time for healing your court wounds

It's tough living through the stress of litigation. If you win, it's stressful; if you lose, it's worse. You may feel completely drained, need to cry or curl up in bed, need to talk or celebrate with a friend, need to walk off your frustration or energy, or otherwise make the transition from court to routine life. You may want to take a second vacation day from work, for the day after your court date. You may want to arrange for a friend to be on call to take care of the children after you return from court. On the other hand, you may want the children to be with you at this time. It's a good idea to plan for both options. This is a time when your support group, if you have one (see Chapter 9), should be made aware of your court process and either be with you physically or thinking about you as you go through the motions, including the after effects. But just as you can expect the court process to be unpleasant, you can expect that unpleasantness to pass. Time is on your side.

CHAPTER 4: Raising Healthy Children

The friendship cake

Unconditional love

Feeling guilty for being a single mother

Divorce adjustment groups

The no-money guilt trip

Questioning your competence as
   a parent

Self-esteem

The importance of affirming for
   self-esteem

Fostering a sense of security

School

Too sick to go to school

School refusal

Discipline

Developing independence

Letting children be children

Male role models in your children's lives

Homework without war

Child abuse and neglect

Aleen,
New red she machine
why your Mama carry you
ten months and smile smile smile?
Vomit then the runs every seven days
but she don't care. She happy.
Why she want you so bad?

Now you here
all wiggle, peep and suck
you do make a body smile.
Your Mama, you wear her out
she shake her head
her eyes black from no sleep.
You one little thunder horn.
Aleen, why you cry and cry?
What you see up ahead, child
that make you complain so?
Hush now. Let your Mama rest.

What you be ten years on?
You be young willow tree
You be mountain stream
You be girl with woman peeking out
long sun-brown legs
runnin' with the pack
so fast tryin' to get somewhere
you don't even know.

Your Mama, she know about the bomb
she know about flesh rot,
head rot, drug stuff, rape, tears.
She look at you and forget that trash.
She look at you and have faith.
She want a baby, that all.

The friendship cake

No mother I know is perfect, but we may feel we ought to be. That brings to mind the story of the friendship cake that Pauline Rawley of Mount Airy, North Carolina, made for her son-in-law. It takes 30 days to make a friendship cake. First you mix together the fruit ingredients and let them sit for ten days, stirring occasionally. Then you mix in the second batch of fruit and let that sit for ten days, stirring occasionally. Then you add the remaining ingredients to form the whole batter, cook the cake and let it sit for another ten days so the flavors will blend and age just right.

It takes a lot of attention to make that cake. It is a process that is spread out over time. Raising children is like that. They take a lot of attention spread out over time. They are in a process of development and maturation that will never happen overnight. These days, it seems, everybody is used to a Betty Crocker cake-mix solution to dessert. And we would love to have a quick-fix solution to raising perfect children instantly, but that does not exist. The reality is that the process will involve struggle, problems, mistakes, worry and a lot of attention to details. All you can do in helping to form your child into a healthy adult is do a little mixing and stirring. A lot of the process is up to your child, especially in the teenage years. Our job as mothers is to keep on paying attention to the details even as we gradually let go of the controls.

Mothering isn't easy, and single mothering requires extra effort. In the end, we are all struggling together to do the best we can. Perfection is a goal toward which we are working but which we must understand we will never attain. But we don't have to be perfect to be ideal. Read on.

Unconditional love

Being a mother requires a high degree of constant responsibility. When you divorce, that responsibility intensifies. Even if you have joint custody with your ex-husband, when the children are with you they are totally dependent on your time, your energy, your patience, your love. Living with parents, a roommate or a male companion can make your job more complex: you are probably having to run interference between your children and the other occupants of the house, trying to keep the children quiet, trying to keep their "stuff" picked up from around the house, trying to keep them from destroying the other occupant's chair, pipe, books, china or whatever, trying to keep peace.

Children of divorce are automatically under stress. They have two parents in two homes, and they would like to heal the rift, to meld the family into one whole biological unit. It takes a long time for children to give up that fantasy.

According to Sara McLanahan and Irwin Garfinkel, in their book *Single Mothers and Their Children: A New American Dilemma*, (Urban Institute Press, 1986), children from single-mother households are less likely to graduate from high school, more likely to marry as teenagers, have children as teenagers and, later, divorce than those who grow up in two-parent households. Poverty is not the sole cause. McLanahan shows from her research that the negative effects persist even when the mothers' incomes equal those of married-couple families. The stress the mothers feel as they adjust to changes in their economic standards, working conditions and living arrangements affects their children.

Children can cause problems for a single mother. They can call her away from work and social activities. They can sap her finances. They can handicap her attractiveness to men. They can misbehave at home to the point of becoming out of control. They can get into trouble at school and with the police. They can develop serious physical and emotional problems.

Viewed another way, children are refreshing. They've got energy. They are wide-open to the world at every phase of their growth process. They can be funny and fun. They can challenge your established world view and keep you growing in new ways. They can bring new people into your life. As they grow older, they can be tremendous help around the house and, as adults, they can be friends.

Part of single motherhood is the basic acceptance of your children, learning to minimize the minuses while you maximize the pluses.

Above all else, children are family. Someone to come home to after a day's work. Someone to interact with on a daily basis, to rub smooth your rough edges, to give you polish. Someone to share holidays with over time. Someone to invest in and who invests in you. Someone whose blood is your own, the bond that never breaks.

This chapter will deal with children as whole people, with assets and liabilities, who deserve and need tender loving care so that they have an odds-on chance of becoming the wonderful, caring, responsible adults you envisioned when they were born.

It needs to be said that nobody is perfect. Everybody makes mistakes. In addition to ex-partners, this includes children and single mothers. It is important to allow ourselves to be less-than-perfect mothers and to know that we are not going to cripple our children in the process. Depending on how we deal with our mistakes with the children, those mistakes can be great learning tools. Mistakes can allow the children to accept their own imperfections and can strengthen the bond between mother and child. For example, let's take a mother, Margaret, who comes home from work tired. Her daughter, Debbie, says that she has a piano recital the next day at 4:00 p.m. "Why didn't you tell me last Saturday after your lesson?" Margaret asks. Debbie gives some excuse. Then Debbie spills milk on the living room sofa, does a shoddy job washing the dishes and forgets to feed the cat. Margaret yells and sends Debbie to her room. Time passes, and Margaret reflects on the events of the day and evening. She regrets the yelling. She goes to Debbie's room and says those magic healing and bonding words, "I'm sorry." Then Margaret tells Debbie about her day at work and that she was set up for a short fuse. She is able to talk calmly with Debbie about Debbie's responsibilities and how important they are in maintaining a sense of community within their household. Debbie can tell the mother what has interfered with her doing a better job. Mother and daughter have done a lot of disclosing in this interaction, and together they have the chance of better understanding each other's concerns and supporting each other's efforts at harmony. Above all else, the mother has demonstrated true love and concern for her daughter.

In the end, this feeling of love and concern, paired with parental control, provides a solid foundation for our children. If a child feels unconditional love from a parent, the mistakes will be forgiven. The mistakes can be growing experiences, and the bond between parent and child will carry them through many years and many transitions together. And as time launches the child into a world increasingly separate from the mother, that unconditional love will work like a shock absorber to cushion the child against the harsher realities of the world. That love will provide emotional sustenance, the greatest gift of wholeness that a parent can bestow.

So the single mother needs to look carefully at her child and ask the questions, "Do I love my child with a love that is based on more than good behavior and good works?" and "Do I love the core of being of this child, that special part which this child was born and will die with and to which I respond in love, at some deep level, even when I am angry?" If the answer to both is yes, then the single mother can carry on with some assurance that her parenting, which will be sprinkled with "mistakes," will contribute to the raising of a child who says yes to life.

While you, as a mother, are a strong influence on your child's life, you are not alone. Other people influence your child as well— and thank goodness. To the extent that your ex-partner loves your child, the child is enriched in many ways. To the extent that extended family, friends, teachers and others invest in your child, the child is enriched again. So to the extent that you can expose your child to extended family and friends in positive interactions and monitor your child's educational experience, the child will profit.

But you have a limited amount of time and energy, and you have considerable needs of your own. That is why it can be comforting to recognize that your own unconditional love for your child is sufficient for the day. To the extent that the rest of the world sees the goodness in your child—and many people will, many who are strangers to you—then the societal system is working.

Feeling guilty for being a single mother

Becky Simpson runs her own non-profit community resource center in Harlan, Kentucky, to serve her poor Appalachian neighbors. Among other victories she can claim, Becky fought and won the first class action suit against a coal company for strip mining the earth off of a mountain hollow and displacing 18 families, one of them Becky's brother's family. Becky's legal and community work has been featured in national and even international media.

Becky has a third-grade education. As she puts it, "I thought for a long time that I didn't have no education and that I couldn't do nothin'. But then I said, 'Well, this ain't right, what the coal companies is doin' to our people. It just ain't right.' So then I started askin' questions and doin' things that I never thought I could of done in my life. I learned that if you don't have a education, you've just got to go on without it. You've just got to go on."

It's the same story with a single mother. Her children don't have their father and mother living together with them. Their family is divided into two parts. Some children relate to their fathers on a regular basis. Others don't know who their fathers are. In these circumstances, it is easy for a single mother to feel guilty for being a single mother and "subjecting" her children to "split" parents or only one parent. But like Becky Simpson, if, for whatever reason, a woman can't offer her children a biologically intact family, she must just go on without it. That probably means she will have to shoulder greater responsibility in caring for her children, but she and her children also, like Becky Simpson, can prevail.

Divorce adjustment groups

Many towns offer periodic courses, workshops, seminars, lectures and counseling groups on the theme of adjusting to divorce. Some of the groups are structured to include children of divorce.

Infants and toddlers would not benefit from these offerings, but as soon as a child is old enough to ask questions about the divorce, he or she is old enough to need some answers.

Divorce adjustment groups can provide children with
- What to expect from divorce as a life circumstance
- A place to ask and get answers for questions
- Other children in the same boat with whom to share experiences.

You can find out about such groups by calling your local mental health association, the YWCA, a school counselor, social service organizations or a clergy member. Announcements of such events are often made in newspapers and on library bulletin boards.

If you can't find a divorce adjustment group for children in your town, you can suggest to the resources above that they create one.

The no-money guilt trip

You look at your sleeping child and think, "Poor baby. I can't afford the same lifestyle for you that I used to be able to afford when your father and I were living together." Your underlying thought is, "I am failing to provide for you, and you are suffering for it, my child."

In the section above, we dealt with unconditional love as a measure of your contribution to the emotional health of your child. However, unconditional love does not pay for designer jeans or tennis lessons or prom dresses or even diapers and good day care. The average standard of living for women goes down when they divorce, while their ex-husband's standard of living goes up. So if your financial resources have been reduced by separation from your partner, you are following the normal pattern. Considering that women usually care for the children after a split, that decrease in money creates considerable financial strain on both women and children, the largest segment of our nation's poverty class. And until women secure—through persistence or demand—the same opportunities and salaries as men in the workplace, this pattern will continue.

Dealing with a reduced income is never pleasant. Single mothers can, however, be creative about compensating for that reduction. A woman who loves to have company can switch from preparing dinner food herself to inviting guests to contribute to a pot luck supper, which saves the single mother the cost of food and the time in having to prepare it. She can collaborate with the children in making hand-made holiday cards, give gifts of time, buy fewer clothes or fewer store-bought, new clothes. And though her teenagers might not like the clothes she can afford to buy, she can encourage them to get jobs so they can buy their own designer clothes and begin to learn useful lessons about the working world. In many small ways, the single mother can "make do" without there being a significant negative impact on family life.

It is often the bigger ticket items that frustrate single mothers. Your child may have to move from a house into an apartment. He or she may not get the dance or art lessons you dream of and might not get to go on the school trip to Washington, D.C., that costs $269. If your child's bicycle is stolen, you may not be able to replace it this month—or next month, or possibly until next year. And God forbid that the refrigerator should break down. Or the car.

One evening, a woman I'll call Liza spoke to a group of women about her anguish over her limited financial resources. Liza was an artist doing mostly commercial art. She had given up a good-paying job to go into business for herself. In spite of her high energy and hard work, her capital on hand couldn't carry her business along until she was in the black. The business failed. She was forced to move into a leaky duplex with her two children while she was looking for another job. Meanwhile, she was scrambling to meet her daily expenses.

Liza's ex-husband owned a spacious home in the country. A creek flowed across his property. The children enjoyed visiting him on weekends, exploring the small wooded area, going out to dinner and riding with him on his motorcycle. Liza worried about the motorcycle, but in other respects, she felt, her ex-husband seemed to be a good father. "Sometimes I think I should just give him custody of the children," she said in despair. "He can give them so much more than I can."

The other women encouraged Liza to ride out her financial difficulties. In many ways Liza was a loving, caring mother. The children were as well off with her as with her ex-husband, the group maintained, because they were family together. And the children needed Liza's mothering.

It is hard to let go of feeling guilty because you can't provide all the material things you would wish for your children. But it is important to remember that we all live within limits. That father with the country home has his limits, as well. He cannot afford to go to Europe every year, drive a Porsche and keep up a winter home in Florida.

We may think, "Well, those are hardly basic needs." True. And the point is that life is full of struggles in so many ways. One of those struggles is learning to accept our limitations, to make the best life we can from our circumstances while we are working to improve them for ourselves, our children and our communities. Our children need to learn to accept limitations, as well. Single mothers can be excellent role models in showing their children how to live within financial limitations and still maintain quality in life.

In the end, basic needs are still food, shelter, clothing and love. If you can provide those basic needs for your child, you are doing your job. People live through good times and bad together, and they grow stronger for it. It's easy to dance and sing when times are good. The quality of endurance is measured in part by the woman who can dance and sing when times are bad.

I remember the story of my grandfather, a farmer in Nebraska. One year, all the farm crops failed due to lack of rain. My grandfather piled his family of six into the car and headed out to explore the Black Hills of South Dakota. Other farmers thought he had lost his mind, but he said, "Well, if you can't harvest the crops, you might as well take a vacation."

To the extent we and our children can learn to accept limitations and take a vacation within the context of difficult financial times—a walk to the park, a shared meal with friends, dancing to the radio—we can overcome the weight of circumstances, get our day's job done and move forward as a family.

The bottom line for carrying through is self-esteem, which says our lives together, our futures, our potentials are more important than this broken toaster or this overdue bill or what happens financially in the next six months.

Questioning your competence as a parent

Joyce confided to a friend one day, "Sometimes I feel like I'm flying by the seat of my pants. I don't know whether I'm helping or hurting my kids." Joyce had tough decisions to make about housing, about her job and how a change would affect the children, what to do with a son who was bringing home failing grades, etc.

When you don't know what to do in a situation, get more information. Call friends, read books, call up the school or other professionals. If you have made a decision you are unsure of, get a second opinion in the same way.

After you have instituted a new rule, tried a new intervention technique, initiated a new family tradition, take time out to reflect on it. Think through and evaluate how successful it was. How could it be improved the next time? Formulate a new, revised action plan, and try that out. Reflect again on the situation. Are things getting better?

Learn to trust your instincts. If you sense trouble, confront the situation yourself or get help. If you sense a child is out of sorts, sit down with the child and ask, "What are you feeling right now? Do you want to tell me about it?"

From time to time, you can even ask your children, "How am I doing as a mother?" and they will probably give you some interesting feedback. Reflect on that.

Remember charity with the children. Give yourself a break, you're probably doing a good job. And when all else fails, call a friend.

Self-esteem

Self-esteem is a very important personal quality. People who feel good about themselves tend to do well in life. People with low self-esteem are more likely to fail. Your child's self-esteem will play a critical role in how he or she performs in school, at work and with his or her peers throughout life.

Use **high-esteem words and phrases** with children, such as

"great"
"good job"
"thank you"
"you're wonderful"
"I'm proud of you" and
"I love you."

Self-esteem is the extent to which a person believes herself to be capable, significant and successful. People who have low self-esteem feel unworthy, incapable, or unimportant. People who have high self-esteem feel they are liked, talented and successful.

Some characteristics of high self-esteem are: feeling good about yourself, being cheerful and friendly, thinking such positive thoughts as "I am me, and I am OK," having a sense of humor, having a high energy level and helping other people feel good about themselves.

Some characteristics of low self-esteem are: constant anger, destruction of one's own property or that of others, inability to get along with others, poor decision-making skills.

Children's self-esteem can take a major dive through the process of divorce. As children of divorce question the stability of their family, they question their own worthiness. Children are emotionally bruised, in various degrees, by the divorce process. The single mother, therefore, must provide tender, loving care to her children in order for their self-esteem to climb back up.

When we treat children with dignity and respect, they will find ways of solving their problems and facing disappointments and setbacks. With high self-esteem, your child will have the courage and determination to achieve his or her goals in life.

Some ideas to help improve your child's self-esteem:

◇ Celebrate your child's birthday.

◇ Find other important events for your child to celebrate: a new tooth coming in, a school performance, making the team.

◇ Provide opportunities for your child to help others. Older children and teenagers can be responsible for a regular "volunteer" activity, such as reading to a blind person, helping serve food at a soup kitchen, tutoring younger children after school, visiting a senior citizen for 30 minutes each week. "Help your sister/brother/me," is an easy request for a child of any age.

◇ Ask for and respect your child's opinions.

◇ Spend quality time doing things with your child, such as playing cards or other indoor and outdoor games, walking to a park, telling stories, reading a book.

◇ Provide opportunities for your child to experience success. Helping you around the home with manageable tasks which he or she does or can learn to do well, for example, reinforces that child's self-image. If you find out what your child does well and encourage situations which enable him or her to use those talents, your child will succeed.

◇ Be sensitive to your child's physical and personal needs.

◇ Encourage your child to perform at school or at events in your community.

◇ Take time to visit your child's school. Most schools have evening orientation programs for parents in the fall. If you work in the evening, you can visit the school during the day. Some mothers work close enough to their child's school to have lunch with them from time to time.

The importance of affirming for self-esteem

Children love positive attention. So do we all. And giving children that positive attention is not as easy as it sounds. Positive attention requires enterprise, in a way. Part of how we operate as single parents is "Don't rock my boat." We want our children to pick up after themselves; keep themselves clean; refrain from crying, whining, failing, and fighting; do what we ask them on the first request, and do it well; and give us some time and space of our own. When the children don't come through for us in these ways, they are "rocking our boat," and we have to get up and deal with the problem or live with it. So when two children are fighting with each other, we may physically pull them apart, if they are young, and yell, "Stop fighting!" If they are older, we may offer, "Give me a break!" or "Go to your rooms, both of you!" Often we are dealing with the problem the fast way because we have been dealing with problems all day, at work and at home, and we are just plain tired of problems.

But if there is no problem, if Megan and Bret are playing a quiet game of cards, our mind is free to deal with other matters. It takes some objectivity to look and the children, think, "Well, this is a nice quiet time," and some energy to say, "You children are playing so nicely together. Watch out, now, you may be growing up!" I guarantee you they will like the attention. You can almost see their chests puff up.

Build self-esteem through positive reinforcement:

❶ *Mother makes a request (optional)*
❷ *Wait for child's response*
❸ *Offer affirmation /praise*

Example 1:
❶*"Do the dishes."*
❷ Child does this on first request.
❸*"Thanks for helping out on the first request. It means a lot to me and to the family. You did a good job, too."*

Example 2:
❷ Sibling A brings sibling B a glass of ice water, without being asked.
❸*"What a nice thing to do! You're a thoughtful brother/sister."*

You've got to take the initiative in these good-behavior situations. What you are doing is building self-esteem through positive reinforcement. It contributes to behavior modification toward the good.

You can praise a child at the moment of the good behavior, or you can save the praise until later. One time to comment on your children's behavior is when you sit down in the evening to relax and reflect for a minute. You create a lap into which a young child will probably crawl and offer a warm body next to which an older child will want to sit. Then you can pick out some "good news behavior" to comment on to the children. Another time to do this is at bedtime when you say good night to each child. If you always leave them with a positive comment about a specific behavior, their heightened sense of personal worth will do as much for them as a hug and a kiss to make them feel loved. Once you begin looking for opportunities to praise your children, the positive reinforcement becomes a habit, one you'll enjoy and which can become one of your best tools for raising children who feel good about themselves. But you have to keep in mind the technique. When the children are not rocking your boat, that's the time to pay attention to them.

Remember to avoid such low-esteem words and phrases as "stupid," "dumb," and "you can't do anything." Instead, use such high-esteem words and phrases as "great," "good job," "thank you," "you're wonderful," "I'm proud of you," and "I love you."

Fostering a sense of security

Sad things happen when children don't feel secure. They can begin to tell lies because they are afraid people will not accept them if they are not perfect. They can turn from outgoing children to withdrawn children because they question their own self worth. They can become reluctant to form trust friendships because they are afraid people will leave them or turn on them and hurt them. They can become obsessed with consuming things, attention and time because they feel a lack of something necessary in their lives: loving people who stick with them over time.

Giving your child a sense of security works against these ills and for your child. Unconditional love is one element in building security.

To help foster a sense of security in children:
◊ Always let your child know where you are and how to contact you.
◊ Make sure your child knows how to contact his or her father or other available, caring person in case of an emergency.
◊ With young children, always say goodbye when you leave them with a babysitter, their father or anyone outside your home, even if the child cries.
◊ Reinforce the idea of family and the importance of family by talking about this with your child.
◊ Let your child have access to the family photo albums. Look through them together from time to time.
◊ Frame a picture of your child's father even if he is gone from your child's life forever, and hang it or otherwise display it somewhere in your home, perhaps in the child's room on a desk or dresser, if that is where your child wants to put it.
◊ Present your child's father as a well-meaning person to your child.
◊ Let your child enter into some of the decision-making in the family, such as helping to choose a vacation spot. This will give the child a feeling of control over and ownership in his or her place on earth—family.
◊ Give your child a territory he or she can count on for privacy—a bedroom, a drawer, whatever. And let the child control that territory.
◊ Allow your child to ask questions and answer them truthfully. Get more information if you need it in order to answer them. If the questions are painful, share the pain.
◊ Always be honest with your child. He or she needs to trust you.
◊ Try to keep your home life as stable as possible. Minimize the number of moves you make, the number of babysitters you call on, the number of men you introduce you child to.
◊ Always give your child a good night kiss and hug and say "I love you," even if he or she is 18 years old. Do not wait for your child to initiate this; you initiate it. Make it a ritual.

School

Schools are bureaucracies, and school systems are set up to deal with biological family units—Mom, Dad and the kids all living in the same house. All schools have information forms made out for each student. When your child enters a new school, you should check to make sure that the information form accurately reflects your child's situation. If you have joint custody, for example, does the form reflect both addresses and, assuming there is a regular schedule, tell when the child is at each home? If you, your ex-partner or whoever is listed as an emergency contact on the form changes jobs or moves to another location, this will mean new phone numbers and schedules for that person; you need to phone such information in to the school office.

Some of the things that happen due to inaccurate information: School newsletters go to the wrong address; room teachers call up the wrong parent to ask that cookies be brought to school Monday morning; your child has a fever, and the school can't reach you to ask that you pick your child up. In all of these cases there is a communication breakdown that you want to avoid for everyone's sake. And in case of an accident, some hospitals and emergency rooms will not treat minors without written permission from or the presence of a parent or legal guardian.

Be aware that your child's school performance may be affected by separation from your partner. Children can become occupied with their parents' problems to the extent that it affects their ablity to concentrate in school, and their grades may drop. Or children can begin to "act out," or behave in unsatisfactory ways.

If signs appear indicating that your child is in trouble at school, you need to call the school right away and deal with it. You probably will talk with a teacher, the principal, a guidance counselor or a social worker attached to the school. Talk with anyone who will listen. Find out what resources—people and programs—your school system has available. It is a process of getting to the source of the problem, and working with school personnel to try to intervene. It is the job of the U.S. public school system to provide an education for your child which meets his or her needs, to prevent emotional damage and to prevent your child from dropping out. The majority of educators believe in these goals, but they are busy people. In spite of the fact that single mothers are busy people, too, they need to make their child's performance at school a priority, because that child is in school about six hours a day, and that's a lot of hours to be miserable.

As often as not, if your child is having a problem in school—and junior high school children are famous for this—it will take some effort to work out. It will take patience, faith in the system, challenging the system, hope, love, charity and time before the worst is over. If your child knows you are concerned enough to be working on "the problem," you will be sending that child the message that you love him or her and will stick with him or her through thick and thin. Whatever else happens in school and out, your child needs that message.

School refusal

A minority of children develop physical symptoms, such as vomiting, which appear in the morning before school and lessen or disappear in the evenings and on weekends. These symptoms are caused by anxiety related to the school experience. Children might be frightened of the overall experience, they might dislike their teachers, they might feel isolated from or pressured by peers, they might find the academic work too challenging. The greatest numbers of these children are in elementary school, but school refusal also happens with frequency as school opens in seventh grade and the first year of high school.

A parent should be concerned enough to take the child to a doctor if there are
- Recurrent, vague physical symptoms (headache, diarrhea, palpatations);
- No physical cause found on careful evaluation;
- Symptoms predominate in the morning on school days;
- Child has missed five or more days of school because of these physical symptoms.

Too sick to go to school

Many school-age children try, at one time or another, to stay home from school, whether or not they are feeling ill. This is usually a minor problem, but a mother can feel some distress in knowing how to evaluate whether her child is ill enough to stay home. If her child is recovering from an illness, once again, a mother needs to decide when her child is well enough to go to school. For these lesser health problems, pediatrician James W. Cheek, M.D., offers the following medical advice:

Objective Criteria for Keeping Students Out of School

◇   **Fever** of 101 degrees or more.

◇   **Repeated vomiting** to the point of being unable to keep down clear liquids. This is in contrast to single episodes that may occur due to stress over projects, tests, presentations. In cases of stress- or anxiety-related nausea or vomiting, a cool, rational discussion as to the reasons for the upset along with reassurance and moral support on the part of the parent are a necessary part of teaching the person the importance of fulfilling even unpleasant responsibilities.

◇   **Other gastrointestinal upset,** i.e., diarrhea.

◇   **Headache** or other pain sufficient to prevent appropriate concentration on school-related activities, including reading and calculations.

◇   **Evidence of contagious disease,** e.g., chicken pox, strep throat, influenza.

◇   **Common cold** causing frequent coughing and sneezing, runny nose or badly congested sinuses. This is a judgment call by the parent. If the child cannot profit from going to school in this condition, or if he or she will be an obvious health hazard to others, it would be better to keep the child home to rest for a day.

◇   **Severe menstrual cramps or earache:** child should stay home from school and see a health provider.

Activities: When a child stays home from school due to illness, he or she should stay in bed. If the child is well enough to watch TV, he or she should engage, instead, in reading or studying school subjects in order to keep up with classroom assignments and the overall aim of education.

Extended illness: Any illness which prevents pursuit of normal activities for more than 48 hours usually requires at least a telephone contact with a medical provider, such as the family doctor or a hospital emergency room, to determine the need for a formal evaluation.

Discipline

Children need someone to be in control making decisions. You need to be that person. Above all else in dealing with your children, your word must be law. If not, you leave yourself and your children wide open for catastrophe.

Diane was a single mother whose son Scooter was three years old and out of control. Diane would say, "Don't throw the coffee cup." "Don't hit your sister." Don't. Don't. Don't. But Scooter would do it anyway. He was a charming and bright little boy who simply was not old enough to set his own limits, and Diane did not know how to help him.

> ❦ It's OK to express anger. Use words that express your feelings instead of attacking the child:
> *I feel very angry about . . .*
> instead of:
> *You make me so angry when you . . .* ❦

Another single mother had a teenage daughter named Susan who stayed out all night whenever she chose to do so, against her mother's wishes.

Both Scooter and Susan were out of control, and their mothers clearly were not in control.

Discipline is a very personal subject to parents. Here we are talking about discipline not as punishment, but as control. And it becomes a crucial subject for single mothers because they do not have their child's father to reinforce their authority and to follow through with difficult interactions when the mothers cannot.

When you have reached the end of your patience with your child, when your child has crossed over the line of demarcation between what is OK and what isn't, when your child has begun to push all your buttons and you are frustrated and angry, there are things you can do:

Expressing anger. It's OK to express anger, just be careful how you express it. Use words that express your feelings instead of attacking the child: "I feel very angry about . . . " instead of "You make me so angry when you . . ." Try to find out how the child is feeling, and why. After the feelings are out on the table, you can talk about the issues more calmly.

Using Time Out.

"I think you need Time Out. Your behavior is clearly out of control. You need to go to your room [sit on the chair, etc.] until you regain your control [cheer up, etc.]," <u>or</u>

"I need time out from you. I've lost my patience and my control. Your behavior needs to change, because I can't deal with this. Go to your room [I'll go to my room] until we both regain our control."

Separating yourself from the child gives you time to cool down and think about what you'll say when you see the child again.

Taking away privileges.

"You don't have to eat your green beans, but you can't have your ice cream until you eat your green beans."

"You can't go outside to play right now because you hurt the dog."

"No TV/ telephone until you clean up your room."

"Sorry, I don't feel like sitting by you right now. You can't be disrespectful to your piano teacher and then expect me to give you a hug. I love you, but I'm upset."

Work Consequences. When you establish a rule and the child does not carry out his or her responsibility to obey it, you can give the child a consequence. You both understand that the rule has been broken, and the child knows that he or she will have to do some chore to pay for breaking the rule.

♦ *"Since you didn't do the dishes last night, you can do them this morning before school, and after school you can scrub out the tub, too."*
(Rule: Do the dishes before you go to bed.)

♦ *"Since you two are fighting, Jake, you can take out the garbage and Laura, you can bring in firewood. You can both work off some of that energy in a more productive way."*
(Rule: Don't fight.)

It's a good idea to write the rules on paper, go over them with your children and then post them somewhere.

If the child does a poor job with the consequence, you can say, "Since you did a poor job with the garbage, you can clean up your mess and also sweep off the driveway." Very quickly your children will understand that the path of least resistance is to do what Mom asks. However, there may be times when they choose to break the rules. No problem. They understand they have to accept their consequence, and you get the garbage taken out.

> ❝ You both understand that the rule has been broken, and the child knows that he or she will have to do some chore to pay for breaking the rule. ❞

Because you get a cleaner house, this technique diffuses much of your own anger toward the child who chose to disobey the rule. You can forgive the child more easily because in the consequence the child is helping you clean the house!

Consequences are appropriate for children ages five and above. A list of consequences could include almost anything. You can post them on your refrigerator like this:

◇ fold laundry	◇ set the table
◇ wash windows	◇ scrub out the bathtub
◇ vacuum carpet	◇ straighten bookshelves
◇ sweep walkways	◇ go to the grocery store
◇ take out garbage	◇ wash out the dog dish
◇ dust furniture	◇ wash baseboards
◇ empty dishwasher	◇ wash mirrors
	◇ water plants

If you are unable to establish clear control over your children, seek help. Some sources are your child's school counselor (free), books on child care (free in library), a private counselor ($), or an organization called ToughLove (see page 110).

Natural and Logical Consequences. There is at least one primitive tribe which allows its young children to crawl toward the fire when they get curious. They do this only once. The fire burns them, and they learn to respect their distance from it without an adult ever having to say, "Don't go near the fire."

In our technological society with the hazards of electrical sockets within reach of our toddlers and habit-forming drugs all too easily available to our teenagers, it would be dangerous to allow children free access to everything about which they are curious. But by finding situations where natural and logical consequences teach your child a lesson, it will be a lesson well learned. And you will not have to play the "bad mom" who says "Don't" or who nags. For example, your toddler continues to ride her tricycle too fast around a corner. You stop saying, "That's too fast!" Before long, the tricycle turns over, and she scrapes her knee. She slows down the next time. Or your teenager wears dirty clothes to school because they are "my favorites" in between washings. One day someone at school says, "You stink!" and the teenager learns a lesson in cleanliness.

In both of these cases, the children will learn on their own that their actions were not the option which worked best for them, and they will alter their behavior the next time. These are lessons that we all look back on and say, "I learned it the hard way." And they are usually lessons well learned.

The problem with this method of discipline for parents is that we want to protect our children from pain, rejection and failure. And we would like to avoid embarrassment by association with our children when they are making mistakes. We can say to our children, "I think you should do _____ in this situation. However, you do what you think is best and take the consequences." In some situations, the children turn out to be right, after all! One straight-A student who had some social problems wanted to go into the Army after graduation. His mother wanted him to go to college, but she accepted the Army decision with little complaint. The boy enlisted and stayed in the Army for two somewhat tough years. He did a lot of maturing, and when he was honorably discharged, he was able to pay for his own college eduation. For him, it was a good decision, in part because he bought into it.

Allowing children to make their own decisions is one way to foster maturation, since as adults they will be totally responsible for their own decisions and their consequences.

Rages. Some children have tantrums and otherwise rage uncontrollably from time to time. In both cases you can isolate your child from everyone else and let the child let off some of that emotional steam. One woman I know told her nephew, who growls and yells when he gets wound up into a hyperactive frenzy, "It's OK if you need to yell. But you can do it in the back bedroom, and then, when you are finished yelling, you can come back out and be with us." He did go to the bedroom and yell until he tired himself out. Then he rejoined the group and was fine. His father disapproved when he heard what the aunt had done. He felt the boy should learn to control himself at all times.

The bedroom solution could work as an intermediary step between the "Terrible Twos" and adult control. It worked with no harm done to persons or property. Whatever works for you and your child should be seriously considered as an effective control tool. Think of safe options.

Developing independence

The children of single mothers are more independent, on the average, than their peers who live with mom and dad together. They have to be, because mom needs their help in big ways. To the extent that the children can dress themselves, care for their bodies and their possessions and help with chores around the house, the single mother's time and resources are extended. When a single mother asks her child to wash the car, it is a more serious request than when a married mother asks the same thing, because the single mother *has no husband to back her up, has no husband to do the job for her if the child fails to do it, may have no time or energy to do it herself, and may have no discretionary money to get it done at a carwash.* Even a toddler who learns to put on a coat in the wintertime is making a valuable contribution to the energy resources of the single mother, and the mother conveys that gratitude.

> 66 Independence is more than learning tasks. It includes the confidence to launch out into the world separate from family, to risk failure in order to find success. Unconditional love and self-esteem contribute to the confidence to risk in order to succeed, and thus to become independent. 99

But independence is more than learning tasks. It includes the confidence to launch out into the world separate from family, to risk failure in order to find success. Unconditional love and self-esteem contribute to the confidence to risk in order to succeed, and thus to become independent.

Single mothers are in a tug-of-war with themselves regarding the independence of their children. The children are sometimes a too-heavy responsibility. They are also sometimes oh-so-wonderful company. They are a burden, and they are family. One single mother tells her children, "Just remember, when you're 18, it's up and out of this house!" She also tells them, "Oh, don't grow up so fast. Who is going to stay with me when I am an old lady?" She tells them this in humor, but in all humor there is an element of sincerity, of truth.

As single mothers, we need to encourage our children to be independent, to go to kindergarten, birthday parties, clubs, teams, jobs, proms, college, the world when they are ready for each step. To the degree we can feel they are ready for the next step and help them through it, we will be making their path in life smoother. They will carry on with or without our help, but our job is to let ourselves let them go, to provide help when we can, and to wave them on with pride.

Letting children be children

Sometimes we push too hard. We expect too much from our progeny. We need them to be responsible, always. We need them not to make mistakes. But they will make mistakes. They will forget to take books to school, they will forget to tell you someone called, they will forget to pack their toothbrush for camp. They will wet their pants. They will spill, stain, break, be silly or obnoxious, and do so many things that you know they could avoid if only. If only they were always careful, thoughtful, thinking, sensitive. Well, we need to remind ourselves that the job of children is *to become* careful, thoughtful, thinking, sensitive. When they have done that, we call them adults. Meanwhile, they have a lot to work on, and we have to give them some slack in what we expect of them.

If you find yourself snapping at your children a lot, if they make you more angry than pleased with them in general, then something needs to be fixed in that relationship. The relationship is disturbed. And you need to reflect on whether the child is not following through with responsibilities normal for his or her age group, or whether you are expecting too much of your child. It's a question well worth asking from time to time, especially in regard to your expectations of your oldest child, who paves the way for younger siblings.

One thing single mothers have to watch out for is that they do not allow their children to become their caretakers or their counselors. If you have a problem with alcohol, drugs or your emotional health, you need to get help for yourself from a professional trained in that area. To delay getting help is to put a burden of "taking care of Mama" on your child, a burden which may adversely affect his or her relationships when it is time to choose a life partner, for example, and your child chooses a person who needs to be taken care of—just like Mama.

If you've had a hard day at work, it is fine to come home and say to your child, "I've had a hard day at work. I'm beat. My boss/secretary gave me a hard time about a project." It is a mistake, however, to involve your child in your problems at work or with the child's father—or whatever—to the extent that the child feels you can't handle the problem and the child needs to find a solution.

Sometimes you can do this and not even know it. Bridgette, for example, had been having financial problems since she left her husband, five years earlier. She and her daughter, six-year-old Kerry, were living in a house with a broken window, faulty plumbing, etc. Bridgette's dismal living conditions did not stop her from writing inventive romance stories, using her considerable imagination. Kerry was the practical one. She reminded her mother to lock the door. She reminded her mother where she had put and forgotten little things around the house. She wrote out a Christmas list for Santa Claus which included a play sink, stove and refrigerator, along with a tool set to fix all the things that needed fixing around their house. Was this a case of a mother inadvertently allowing her daughter to carry too heavy a burden of their problems? You call it.

Male role models

Whatever your relationship with your ex-partner, you will probably want to expose your children close-up to other male role models. Family, friends and lovers are the three options over which you have control. From these categories you can pick and choose those you know have a genuine interest in your children, who like to spend time with them. Some do, some don't. The single mother quickly learns which men she can invite to enjoy dinner at the house with the children, and those who see her children as an interruption, an irritation. The children know who likes them and who doesn't. And it is best to keep your social relationships separate from the children when they involve men who do not enjoy your children.

If you feel your son, especially, needs to have a special relationship with a man where the man and your son spend time together away from you, you can suggest that to a relative or a friend. Lovers will probably get uncomfortable with that kind of a responsibility because it hints of commitment.

If you can't find an available man to relate to your children in this way, there are buddy programs set up in many cities to provide male role models for children, especially boys. Big Brothers International is one such organization. They will be listed in the phone book. They often have more requests for big brothers than they have volunteers to fill, but you can ask that your child be put on a waiting list. This is a good opportunity to match your son with a caring man. Some of these relationships last for years.

Some boys who play team sports become very close to their coaches, particularly when the coach's son is a friend. Other boys find role models in scout leaders, their best friend's father or older brother. And mothers can take advantage of teenage boys as babysitters who will serve as role models for their sons.

Just as mothers and daughters share gender concerns and world views, so a son can profit from the same with a male role model. And while a boy relates to other boys as he grows up, it is a good idea to have a mature male with whom to talk over concerns—A kind of sponsor and mentor, whose values and motives are approved by you, guiding him into the world of men.

Homework without war

One Atlanta single mother who has grown children says this about homework for junior high and high school children: "It's even more important for older children that it be done before anything else (no telephone or TV) and that the groundwork has been laid for self-imposed good study habits before children are subjected to the incredible peer pressure which begins at 11 or 12.

"Get involved! Crack a textbook or two yourself so you can discuss the Magna Carta, isosceles triangles and cell division. Keep kids talking and their world view will reach to Tibet. You'll also end up discussing what Susan said about Karen, why all the guys hate the new Phys Ed teacher, how gross the lunches are. You want curious, fired-up kids who love learning? Teenagers who are not secretive?

The homework basics for children are to
◊ Set up a study area, even if it's the kitchen table. Make sure it is well lit.
◊ Choose the right time to study, then stick to it.
◊ Get rid of distractions. Some children need quiet, others like a radio playing softly.
◊ Find a motivation for doing well, such as receiving praise from a teacher or parent, or feeling good about yourself.
◊ Do the hardest work first.
◊ Repeat it out loud. Verbalizing helps you use hearing to learn.
◊ Take breaks. After 15 minutes for first graders, longer periods for older children. Stand up, stretch, get a drink or a snack.
◊ Check your work.

The homework basics for parents are to
◊ Help your child set up a system which works for him or her.
◊ Monitor your child's homework habits from afar, once the pattern is set. Avoid criticizing the child's methods, as long as the work gets done.
◊ Let your child know that homework is a top priority in your home. It comes before friends, TV or other recreation.
◊ Stop by your child's homework area and pat him or her on the back from time to time.
◊ At the end of each session, ask your child to show you what she or he has done, show genuine interest and praise the effort.
(from New York Times *columnist Dr. Lawrence Kunter)*

"The point really is, if their homework is interesting to you, if they perceive their job—and school is their full-time job—is as important as your sense of productivity is in yours, they take responsibility. Yours is to get them to that point, not to be drudges or scholars but to realize as teenagers their future is really in their own hands. It helps if their father helps pay for college. But if not, they can do it if they want.

"You can't preach educational values; the kids instill them in themselves early on. Your part is the cheerleader, the self-esteem booster. Not stressing the grades but the knowing and wanting to know more."

This same mother encouraged her own children to watch local and national news on TV, to read newspapers beyond the sports page and comics and to read books for fun.

Child abuse and neglect

Child abusers have low self-esteem, and many single mothers suffer from low-self esteem due in part to difficult circumstances at work, at home and with their ex-partner. The pattern is, the boss yells at the mother, the mother comes home and hits the child, the child kicks the dog. It's a pattern of violence that needs to be broken before it gets to the child.

Sometimes even the most rational of mothers feels dangerous and destructive urges toward her children. *"I felt like I was going crazy. I was sick of the kids, sick of talking to them, sick of seeing their faces. . ."*

For a single mother, children are a double burden of responsibility, since her partner is no longer on site to help with child care. It is usually the mother who has full custody of the children and whose inner resources are stretched to the limit. The needs of her children can overwhelm her. She needs only one irrational moment to lash out at a child—emotionally or physically—to damage that child. And her own need for sexual intimacy may, in times of extreme fatigue and stress, cause her to reach out to her children for sexual gratification of one kind or another.

When the single mother lives with a man, who by his presence in the home takes on the role of stepparent, this man may or may not have the best interests of the children at heart. He may become an emotional, physical or sexual abuser. The mother may suspect this but turn the other way because her own needs for a companion are strong. And the children seem to survive one way or another.

The first function of a mother is to protect her children from harm. This includes hunger, overexposure to weather, and *abuse from others and from herself*. When there is child abuse and neglect in our own homes, we as parents are creating emotional scars in our children, scars that will never go away. As adults, children from troubled homes may fall prey to alcoholism, eating disorders, compulsive gambling, compulsive shopping (leading to bankruptcy court), or any other addictions that begin as coping mechanisms. And add criminal behavior to that list.

Often adults who abuse children were abused themselves as children, resulting in low self-esteem and a continuation of the abuse cycle. It is too easy, in the privacy of your own home when no one else is watching, to verbally batter and denounce your child, to hit or beat your child, to engage your child in inappropriate rubbing, hugging and kissing. It happens all the time behind closed doors, but *it should not happen*.

If you know or even suspect that you or someone else is abusing or neglecting your children, please get help today for your child and for yourself. You can make an anonymous call to the National Foundation for the Prevention of Child Abuse (see Resources), and they will help guide you to a better tomorrow.

One caution is that in many states, if you tell a professional you have abused your child, the professional is bound by law to report the abuse to the child abuse authority in your town. This agency may remove the children from your home. So when you are talking about possible abuse, talk about your urges and not about the actual events if they have already occurred. You can ask the professional what the law is in your state regarding disclosure of abuse information.

CHAPTER 5: Children and Community

The family meeting

Consider meeting once a week at a regular time with your children to go over business. Let's say Friday night. You and the children are finished with a week of work and school and are facing the weekend. You can gather together, even if your family is only you and your one child, to discuss whatever is on your minds. If the meeting is run like a usual business meeting, it has the advantage of teaching your child useful business lessons.

The meeting can open formally with, "OK, this meeting is open." There should be a designated chairperson for the meeting, and this can always be the same person or can rotate among the mother and older children to develop leadership skills and encourage a sense of community and ownership in the meeting.

> **A simple agenda includes:**
> ◊ *Weekend plans* (or some variation of short-term plans)
> ◊ *Old business*
> ◊ *New business*
> ◊ *Bad news/good news*
> ◊ *Adjournment*
> ◊ *Refreshments and family activity*

The weekend plans item gives children a glimpse into what you, they and their siblings will be doing in the immediate future. Not only do they know, then, where you are right now, but they know fairly accurately where you are going to be in the next few days. Often they will have questions about the activities, and this is a good time to talk about them. When those activites occur, the children will have a better sense of what's going on.

Old business includes anything that the family has discussed in a previous family meeting. For example, if you and the children discussed a family vacation in the last meeting and you have obtained more information on that in the past week, you can bring that up for discussion. Or if a child is unhappy with a schedule set up last week for doing dishes ("I have to do them on Saturday and Sunday when we use more dishes. Cherrie gets to do them on Monday and Tuesday when we mostly use only dinner dishes.") you can take another look at the schedule based on the new information.

New business is anything that hasn't been discussed before in the meeting. For example, Jeremiah might express his anger that his sister is going into his room and playing with his things when he is not at home. Or a child may confront the mother about wanting to stay up later at night, wanting a higher allowance, feeling angry about being yelled at on a particular occasion—whatever is on that child's mind.

Bad news/good news is a time during the family meeting when each person expresses one thing that happened in the past week that was "bad news" for him or her, for example, "Ronnie Meyers tripped me on the way to school this morning" and then the "good news," "I think my math grade is coming up this time, because I got an 86 on the test this week." Some children have difficulty thinking of bad news/good news. Often, if you give them a few minutes to think about it, they can come up with something. This part of the agenda gives everyone an opportunity to share in the lives of family members outside their family setting. And everyone in the family shares at least two concerns of every other member.

After the meeting is over, it is important to devote some time, even if only a few minutes, for the family to have fun together. This can become a tradition, such as ice cream sundaes after the meeting, followed by looking through the family album, playing a board game, dancing, reading a story or whatever you like to do together.

The family meeting can be a time to set rules and allow the children to negotiate a little. The meeting gives children a forum to discuss problems and feelings with their mother in an atmosphere of more neutral emotion. The children must be able to trust the mother to listen to their concerns and discuss them without becoming angry. If the mother feels herself becoming angry, she needs to table the matter until she can again discuss the issue calmly. This is a time of listening, negotiating, consensus when possible, resolution and sharing.

Initially, the children will not understand what the meeting is supposed to accomplish. After a few meetings, they will catch on. You may hear some resistance from them about the meeting, such as, "Oh no, it's time for the family meeting again." But in truth, if there is an atmosphere of love and trust, the children will greatly appreciate the forum.

Here is one mother's agenda, the list she jotted down during the course of one week to bring up at the meeting. During that week, a couple of incidents involving her children's friends caused this mother to want to take a look at how and when her children related to friends and establish some clearer guidelines with the children:

Family meeting agenda items

◇ Bath rules
◇ When Mom is not at home rules
  ♦ *how far to roam*
  ♦ *having friends over*
  ♦ *asking permission*
◇ Having friends over (supervised)
  ♦ *by day*
  ♦ *by night*
  ♦ *how far to roam (with permission)*
◇ Mail rules
◇ Other new business
◇ Weekend plans
◇ Hugs
◇ Soft drinks
◇ Dancing

Having fun with your children

Kids are great. To the family structure, they bring energy, innocence, a fresh look at the world, skills, talents, dreams and companionship. And they can be a lot of fun. Talking with them

---

FREE AND CHEAP FUN

VCR and popcorn—99 cents on
    Sundays at Pop&Go
Cumberland Museum of Science—
    free on Tuesdays
Tennessee State Museum, down-
    town—free
Airport—watch the airplanes
Story hours at bookstores and
    downtown library
Conservatory at Opryland—
    look around, it's beautiful

Kickball, soccer, badminton
    in the park
Fort Nashboro (free) and other
    historic sites
Junk stores/flea markets
Bike trip with kid carrier and
    picnic pouch
Radnor Lake—walk around
    on trails
Canoe trips for adults and
    older children—$$

Fly kites
Pet store—next best thing to a zoo
Feed the ducks at Centennial Park
Ice skating, roller skating, bowling,
    tennis
Cheekwood Botanical Garden
    and Museum—art and
    nature (feed bread to the
    fish in the ponds)

Scratch your child's back and let
    him or her scratch yours
    (rub feet, scratch heads)
Go for a walk around the block
    after dinner
Pro baseball game ($3 adults,
    $2 children) or a high
    school game
Nature walks and programs
    at parks—free

and spending time with them builds intimacy and sets a pattern for them to be intimate with their own families when they are adults.

With this in mind, the Single Mothers Group of Vanderbilt University developed this list for use in Nashville, Tennessee. Many of the ideas can be adapted for use in other towns:

Miniature golf
Library visit (downtown
  has a great children's
  section)
Goo-Goo candy bar factory—
  free tours and samples!
Squirt bottle tag in summer
Wash the car together with rags
  and buckets in summer
Turn on the music and DANCE
  in your own home

Watch model airplanes at
  EdwinWarner park
Walk around the Steeplechase
  course
On rainy days, cook together
Card games or board games
Craft fairs, street fairs and
  festivals
Visit Fanny Mae Dees Park
  to see the dragon and play

Music in band shell at Centennial
  Park in summer—free
Wade in a creek
Climb trees (the magnolias
  at Vanderbilt are great)
Put on swimsuits and run under
  the lawn sprinkler
Bike ride together in parks

Go jogging together
Sing songs
Fish at a nearby lake
Go tent camping with friends—
  $2 at Montgomery Bell Park
Sit on the front porch at night
  and tell stories
Go on a hike, collect items for
  arts and crafts

The family with others

It's wonderful to have family and friends with whom to share your children. In a larger circle of people, you and your children share larger concerns. You can promote common goals and common values. It reinforces who you are as part of a group.

Within the context of larger groups, you can play together, worship together, do volunteer work together and sleep overnight together with family or friends (except casual romantic friends).

Getting the children to help around the house

Many daily chores, like feeding the cat, can be done according to a schedule and established rules (see Chapter 4, pages 76-77). For those times when you assign the children non-routine jobs, like a Saturday morning "Let's clean up the house," the children may look around and say, "The house looks OK to me; I'd rather play." To the extent you can convince your children that they are contributing to the community of their family, assigning jobs will be easier.

◇ Tell your children you need their help, that you can't do it all by yourself (*"We all want a nice house. We all need to make it happen together"*).

◇ Let them know what specific tasks you expect of them with each job (*"Sweep the kitchen floor. That includes under the table and chairs"*).

◇ If you agree they can do it "later," get them to commit to a specific time (*"I'll have it done by eight o'clock"*) and thenhold them to that time.

◇ Tell them to let you know when they finish each task. You want to inspect the job.

◇ Praise them when they follow through with a job assignment and comment on the quality of the work (*"You've done a good job here"*); the family (*"You're really helping the family"*); personal growth (*"You're carrying through with your responsibilities. You're growing up"*).

◇ Give them a special reward when possible (*"Since we've all worked so hard on getting this house ready for Grandma, let's clean ourselves up and go out to eat"*).

When the above explanations/incentives don't work, try consequences. Remember that all children prefer a neat and clean house, and they need a parent in control.

Creating new family customs

Diane said, "The first Christmas after we split up, I went out and bought the kind of Christmas tree Dave used to get and put it up in the living room. I bought the same kind of lights that Dave used to put on our tree. I bought the same colored balls and tinsel. I started putting all this on the tree, and then I thought, 'I'm doing everything just the way Dave used to do it. This is absurd. I didn't like it then, and I don't like it now. I can set up a different kind of tree.' And then the whole holiday season took on a new sense of beginning."

> 66 A holiday is an obvious time to change some of the traditions to suit the needs of the new family structure. And anything goes. 99

Traditions are powerful framers of our definitions of who we are as family. There can be a sadness, a sense of loss, when family traditions change due to divorce. But it is an obvious time to change some of the traditions to suit the needs of the new family structure. And anything goes. The single mother has complete freedom to design new traditions using food, family, friends, decorations and details as her variables. If you and the children like to go for a bicycle ride every Sunday afternoon, you can do it. If you want to order pizza every Friday night when you come home and collapse from a week of work, you can do it. If you want to invite a foreign college student to share your family's Thanksgiving meal each year, you can do it. Whatever heightens you pleasure in family and life, you can do it. And the family will profit.

Saying good night

If you have pleasant memories of a parent tucking in your bedcovers when you went to sleep as a child, you know how important bedtime can be in conveying a sense of well-being to a child.

From babyhood to age 18, the ritual of bedtime usually declines. What a shame, since bedtime is a nice time for a parent and a child to do some sharing that is important for both of them. And teenagers need attention from their mothers as much as infants do; not physical maintenance, but mothering. *So here are a few things to keep in mind for your children at every age through high school:*

♦ *Read a bedtime story.* Turn off the TV in time to read to them; as they get older, the books just get more interesting. Children who can read may enjoy sharing the reading with you. If you are especially tired one evening, you can ask them to read a short section for you. At age four, the book might be Margaret Brown's *Goodnight Moon*; at age 17, it may be Stephen King's *It*. Select whatever you and your children can enjoy together.

♦ *Tell your child* that something he or she did during the day pleased you.

♦ *Give your child* a kiss and a hug.

♦ *Say "I love you."*

♦ *Tuck them in bed* (for older children, do this for as many years as they will let you).

Societal pressure to have things

It's built into everything from coveting country club membership to toys and cereals advertised on TV with Saturday morning cartoons. Our society is full of overconsumers. Shop until you drop. Teens and pre-teens cruise the malls ceaselessly. Window shopping is an acceptable date activity for adults. Our clothes are useful while they are stylish (especially teenagers' clothes), and then we discard them. Garage and yard sales feature yesterday's treasures which have become today's junk. Yesterday's hi-tech computer has been bumped by the next generation. On and on it goes, the buying and selling of fast-outdated merchandise.

This fast-paced consumption of goods works against the typical single mother who is struggling to meet financial commitments. It helps to value people above things, and we can simplify our lives

- ◆ Recognize areas of our lives where we overconsume and work at cutting back.
- ◆ Value things for their function first and their newness second.
- ◆ Be creative in making our environments attractive and in maintaining quality interactions with family and friends which are not dependent on heavy outlays of money.

The haves and the have nots

You look at your children, and you don't want them to suffer in any way in this world. They have already suffered through the divorce or separation process, and you probably feel some regret about that. But to the extent you can protect them from harm and deprivation, you will. This includes keeping them from feeling poor, even though your income has been dramatically reduced since you separated from your ex-partner.

> **66** I don't know how I'm going to pull off that birthday party, but I'll find a way. **99**

A typical single mother statement is "Mary Beth's birthday is coming up, and I've got to give her a big party. We always give her a big birthday party. But I just paid a car repair bill, and I'm a month behind on two other bills. . . . I don't know how I'm going to pull off that party, but I'll find a way."

It is a tribute to single mothers that they hold their families together financially through hard times, especially in the first five years following a divorce. Somehow, children continue with their allowances, dance lessons, camps, travel and clothing allotments. Meanwhile, their mothers brown-bag their lunches, use fingernail polish to stop the runs in their nylons, skip some haircuts, do not go out on the town at night and, in many ways, cut corners and juggle finances in order to make sure their children do not "go without."

Five to eight years after the divorce, the mother is often in better financial shape because by then she is over the initial financial hump of setting up a new household. She has received promotions or raises or has found a better-paying job. She may have formed a relationship with another man, and she might be benefiting financially from that relationship.

But during those initial difficult years following separation, on those occasions when the mother has to say no to her children, she may feel guilty. Maybe she can't get the allowance together one week, and she asks the children to wait one more week and she will pay them for two weeks then. Maybe she has to reduce the allowances for a while. Maybe she has to buy ice cream bars at the store instead of taking the children out to a soda shop. The best thing in the world for those children is for the mother to explain calmly that she needs to cut a few corners to ensure that she has enough money to meet all their expenses.

One mother told her children that due to her reduced income, the children could pick one new item of clothing for the new school year. The daughter chose a pair of designer jeans. The son chose a jacket with the right brand name and look. The mother purchased the other clothes they needed at discount stores or used clothing stores. The two children valued their chosen clothes much more than the whole wardrobes they had been able to buy before the divorce.

One eight-year-old boy was embarrassed by a tan, second-hand raincoat bought at a used clothing store across town. He was somewhat mollified when his mother explained it was highly unlikely that any of his friends had previously owned the raincoat. She stopped worrying about this when, the next morning, he raised one arm á la Peter Falk and said "Well, Mom, here goes Columbo!" and ran out the door into the rain to catch the school bus.

I remember another mother, Maxine, who sat her two oldest children, ages 12 and 10, down at the dining room table and explained to them with paper and pencil what the monthly budget was. The children saw that every month the mother fell $25 behind in basic expenses. After that, there was much less "I want" this and that and "Why can't I have . . . ?" It was one of the best economic lessons the 10-year-old girl ever learned. She began to respect not only the power of money but the effort her mother made every day when she left for work. That little girl grew up to be the author of this book.

Children are both vulnerable and resilient. If your child is well fed, warmly dressed, safely housed and well loved, a little doing without for a period of time can teach your child about economics, sacrifice, the value of love over things—and the strength of riding through tough times together.

Cheap clothes

- ◆ Discount stores.
- ◆ February and July sales, when you can find new clothes 50-75% off.
- ◆ Used clothing at places like Goodwill and consignment stores. They always carry some designer label clothes which were given away by an affluent family. To be successful at Goodwill, you have to go once a month or so, and it helps to have an eye for good design, diamonds among the coal.
- ◆ Hand-me-downs from relatives or from a family whose children are bigger than your own. You can approach someone you know and suggest a barter arrangement; trading clothes for skills. You can put up a note, with your name and work phone number, at a grocery store in a wealthy area of town. State that you would like to buy used clothes and which sizes you need. You can do the same in the newspaper classified ads one Sunday; this costs money, but if you connect with someone, you save a lot of money very quickly.
- ◆ You can pass on your own children's good clothes to another single mother.

Jobs

When children get to be about ten years old, they may want to start earning their own money. At first, they think any money they make is "a good deal." Then when they start comparing earnings among their friends, they find that some jobs pay more money than others. More good economic lessons.

The first question in most children's minds is, "How much do I charge?" They can ask around at school and get the latest information on fees. Or they can call up businesses listed in the Yellow Pages and ask how much they charge for the same services; these businesses usually employ adults, however, and can charge higher fees.

Babysitting. The American Red Cross has chapter offices in many towns which offer a six-hour course called Babysitting. Girls (and an occasional boy) from age 11 and up are taught basic safety, how to change a diaper, activities and games for children which are age-appropriate, etc. Some chapters offer a referral service to match babysitters with prospective clients who have been screened by the Red Cross. Cost of the course is $10.

It is, of course, the responsibility of every mother to screen your child's potential employers—name, address, phone number, occupation, ages of children, perhaps even references from other babysitters—before you let your child babysit. When you don't know the people, go meet them first, then decide if the family is suitable as a client for your child. As a parent of a minor, you have every right to monitor your child's activities, including jobs. If the first time goes well, then your child can operate on his or her own.

You'll want to be sure your child knows where to reach you, if you will not be at home, and understands how to call for help in an emergency. Fire, police and hospital numbers should be posted near the hiring parent's telephone, even if your town has a 911 emergency hotline, along with information about where the hiring parent is going and the phone number at that location. Some parents do not do this as a matter of course, while others provide reams of notes for their babysitters and call home to check on things during their absence.

When your child wants to start working, with your permission, he or she can call up family friends and go to homes in your neighborhood where young children can be seen playing and offer babysitting services to the parents.

Yard work. Raking leaves, mowing lawns and other yard work is good exercise and can be good money for a child. Again, your child can go through the neighborhood looking for the lawns that need mowing, and offer services. Children should have had some solid practice at home before attempting to do someone else's yard. It's a good idea, too, to find out whether your child might be expected to do heavy lifting beyond the child's musculoskeletal capacities for that age.

Teenagers can design their own summer job so that they can work and play on their own schedule. Two teenagers can team up, post a sign on a telephone pole at a busy intersection (if your town allows this), post a card at grocery stores, put an ad in the newspaper classified section, go door to door offering services (or putting a flyer on front doors). Many jobs require unskilled labor; they may be time consuming, and (in the summer) hot, and some adults are happy to have someone else do it, such as:

- ◆ Walking dogs
- ◆ Feeding pets while owners are on vacation
- ◆ Grocery delivery for senior citizens
- ◆ Washing windows and screens
- ◆ Hauling away junk
- ◆ Fence painting
- ◆ Other odd jobs

Your teen should avoid overstraining (especially macho teen boys 14-18), second-story ladder jobs, roof work, working with chemicals and power saws and overexposure to the sun. Be sure your child has adequate health insurance in case of a work accident.

Hiring out to one employer. Federal law permits children to start working at age 14 for employers who offer minimum wage or more. They can work in non-hazardous jobs (retail work, offices) for up to three hours per school day, up to eight hours per non-school day, up to 18 hours per school week and up to 40 hours per non-school week. They must work between 7:00 a.m. and 7:00 p.m.

At age 16, they can work unlimited hours in any non-hazardous job.

At age 18, they can work in hazardous jobs, as well.

In addition to the federal laws, each state has child labor laws which also work to protect your child from possible labor abuse. Both state and federal labor bureaus deal frequently with employers who break the child labor laws, either by design or through ignorance. It's a good idea for you, as a parent, to know the laws and make sure your child's employer adheres to them.

Some teenagers, especially those who are 16 to 18, can get caught up in working too many hours per week, to the detriment of their schoolwork. If your child's grades start slipping, you can put a limit on his or her work hours until the grades come up. That's a strong incentive for your child to pay more attention to schoolwork.

CHAPTER 6: Teenagers

Teenagers—many books have been written on the life and times of these wonderful creatures. They sometimes seem to come from another planet or a world of their own. All their glands are set on high ooze, like wet butterflies who have just emerged from the chrysalis of childhood. Their energy, ready humor and eagerness for life can be contagious.

In this stage of life, their friends take on almost supreme importance. The herd instinct is strong, and they want to dress like, act like and talk like their friends. They want to be with their friends, sometimes day and night. And when they aren't with their friends, they want to talk with them on the phone.

Get to know your teenager's friends

Make them feel welcome in your home, even if you see them only in the kitchen and on the way to your teenager's bedroom to listen to music and talk. If your teenager goes over to a friend's house, get the phone number and the name of the parents. It is OK to call up the parents and introduce yourself as the mother of _____ and say that you just wanted to say hello, that you think it is a good idea for the parents to have a support network going for their children. Having the names and phone numbers of your teenager's friends and their parents comes in handy if your teenager turns up missing one day (which happens for a number of innocent and otherwise reasons) and you have to track him or her down.

Teenagers need limits

They need to know what is expected of them—how much work around the house, how late they may stay out at night, how often they can use the car, and mothers need to keep those limits firm in order to have peace of mind, keep the teenagers safe and let the teenagers know they love them. Limits indicate love.

Touching

U.S. teenagers, especially boys, don't get touched much by their parents. When society withholds touching, it withholds basic communication. Studies show that it takes 12 hugs a day to promote maximum emotional health in a person. And there are other acceptable ways to touch: hair touseling, a hand resting on a shoulder, a playful punch in the arm, a shoulder or back rub, a foot massage, a kiss on the cheek, even a handshake or hand-on-hand slap. Teenagers get the same kick out of being touched by someone who loves them that we all do. It means "I love you, I like you, I care."

Personal expression

Crazy hair, dress, behavior and music can be irritants to parents. If you go to a junior high or high school, you will see that what looks crazy in your home is quite ordinary at school. Hair may be the biggest issue to parents. Girls and boys may wear their hair so that one eye is exposed and one eye is covered up by a falling shock of hair. They may shave part of their heads, spike or mousse hair into strange shapes and otherwise practice teenage head art. You can fight it or not; that is a personal decision. But to the extent you can allow them to express their individuality (or their group identity) through dress, hair, music, you can save more energy to fight larger battles—such as grades, drugs and sex. One rule to consider is that as long as it doesn't hurt them or someone else, or violate your moral standards, they are free to experiment. And that is, after all, what they are doing. If they confine their experimentation only to dress, hair and dance, then count yourself lucky.

Experimenting with values

Teenagers may love their mothers, but it is their job to create identities separate from their parents, and so there is an emotional drawing away at this time in their lives. It is easy for parents to let go too soon, to stop monitoring their teenagers who seem so able to take care of themselves. Or if the teenagers are experiencing trouble signs, it is tempting to hold your breath, shield your eyes and hope whatever it is will go away. But while teenagers are able to care for their own bodies and get around town by themselves, they do not always make wise choices about how they spend their time, experimenting, as they are, with alternatives to your value system.

The story of Laura's blue year: Laura, a straight-A, seventh-grade student, brought home a report card one day with an F. Her father—the parents were divorced with joint custody—was astounded. It was as if his world had turned upside down; grades were very important to him. When he asked his daughter why she failed, she told him, "I just wanted to know what it was like to get an F." However creative that response might appear, Laura's father was not amused. Her mother was more curious than angry. Both parents were concerned. They met with Laura's teachers and the school counselor, who said, "Many of our students run into problems in junior high. Sometimes it seems like it is the norm for passage on into high school."

The father arranged for regular counseling for Laura, insisted she do more homework, bought her organizers, and did all he could think of to help his daughter get back to her straight A's.

All of this did no good. She made poor grades for most of the year, to her father's frustration. And she was frustrated with her home situation at her father's house. Near the end of the year, her teachers told her that if she did not pick up her grades, she would not be able to participate the next year in the program for gifted students that the school offered and in which she was currently enrolled. Like magic, all her grades broke 95, and she was back on track in school. Even so, her problems continued at her father's house, and at one point she suggested to her mother that she might run away. Then summer came along, with camp, vacations, free time. Fortunately the communication problem between Laura and her father's household resolved itself, and she started her eighth grade year in better shape all around.

Like measles, some adolescent difficulties simply have to be borne and worked through to resolution. As with physical diseases, some children will suffer more than others. Beginning in junior high, teenagers can have problems. **The biggest concerns that teenagers voice, as a group, are**

♦ Pregnancy
♦ Sexuality
♦ Sexually transmitted diseases (AIDS)
♦ Relationships
♦ Birth control

Teenagers are looking for guidance in these areas, and the mother who is knowledgeable and informed about these issues can look for opportunities to bring them up for discussion in a natural way—in response to a television program, a newspaper article, a popular song on the radio.

Sex

This is a subject which each parent handles in a different way. Most teenagers have their first sexual encounter before they graduate from high school. With this high level of sexual activity, it makes sense to give teenagers solid information on venereal diseases, especially AIDS, condoms, safe sex and birth control.

Teenagers bear nearly 20 percent of all babies born in the United States; 96 percent of unmarried teenagers keep their babies (Consortium on Adolescent Pregnancy and Parenthood, Nashville, 1989). Again, it makes sense to educate both girls and boys about their sexuality, how pregnancy occurs and how to prevent pregnancy—every method from abstinence to birth control pills. Planned Parenthood is an organization which has specialized in sex education for years. Local offices have free brochures available, and classes are offered from time to time on sexuality and communication themes.

Ina May Gaskin, writer, lecturer and director of The Farm Midwifery Center in Summertown, Tennessee, writes, "From my perspective, there seem to be three distinct ways of dealing with sex education . . . *you don't tell them anything* and they learn what they can from the barn [or the streets]; *you don't tell them anything* but let them watch "Dynasty" and "Dallas" [sex without the hard work and consequences]; and *you tell them a lot.*"

Just say "No"

Peer pressure is strong in teenage years, strong enough to override what your child knows you want him or her to do. With sex, as with drugs, your child is going to make up his or her own mind. Once you have outlined the physical dangers, the legal risks, the moral teachings and the societal consequences of drugs and sex, that's about all you can do.

One of the best responses for a boy or girl under pressure to have sex is "I'm not ready for that yet." To a rebuttal, they simply reaffirm, "But I'm not ready for that yet." It's a nice way of saying no. If someone turns away from your teenager because your teenager says no to drugs or sex, that person does not respect your child's right to make his or her own decisions and is not a worthy friend.   Your child already knows the risk in losing a friend by saying "no." In fostering your child's self-esteem, in listening to your child, in praising your child's efforts to question authority which, in this case, is the peer group, you are supporting his or her efforts at autonomy and the triumph of selfhood.

Listening to your teenager

Whatever your teenager says is important to him or her. The best way that you can encourage your children to open up to you is to take what each child says seriously and respond with respect for his or her personhood. Try not to be personally offended by what your teenager says. One Washington State mother says of her daughter's teenage years, "I learned not to let her bait me." Where you disagree, state that calmly and coolly, along with the reason why. By the time teenagers are 14, they are making up their own minds about things, and all you can do is continue to present your values, your reasons, your life view in a calm and consistent manner and hope that you and your child can maintain an open line of communication. Where teenagers are concerned, as one father said, "Make every effort to keep up that communication with your child, 'cause you can lose it quick."

It helps to keep your own sense of inner balance through these years when your teenager seems so serious about life, so emotionally charged, so cocky and so frightened. Both you and your teenager need that balance, plus a little humor wherever you can find it to lighten the atmosphere and enjoy each day just a little more.

Signs of trouble

When you can't get your teenager to behave in ways which are acceptable, you've got trouble. Typical problems parents agonize over are low grades, lying, bad-influence friends, drugs, sex, not knowing where their children are or what they are doing, materialism, skewed values.

The following is a letter from a woman to her friend whose teenage son was showing signs of trouble:

"I know many junior high and high school kids who have a hard time. My neighbor's daughter, for example, good-time Kimberly, has been arrested for shoplifting, has been suspended from school and has sneaked out of the house at night to spend the night with friends on the prowl. Her mother is afraid she will pair up with her friend and run off to another city for an adventure at some point. The mother is talking about the painful possibility of her daughter having to move to a home for troubled youth because the mother can't control her.

"The majority of prisoners with whom I work were hot-blooded young men when they got into trouble. School was a bore. Warm-hearted women and fast money were strong on their minds. They were looking for short cuts and were willing to take big risks and break rules. They were not asking 'What's right?' or 'How will this affect my loved ones?' but 'How can I have a good time, get what I want and not get caught?' They made mistakes because they weren't willing to walk away from trouble—but that's the price of freedom.

"A few of the inmates are very bright. Prison is a kind of time out to reflect on how they intend to live their lives in order to achieve their goals. That's somewhat idealistic, but operative. But as one of my favorite inmate friends says, 'Hell, after I was in here for a week, I knew I wasn't going to do something to get me back in prison again. They could have let me go.' He has been incarcerated four years and is up for parole next month. In so many ways, he's a nice guy.

"All I know is that teenagers have to go through their own processes. They are making their own decisions. By age 16 they are already set in their world view until a pivotal experience comes along to jar them into rethinking that world view. I think one of those pivotal points is moving out of their parents' house. Another is having a child. It all works on us to sand off the rough edges. Here I am 41 years old, and I'm still learning, still trying to fine-tune my own process."

If you suspect your child is headed in the wrong direction—through "acting out," withdrawing from family and friends, refusing to go to school—you can explain your concern and get information from a counselor at your child's school, your child's physician, the police department, drug testing centers, a shelter for runaways or other residences for troubled youth. Professionals who are used to dealing with troubled youth will be able to give you some immediate feedback about your problem and give you some helpful options in dealing with the situation. Keep on calling different resources until you get some answers that make sense to you in your situation.

ToughLove is an organization for parents who are having trouble controlling their children. The book by the same name (in paperback) has an introduction by Ann Landers. The idea behind ToughLove is that being "tough" is sometimes the best expression of love. For children who will not abide by your house rules, ToughLove has some answers. Each local chapter conveys the message that "ToughLove may not work for every child, but it works for every parent." Parents find support from other parents in the same boat, and they find helpful options to try which have worked for other parents: behavior modification techniques, learning how to enforce loving limits for your child, phone numbers of other ToughLove parents to call in an emergency and much more.

Your troubled teen can benefit from talking things through with other troubled teens, expressing anger, sorting out values, admitting problems. Teen support groups led by competent counselors exist in many towns.

A happy ending

Gina was out of control. At 16 she had been in trouble at home, at school, with the law. He mother was unable to set effective limits on her behavior. After the third time Gina ran away, her mother took her to court and had her declared uncontrollable. She became a ward of the State's Department of Human Services with a social worker assigned to her case. That same day she was given a drug test which determined she was using. Her social worker placed her in an in-patient drug rehabilitation facility in a rural area, paid for by the State. After seven weeks, Gina had completed the program (including some school make-up work), and she was moved to a highly structured group home with a home school and intensive counseling which the hospital determined was the next important step toward Gina's taking responsibility for her life. While in the hospital, Gina told her mother, "If I had not come here, I don't know what would have happened to me. I felt like I was going crazy. I didn't know how to stop."

Through no fault of her own, Gina's mother had to entrust her daughter to the care of professionals who were able to help. Though mother and daughter both missed living together, they also knew that it would not work for them until Gina went through a process of recovery. Giving up custody did not mean giving up loving or giving up communicating. Both mother and daughter gained from the process.

The clock keeps ticking

By the time your children are teenagers, it is clear that you have only a short time left with them. Your goal is to raise them to lead independent lives, which means they will probably move away from you, possibly at about age 18, when they are no longer minors, some to work, others to college. Sometimes remembering how soon they will be gone gives you a little more patience, a little more understanding, a little more grace under fire.

Where teenagers are concerned, as one mother said, "It's amazing how smart I'll be by the time they are 25." Another mother says, "My children put me through the grinder and polished off all my rough edges. I'm a different person, and a better person, for it. Now I'm in good shape to enjoy my grandchildren, too." For most of us, it all happens in a blink. Enjoy your teen.

CHAPTER 7:   Child Care

Choosing a preschool or child care center

Without child care, a mother with young children can't work outside the home. But finding quality care in your area at an affordable price is difficult. Many single mothers are forced to choose child care on the basis of 1) price; 2) an available space at the center; and 3) quality—in that order.

True stories: When Mandy went to pick up her daughter at her babysitter's house one Tuesday evening, the babysitter said she was closing down her operation that very evening. Mandy would have to find another sitter because the babysitter had gotten a job outside her home.

Neb, who worked nights at a convenience store, was in danger of losing her job if she couldn't find a new sitter for her daughter right away. A friend told her about a family on her street who took care of kids. Neb took her daughter over there that night. There were no other children. Neb felt funny about the home and called two hours later to check on her daughter. No one answered the phone. She left work to check it out. When she got there, another neighbor said that the people "took the little girl and left in the car." Neb panicked. She called the police. Later, they found the couple at another house in the general neighborhood. Neb snatched her daughter out of the clutches of those people who, she feels to this day, were going to ferry her daughter away to be sold for adoption.

A printed flyer on a university bulletin board read: "Quality care offered in my home for a few special children. Tender loving care by professional with degree in early childhood education.

> 66 A printed flyer on a university bulletin board read: *Quality care offered in my home for a few special children. Tender loving care by professional with degree in early childhood education. Attention and guidance given to motor and cognitive development. Daily journal kept on your child's activities and progress. $500 per month. Call _____.* 99

Attention and guidance given to motor and cognitive development. Daily journal kept on your child's activities and progress. $500 per month. Call _____."

As mothers, we need to shift our priorities around to looking for quality care first and second for an affordable price. If we have to settle for less than ideal care at some point, we can still look around for another solution at the same price which will upgrade our child's day care.

Make appointments to visit the centers in which you are most interested. After you find a program that you like, drop in unannounced and review the facility again. Plan an extended visit to the center or home with your child before his or her first full day so that you and your child will get to know the caregiver. This visit will ease your child's adjustment into the new program.

Ways of locating programs include
◊ Making a list of child care centers and providers you already know of in your community or near your work.
◊ Asking for recommendations from neighbors, friends, co-workers.
◊ Calling the Department of Human Services for a list in your area.
◊ Checking the Yellow Pages listing.

When you call a potential child caregiver, find out
◊ The availability of care (there may be a waiting list)
◊ Hours
◊ Fees (usually $50 - $125 per week; discounts for second child)
◊ Additional costs, such as supplies or overtime fees.

Evaluating the facility

Licensing. All programs providing care for five or more children are required to be licensed by your state (except in a few states which do not yet have licensing requirements). These state licensing standards are for the protection of your child. You can find out what constitutes these minimum standards by calling your state's Department of Human Services. Make sure the center you are looking at has a current license.

Centers with fewer than five children are usually operated in private homes. Some of these caregivers apply for licenses, as well, for business reasons. If you are considering a home setting that does not have a license, you will have to monitor standards yourself.

Staff. Check the qualifications, training and experience of the director and staff. Ask about annual training, staff development, staff turnover and how employee references are checked. Day-care staffers rank in the lowest ten percent of U.S. wage earners, making less than a parking lot attendant—a fact that contributes to an average staff turnover rate of 36 percent a year.

Adult-child ratio. State licensing requirements vary. A guiding principle is the smaller, the better. The State of Tennessee offers the following:

Age	Required	Recommended
6 weeks-15 months	1:5	1:4
15 months-35 months	1:8	1:6
3 years	1:10	1:8
4 years	1:15	1:10
5 years	1:25	1:15
6+ (after school care)	1:25	1:15
Group sizes		
3 years	20	10
4 years	20	15
5 years	25	15

Operations. Look for posted menus, planned activities and daily schedules. Ask about written policies, discipline policy and emergency procedures. Ask to see the kitchen while a meal is being prepared and check out the bathroom the children use.

Outside play. This is important for each child's well-being. Inspect the playground and equipment for safety and maintenance. Ask if children go outside each day. Make sure they are never left unattended while outside.

Field trips. Ask if you are notified before any field trip or activity away from the center. Check transportation safety. Are there seat belts or car seats? The number of adults supervising a field trip should be twice the number for that group at the center.

Parent involvement. Ask about opportunities for parent involvement and communication. Do you feel welcome when you drop in early? Can you have lunch with your child? Are parent conferences encouraged? Is there a newsletter?

Special activities. Many large programs offer dance, music, gymnastics, computer classes, etc. Are the teachers in these enrichment programs trained to work with children?

Your child's temperament. Will he or she enjoy the benefits of a larger program with more activites or be more comfortable in a smaller environment?

Trust your own instincts. Does the caregiver seem like a competent, dependable and caring person with whom to trust the care of your child?

Infant-toddler care assessment

◇ Every facility should have a professional overseeing the facility —a person who knows about infants and how they develop.

◇ A consistent relationship with one adult is very important for infants. Positive bonding and attachment provides them with the emotional security and energy to develop well. High staff turnover is detrimental to bonding.

◇ No physical punishment of any type should be used on infants and toddlers.

◇ Are bottles propped or lying in cribs or playpens? Propped bottles can cause ear infections, strangulation and an insufficient food intake.

◇ Are parents required to label bottles and food to avoid mix-ups?

◇ Is there a refrigerator in the room so caregivers don't have to leave children unattended to get bottles and food?

◇ Are the crib sheets changed and laundered as needed?

◇ What is the procedure for toilet training? Children should not be forced to sit on the potty for long periods of time.

◇ Is there a specific diapering area? Is it located close to a handwashing facility?

◇ Is there a tightly-covered container with plastic liners that are used for diaper disposal? Is this inaccessible to toddlers? Is this container emptied twice daily into an outside garbage receptacle?

Three- to five-year-old care assessment

◊ Are positive self-concept and independent growth promoted through self-help skills, decision making and problem solving?

◊ Is language development fostered by encouraging children to participate in conversations and discussions, activities with books and flannel boards, opportunities for dramatic play and questioning?

◊ Are children allowed creative expression through arts, music, exploration of environment and play?

◊ Is art a form of self-expression involving creative exploration of materials, with limited use of worksheets and teacher-made products?

◊ Are there opportunities for community awareness through field trips, parental visits and teacher use of community resources?

◊ Do teachers, through observation of children, develop a curriculum that is challenging and based on individual and group needs, interests and abilities?

◊ Does the program emphasize sharing, waiting turns, enjoying being an active participant in group behavior?

◊ How do kindergarten and first-grade teachers in public schools rate this facility in terms of other children's school readiness after having attended the facility? You can call or visit with the principal of one or more schools in your area to find out.

Health care provisions

Find out about the center's policy on children who become ill on the premises. Is there an area where they can isolate a sick child from others? Are children encouraged to wash their hands, especially those with runny noses? Are all parents notified when communicable diseases become apparent among children who attend this program?

Sniffles day-care program

More and more cities are offering day-care facilities for children who are mildly ill with earaches, stomachaches, colds and, sometimes, flu, chicken pox and measles when children are no

Before- and after-school care assessment

◇ What are the hours of operation? What provisions are made when school is closed because of holidays, snow, school vacation days and teacher professional development days?

◇ Does the care center provide transportation for the child to and from school?

◇ What are the fees? Is there an extra charge for extended days? (Extended days are when the center is open all or half of a normal school day due to early school dismissal.) Is there a late fee when you pick up your child after the center closes?

◇ What is the daily schedule? How does it change on extended days?

◇ What are some of the planned activities? Are children required to participate in planned activities or do they have a choice about how to spend their time at the center? Are they encouraged to do their homework before they play? Can they watch TV? If so, what programs do the children watch regularly?

◇ Are there toys, games and books available which interest your child, and are they age appropriate?

◇ Are there opportunities for learning new skills? Taking responsibility? Being involved in community activities such as Scouts, sports teams, music or drama lessons? Doing homework? Being alone? Choosing between active and quiet activities?
(*Source*: The Nashville Association on Young Children in cooperation with the Department of Human Services).

longer contagious. A registered nurse oversees the children. Regular day-care centers will often know of the sniffles program, if one exists in your area.

Babysitters

Professional babysitting services are expensive, and most single mothers find other solutions. If you are lucky enough to have relatives to help with babysitting, treat them like solid gold. The remainder of babysitting is usually done by junior high and high school girls, and sometimes boys, looking for spending money.

Babysitting is often the first paid job outside the home a girl has. The Red Cross offers a class called Babysitting to children ages

11 and up, the earliest age at which a child can be responsible as a caregiver for a short period of time. When a girl turns 14, she is eligible to work for minimum wage establishments and may give up her lower-paying babysitting jobs to scoop ice cream at a local soda shop. If she's your babysitter, you have to look for another one.

Ways to find sitters include asking girls who live in your neighborhood, looking for advertisements posted on bulletin boards at local grocery stores or apartment complexes, advertising for a babysitter on the same boards, asking for referrals from other parents in your neighborhood, calling the junior high or high school in your school district where the guidance or vocational counselor may keep a list of students who babysit. You can also try calling job placement offices at your local college or university; this is usually more expensive, but check it out.

Your community may have a babysitting exchange in place. This is a group of parents of young children who babysit for each other for free. There is a system of exchanging time so that each family does an equal amount of providing and receiving babysitting services. Depending on the exchange rules, you can take your child to the sitter's home, have the sitter come to your home, or a combination of both. The sitter may or may not bring his or her children along. While time-consuming, this is a family-oriented and free way to approach babysitting. The children are getting excellent adult care by experts—other parents. And fathers often provide care as well as mothers. If your community does not have one, you might think about starting one. Even two mothers can set up a free exchange between them.

When is a child old enough to stay alone?

There is considerable pressure on single mothers to leave their school-age children without adult supervision because the cost of child care is almost more than the purse can handle. Called "latch key" children because they carry house keys, many begin staying by themselves after school before they are really ready; and their mothers often feel guilty. Women's groups have long fought the battle for better wages for women and sliding-scale fees for child care based on income. When that battle is won, single mothers will not have to make latch key children out of their offspring due solely to financial considerations. Many children of more affluent families care for themselves, even when money is not the deciding factor. In all families, the decision to start the child in self-care should be made by considering the best interests of each child.

Whether a child is ready to stay alone depends on the maturity of the child, the time of day, the length of time the child will be alone—and the willingness of the parent to risk it. Your child needs to be emotionally ready to handle the aloneness; if the child is afraid, he or she is not ready. One way to test the waters is to leave your child alone for half an hour on a Saturday. Then increase that time gradually until you stay away for two hours or however long your child would stay alone after a typical school day. Always make these daylight sessions. Children, even teens, often fear staying alone at night.

You want your child to be physically safe. This means teaching your child safety precautions about strangers at the door, strangers on the phone, fires, knives and scissors, tornados, earthquakes. More than learning facts, your child needs to deal with "What if . . ." situations, such as, "what if a man came to the door with a briefcase in his hand and asked you to open the door." This game-plan development strategy will program your child for a similar emergency situation, should it occur in real life.

Have your child call you at work as soon as he or she gets home. You need to know where your child is at all times. Use the telephone for frequent communication between office and home. Have emergency telephone numbers posted at the telephone, and make sure your child knows which number to call for what: your work number first, an adult friend's number, your ex-partner's number or other relative (if appropriate), police, fire, hospital emergency, other crisis call numbers in your area. Have your child call the adult friend's number as a role-play activity. It is best if that friend is a neighbor who lives nearby and is usually at home in the afternoon.

Emergencies will not be your child's greatest concern. Loneliness and boredom will be. You need to work up a list of activities with your child which he or she can do to keep busy. Remember that after-school centers have a daily schedule of activities for the same purpose. Limit the time your child can watch TV. Reading, drawing, working on the computer, fixing a snack, washing the dog, putting away the dishes, talking on the telephone with a friend—all these and more will help keep your child happier.

Other self-care concerns are rules about having friends over, going out to play and fighting with siblings. When two or more children are in the home after school, is the oldest child in charge? Is this responsibility too great? I strongly suggest any mother considering self-care for her child get the paperback book, *Alone After School* by Helen Swan and Victoria Houston (Prentice-Hall, Inc., 1985). It can help make your decision easier and the resulting self-care situation more satisfactory.

Summers: beyond day care

Whatever your plans are for summer, start forming them in January. Get on the phone with your ex-partner and broach the subject about his vacation plans and how the two of you can fit plans together. If your ex-partner is the type who says, "I don't even know what I'm doing next week, let alone next summer," you've got to work with that. Make your plans and double-check them with him before you put your money down.

When your child no longer goes to after-school care during the school year, he or she may resist going to a day-care center in summer. What your child doesn't grasp is that while it is pretty easy to be lonely or bored in the two hours after school, that is a certainty when staying alone all day long, day after day, in summer. Your word should be the final word, and if you decide on day care, that's it.

There are some options. You may want to split up day care with self-care, such as day care on Mondays, Wednesdays, and Fridays, and self-care the other two days. Some centers will allow this, especially if you can pair up with another parent whose child needs care on Tuesdays and Thursdays. That's a compromise solution that can work well because the child never gets too bored with either situation.

A nice way to think of your child surviving the summer without boredom is like an orange—in sections. If you fill each section with a different activity, you will be helping to pace your child through what could otherwise be a tedious three months. Choices for what to do with your child include day care, self-care, paid jobs, volunteer jobs, camps, visits with relatives, visits with friends, family vacations.

Day care, self-care and paid jobs are discussed elsewhere in this chapter.

Volunteer jobs are good opportunities to serve other people, which promotes self-esteem. Hospitals, day-care programs, museums and other organizations use teenagers and sometimes younger children as volunteers. In some towns, the American Red Cross has a list of volunteer opportunities approved for teenagers. Other sources are your mayor's office, the YMCA and YWCA, your child's school counselor and some county or municipal agencies. Think about your child's interests and how he or she might apply one of them to a volunteer situation. Some volunteer jobs turn into paid part-time jobs as the child gains experience.

Camps—their name is legion, and their prices can vary from about $65 a week to over $250 a week. There are day camps and overnight camps. You can find out about camps in your area from talking with other parents: of your child's friends, in the neighborhood and at work. The YMCA, Boy Scouts and Girl Scouts all offer summer camps. Area churches and synagogues often have summer programs, some of them free. Many day-care centers offer summertime activities which are more like day camps than sitting services. Children are taken to swimming pools, movies, on excursions to zoos and play sports and other outdoor activities—all at prices less than private camps.

These are the variables with camps: price; number, sex and age of campers; length of stay; activities available; facilities (cabins, tents, river, ocean, mountains, bathrooms, etc.); structured or non-structured (free-choice) time; and adult-child ratio.

Some camps hire former campers to return the following summer as "Counselors in Training," or a similar title, with a camp fee reduction in lieu of wages.

Visits with relatives and friends are wonderful ways for your child to stretch his or her travel wings in a supportive environment, and airlines are wonderful about giving children who travel alone airport-to-airport supervision. For older children, bus or train travel can work well for short trips. Call Greyhound Bus Lines' and AMTRAK's toll-free "800" numbers for more information on age and other restrictions for children traveling alone.

Family vacations bond the family together. And everyone needs a vacation, a time to get out of town, away from the telephone and heavy responsibilities. Even if you are low on cash, you can borrow a tent and do a two-day trip to a state park with the children for very little money. If you do it with a friend and her children, it's guaranteed fun for everyone. Let the children help plan all the details, help with the packing and help pitch the tent! For a list of your state's parks, call or write your state tourist information bureau; you can get the address from the public library reference librarian. While you're at it, ask for information on tourism throughout your state. Your local Chamber of Commerce and AAA Auto Club, if you are a member, also have travel information.

Traveling can become a source of stress, so to maximize your pleasure:

◇ Prepare well in advance.
◇ Notify your employer as early as is practical.
◇ Don't overload yourself with extra work before or after the trip; leave written notes for others to handle your projects while away.
◇ If you have to leave a phone number where you can be reached, make it clear that you should be called only in an emergency, and define an emergency.
◇ Resist the urge to call the office to say hello.
◇ Allow a day before you leave to pack and another day before you return to work to unwind and relax.

CHAPTER 8:   Life with Dad

Talking about your ex-partner

Love game

Tales of two houses

When your children don't want to
   visit Dad

Maintaining communication when
   the children are away

Fourteen-year-old Michael said to his father, "My life has been kind of rough—you and Mom arguing and all, and then you left us." The facts are that Michael's mother left the father and took Michael with her. So while physically, it was Michael who moved out of the house, his perception is that his father left him. Secondly, Michael sees his father every weekend, yet his perception remains that his father in some way is gone.

Seeing your father part-time is not the same as living with your father full-time and riding out all the daily highs and lows together. So there is a justifiable sense of loss when a child enters into a part-time relationship with a father. This sense of loss is intensified if the father lives in another town, physically removed from the child for long periods, or even when he lives in the same town if visits are few or irregular. And the loss is greatest if the child has no communication at all with the father. It is natural for the child to feel abandoned. To feel cheated. To feel unloved and unlovable. That is why it is so important for the single mother to find ways to support the relationship between the child and the father.

Talking about your ex-partner

When you talk about your ex-partner—and his new wife, if there is one—separate your view of him from your child's view. That is, you might honestly say, "Your father loves you. He does the best he can for you," even though you have major communication problems with him. To "bad mouth" your ex-partner to your children will hurt the children. As long as your ex is not dangerous to the children, you can scrape up a positive image—not perfect, necessarily, but positive—for the children. Even if he has abandoned your children, you can say, "Who knows why people leave? I know it wasn't because you are not lovable. Sometimes, people like your Daddy have problems that take them away from people they love."

Love game

Children may try, consciously or not, to work you and your ex-partner against each other in several ways. They can say, "Daddy lets me ride my bike across the street [so why don't you?]." "Daddy takes us to get ice cream cones every day [so why don't you?]." "I never have to make my bed at Daddy's house [so why do you make me?]." The unfavorable comparisons can go on and on, and the underlying implication is, Daddy loves me more than you. But that's not true, of course, and one way to deal with it is to acknowledge the differences. "Your Daddy has more money that I do, but I love you just as much." "Your Daddy has his rules, I have mine. We both love you."

Tales of two houses

Sometimes children will stretch the truth about what Daddy does or doesn't do. That's one reason why the more communication you have with your ex-partner, the better off you both are. At his house, he may be hearing, "Mommy never makes me take a bath at night; I take it in the morning." And maybe that's true—or maybe not. The next time you talk on the phone with your ex-partner, you can ask, "By the way, do you take the children out for ice cream cones every day?" If so, no problem; if not, then the two of you might want to discuss other tales of the two houses just to see how far your children might be stretching the truth. Then confront them with the discrepancies. False statements will become less frequent if the children know you are double-checking on them.

When your children don't want to visit Dad

I hate it over there. There's nothing to do.
All my friends are here. And there's going to be a great party at Jennifer's house Saturday night. Do I have to go?
Dad just doesn't understand me. It's like, I never do anything right over there.
Sometimes over there I feel like my head is going to burst and I just can't take it anymore. I've thought about, maybe, hiding.

It's painful to think about your child going into a situation that is either boring or harmful. It throws you into confusion. On the one hand, you could use a parenting break. On the other, you want to protect your child. Immediately, questions arise. "Is he neglecting our child?" "Is he mistreating our child?"

What you need is more information. You can get it from your child and from your ex-partner.

When your child doesn't want to visit Dad, ask such questions as
◇ Can you give me specific examples?
◇ How often does this happen?
◇ When do you remember feeling this way the first time?
◇ Are there things about your father's house that you do like?

Tell your ex-partner what your child has said, and ask for his response. You might give him some support by saying, "Look, I'm not trying to criticize you, I'm just aware of a problem with Rick, and I think we need to find out more about it so that we can help change his attitude for the better. What do you think?"

Your ex-partner might make a few trial changes based on what the child has said. He might want to talk with your child on the phone about the problem or in person on the next visit. You and he might agree to reduce the length of the visit temporarily to see if that helps, or to break up the single long visit into two shorter visits. Or in the case of having to miss Jennifer's party, to reschedule the visit and let the child bring a friend along the next time for a change of pace.

Children and parents sometimes go through difficult communication spells that pass, and part of the ongoing tension of family unity is living through the tough times together. The bad times count, too. During those times it is best to listen to the child, sympathize with the child's feelings, but don't make a judgment against the father. Instead, say, "I need more information. Maybe there's a way we can work this out. I know your father loves you, and that you need to be with your father."

At some point counseling may be necessary for the father and child. Try whatever works. If nothing works, and you feel strongly that it is warranted, you can deny visitation and see a lawyer.

Always the goal is not to separate the child from his or her father, but to promote a family relationship in his household, as well as in your own home. Children need fathers.

> ❝ Always the goal is not to separate the child from his or her father, but to promote a family relationship in his household, as well as in your own home. Children need fathers. ❞

Maintaining communication when the children are away

We all like to get letters and phone calls from loved ones far away. When children are away from home for an extended period for holidays, camp, vacation with Dad, visiting other relatives, they need to hear from you. **Here are a few suggestions that have worked for other mothers:**

- ◆ **Call them,** and be sure they are allowed to call you, collect if necessary, when they need to for any reason. If they are too young to talk, sing to them or recite nursery rhymes. While the father may initially resent this intrusion on "his time," without some opportunity for contact by the child with Mom, the child can feel cut off from her.
- ◆ **Send books.**
- ◆ **Send T-shirts.**
- ◆ **Write letters** to them. One mother puts four letters in one envelope to avoid any of her four children getting a letter later than the others.
- ◆ **Draw stories** in pictures to send to younger children.
- ◆ **Cut out pictures** from magazines, glue or tape them to paper, and make up a story to go with them, perhaps offering a choose-your-own ending.

- ♦ **One mother chose a theme:** bears. She sent a series of bear cards every few days.
- ♦ **Send a photo of yourself.** One mother sent a photo of herself taken by her daughter in the park where they often to go play. Another child said on the phone to her mother, "Mommy, I can't remember what you look like!" The mother sent her picture to be put by the child's bed.
- ♦ **Send a storybook** with a cassette recording of the book which you have read onto the tape. For older children, send a cassette recorded letter. They can send you one back on the same tape.
- ♦ **Send a videotape.** Get someone to run the camera to "shoot" you, then you can take over for a film tour of the house, or whatever. Often schools have video equipment, and sometimes they will loan a camera to you for a special event. You can also rent cameras. Check in the Yellow Pages under Video Rental.
- ♦ **Visit them for a few hours** or overnight. This is especially important for preschool children when they are gone for more than two weeks so that they can "see" you and they will not fear you have abandoned them.
- ♦ **Write letters to them that you don't send,** journal-type letters that you just keep, letters which allow you to bare your soul to yourself and your child—even if he or she is too young to understand. It helps you feel connected with your child. Ten or twenty years later, share them with your child.

Communicating with your children in person and while they are away is so important for each child. It is equally important that their father do the same. And in your child's heart, there are no territorial privileges. There is ample room for everyone who loves the child. With that in mind, whenever you find a useful new idea to promote communication between you and your child, you might pass along that idea, for the child's sake, to the child's father.

CHAPTER 9:   Taking Care of Yourself

Fourth of July—
bombs boom in my ear.
Firecrackers crackle and dance.
The street zings alive with freedom.

I'm waiting for tomorrow.
Light up the sky with L-O-N-E-L-Y.
Let the chemicals of my frustration
burst upon the sky in green orange red.
Send up a rocket for my children to ride
high beyond the limitation of their mother.

Fire cracker snapper
spill your pungent smoke
upon the wide-open black night
and FREE Free free ME Me me NOW Now now

"No wonder I'm frazzled!"

A typical single mother's day might look like this:

♦ **Get yourself and the children ready** for work/day care/ school (*"Who left their dishes on the table?" "Have you brushed your teeth?" "Where's your other shoe? Has anyone seen Joey's shoe?" "We're late. Hurry, hurry, hurry."*);

♦ **Overload at work,** gossip, misunderstandings, meetings;

♦ **Go to K mart on your lunch break** to pick up a couple of sale items, then on to the bank, even though you are due back at work;

♦ **Rush to the day-care center** after work to pick up the kids;

♦ **Stop at the gas station** to fill up so you don't have to do that in the morning (the kids are saying, "I'm hungry Mama, what's for dinner?" and you don't know yet);

♦ **Drive home,** pick up the mail, get everyone and everything inside the house;

♦ **Dump the mail and the packages,** thinking, "I'll deal with that later" (meanwhile, the children are dumping their coats, shoes and school items in the same manner);

♦ **Check out a quick-fix dinner** in the kitchen, get that going; and

♦ **Thirty to forty minutes later, everyone is sitting down eating.** The kids are talking over their kid days, laughing, fighting, spilling or saying nothing. In ten minutes, they are done and gone from the table. You eat on in silence. "Can we watch TV?" the children ask. "Yeah," you answer;

♦ **What's left** is dishes, children's baths, bedtime routines, maybe laundry and ironing. You may or may not do these, depending on how you feel;

♦ **When the children are in bed,** the house is quiet. Maybe peaceful, maybe lonely.

Throughout the day, you have been planner, organizer, manager and support staff. You have been mother, father, teacher, nurse, chauffeur, detective, judge, employee or employer, consumer and friend. You are tired. And you know that tomorrow you will get up and do it all over again.

Thank goodness mothers are generally young, because they need all the physical energy they can get to last through all the responsibilities of their days. And, of course, single mothers shoulder those responsibilities alone. On some days, you wind down before your responsibilities do. It happens to everyone, though everyone tries to prevent it.

In order to maximize your energy level for every day, you need to understand and take care of your most important asset: yourself. It is your emotions, your spiritual self, your body and your intellect working well and working in harmony that will enable you to do your best. Single motherhood is like driving through thick fog, especially in the first raw years and when the children are young. But if you can say at the end of the day, "Well, I did my best," then you have prevailed for that day. We all live just a day at a time.

Support group

Our society has overdosed on the "I, me, me, my" philosophy. "I get mine first, and if there's any leftover, you dogs can fight for it." We are urged to be strong and "Do it yourself." Children grow up and move away. Commercials plant self-indulgent appetites in us. And TV programs and movies push violence and sex as ends in themselves. All these things promote the individual as opposed to the group. Yet there is great strength in belonging to and relating to a group. When you are weak, the group can carry you along until you regain your strength. And you find companionship in a group, people with whom to share the human condition and your personal feelings. Having a group to relate to makes the journey of the single mother so much more comforting,

66 *There is great strength in belonging to and relating to a group.* **99**

like salve on a burn. Single mothers often feel isolated. Their need for group support is as strong as at any other time of their lives. Yet, too often single mothers remain isolated, not knowing how to locate—or risk identifying with—a support group. And they suffer needlessly.

For a solid support group, you need to identify five or more good people with whom you can spend time, even by phone, and talk over your problems. These people should include at least one man as a support friend. And they should include at least one other single mother, because she knows exactly what you are going through. Write their names down on paper; if you can't name five, then you need to recruit a few more. Look around at people in your community who warm up to you, people who have befriended you in the past, people whom you trust. Approach them and start a conversation. If they listen to what you say and are genuinely interested in you, and you respond in kind, you are already developing a support relationship. When you have five total, then when one is out of town, one is sick and one is not at home, you still have two to call.

These are the people with whom you can share your deepest, darkest secrets, your fears, your questions, your complaints, your uncertainties, and they will not turn you away or turn away from you. Because they care about you, they are willing to invest in you. And you will invest some time and energy in them, as well. They will act as your emotional shock absorber, so that if you feel high or low, you can call on them to listen and give you feedback. Having a group of people in place to tap into is great. Use them for emotional burdens, friends to go places with, one to exercise with, one to worship with, all to call on in case of an emergency—whatever your support needs are.

Self-esteem

If your self-esteem did not take a severe dive when you separated from your partner, you are the rare single mother. So much of who you were, your sense of personal identity, was tied up with the life you led with your ex-partner that you need to redefine yourself. When you can let go of the past and redirect your view to the present and the future, then you are in control of defining your important new roles. The healing process takes time. Allow yourself time. Learn to value the little things you do. Even getting out of bed in the morning is an accomplishment. Discover yourself all over. Ask yourself, "What do I like?" and give yourself pats on the back for many many jobs well done. You can look at the new you and say, "This is who I am, and I like this person." If we get all our self-value from what we do for other people, thinking that the good works will come back to us, we err. We need to be our own best friends.

A sense of self

Educator and theologian Howard Thurman, who died in 1981, talked about a healthy sense of self being composed of two dimensions of experience:

> *Self-image*—*what we get from interpersonal relationships, seeing ourselves as others see us, and*
>
> *Self-fact*—*that immutable piece of self that undergirds all of our life processes; who we are when we strip away our partner (or ex-partner), our family, our friends, our job, our home and car and all our possessions; who we are that does not change with the years.*

So this healthy sense of self is really two parts in tension—the self-image and the self-fact—weighing against each other. We can go too far in either direction, relying too much on other people's opinions of us or engaging in narcissistic "navel gazing," relying too much on our own view of ourselves. What other people say is important, but ultimately that is a measure against self-fact, a test, and both the inner and outer view are important in defining the person.

It can be a worthwhile exercise to spend two hours all alone and without distractions meditating on "Who am I?" the self-fact question mentioned above. One woman's description of herself after a two-hour reflection session was, "I am a person for whom truth and beauty are essential. I love art. I need gentleness and peace in my life. I shy away from people, but I watch them all the time. I believe in the goodness of people, and that in the end, goodness will prevail. I am not very disciplined, but I have a strong will. I am a strong person. I have certain talents. I care about other people."

Often we hear more from other people about who we are than we hear from ourselves. But only the self can fill in the second dimension of self-fact to balance our view. And knowing more fully who we are enables us to better experience and appreciate our unique personhood and to make life choices that are in harmony with our selves.

Euphoria

Just following a split from their partner, women often feel free, with the wide wonderful world waiting for their golden touch. There is no doubt you are walking into adventure, but the territory is totally new for you in many ways, and you miss the familiarity of the old which is now gone forever. And you may be glad that it is gone forever, but you will begin to grieve for it anyway.

Grief

Every single mother goes through a painful, yet standard, grief process because she has lost her partner. She may also have lost her home, her car, her neighborhood—an entire way of life. Elisabeth Kubler-Ross, a psychologist who has studied and written about grief, lists five basic stages of the process:

1. Denial
2. Loss and depression
3. Anger and ambivalence
4. Establishing a new identity and lifestyle
5. Acceptance of self and others
(*On Death and Dying*, Macmillan, 1969)

This is normal, expected behavior, and it is helpful to know that in going through this grieving process, you are OK and your feelings—all the hurt, rage, frustration, futility—are OK. There are, at the time of this writing 14 million American women divorced or separated from their husbands who are going through, or have already gone through, the same intense emotional experience.

There are so many changes and losses which come automatically with separation, and these take an emotional toll. And the losses continually recur. You might move three or four times, for example, before you settle in somewhere. You are in such a period of whole-life transition that you bounce around a lot, and you experience tremendous mood swings. It's like a body going through a terrible car wreck. It goes to the hospital and gets patched up and sewn up. But it's been broken and bruised, and there is a time of painful healing that has to take place before that body is back to being strong. And that period of painful healing is normal for a body that has just been busted up. Divorce is like that. The grieving/healing process is normal and takes time. Years.

Loss and depression

Janine came to a meeting of single mothers. An attractive, professional woman, she was recently separated from her husband. The time came for Janine to share whatever was on her mind with the group. After three words, she burst into tears and said, "I'm so sorry. I don't mean to be going on like this. I don't usually behave like this. I don't really understand what's happening to me."

"Depression, thy name is Single Mother." Shakespeare didn't say that, but it still holds true that one fact of single motherhood is episodic depression. It comes and goes, depending on the big changes in your life. **Some symptoms are**

- No appetite or eating too much
- Inability to sleep or wanting to sleep all the time
- Inability to function—can't get out of bed in the morning, can't change from one activity to another at work, can't get going
- Somatic complaints—going to the doctor with symptoms for which the doctor can find no cause (internalizing stress, for example, can cause stomach cramps, migraines)
- Feeling sad and hopeless

What can you do about it? Take it a day at a time. Sometimes a step at a time, literally. If you feel you can't move, but you have responsibilities to fulfil, just take that first step, put one foot on the floor. That will get you up and moving.

Find or create a support group of people with whom you can share your emotions, ideally a group of people who are going through the same grieving process.

Give in to your need for isolation. As a part of the healing process, there is a period when you want the world to go away. You feel numb, like a sleepwalker, not emotionally there but going through the motions. Being all alone to reflect on life will help you sort out your experiences and give you breathing room for your heavy-duty emotions.

Make sure you have a regular social life, when you can be with other people, creating new and good memories for your new life.

Turning around a blue day

For the times when your workday turns blue long before your responsibilities are over, try turning it around:

◊ Take a break and think. What are the good things that are happening in your life right now? What do you look forward to in the future—what are your plans and your dreams?

◊ Telephone someone outside of work who loves you and say, "I need someone to tell me they love me." That person will probably say, "I love you. What's wrong?" And you can unload your troubles for a few refreshing minutes.

◊ Laugh. Most offices include someone who knows jokes. Ask him or her to tell you one. Laughter is wonderful medicine, and you don't have to deal with deep, heavy problems in order to feel better fast.

◊ Go for a brisk walk around the building for some exercise and fresh air.

◊ Do something totally different. If you usually drink coffee, get a cup of tea. If you usually take a break with a certain person, invite a third and fourth person to go with you and declare a ten-minute party. Call up a Porsche dealership and ask the price of a brand new car—loaded. Write a personal note to the President of the United States, The White House, 1600 Pennsylvania Avenue, Washington, D.C. 20500. You will get a letter back.

Anger

When you supress anger, it turns into depression. Women brought up in the United States are taught it is acceptable to be depressed and to cry, that it is not acceptable to be angry, that angry women are bitchy women, and bitchy women are not attractive. So unexpressed anger at your ex-partner, your boss, whatever, can translate into somatic illnesses, depression, kicking the dog, abusing the children and abusing yourself.

There is ample reason to be very angry, as a single mother, angry at all the losses you have to endure, angry at your ex-partner, angry at what it means to be a divorced person in our society—"used merchandise," "handicapped," "a failure," "bad news," "second-class."

> 66 Don't carry a grudge. While you're carrying the grudge the other guy's out dancing. 99
> —*Buddy Hackett*
>
> Give it up. Let it go.

It is OK to be angry. Allowing yourself to feel angry and to look at that anger is the first step to getting rid of it in acceptable ways. You can reflect on that anger and follow it to that deep down hurt you feel. Only you can precisely define the hurt—losing your ex-partner, loneliness, no money, no decent job, etc. You ask yourself, "What can I do to make myself feel better?"

First of all, you can let go of your past life. Cinderella did not live happily ever after with Prince Charming. They got a divorce. And once you get that divorce, you need to stop letting the man and the house and the rotten things that happened—and the good—turn into hate which, like acid, will eat you alive. Comedian Buddy Hackett says, "Don't carry a grudge. While you're carrying the grudge the other guy's out dancing." Give it up. Let it go. You need your energy for looking at where you are in life now and forming new hopes, new dreams, new plans—the bricks to build your future.

Exercise is an excellent outlet for anger. If you need to express anger at your ex-partner, for example, one therapist tells her clients, "Get out your lawnmower and whack off every blade of grass as if it were his head. Go bowling, and every pin you knock down is . . ." You get the message. This working out of anger, depression, stress through physical energy feels tremendously empowering. Single mothers have gotten up in the middle of the night, full of anger, and attacked their kitchen floors on their knees, mopping, waxing, polishing. And it works. They end up exhausted, spent of anger, pleased with themselves and able to sleep like babies.

Assertiveness

Some anger is extremely useful in helping us function in life. It enables us to stand up for our own rights, rather than be pushed around by other people. A lot of people give single mothers advice—lawyers, family members, counselors, friends, store clerks, strangers on talk shows, even authors—and much of that advice is probably well meant. But the single mother must ask herself, "What do I want? What do I need?" And when the advice doesn't match those wants and needs, she needs to stand up to everyone and say "No, thank you." If she sees something she wants, or something that needs to be fixed, she needs to confront people about it.

If you have trouble standing up to people, you may need to learn to be more assertive. Many communities have classes in assertiveness training—how to get your own needs met without stepping on anyone else's toes.

Stress

Stress is a physical response to a crisis situation, sending adrenalin pumping through your body to give you the strength to handle the crisis. This is what allows mothers to lift cars off their children in order to save their lives. It's a surge of unusual energy. But when the crisis is another special project your boss just dumped on your desk, the adrenalin can work against you because there is no physical outlet for it.

Stress can manifest itself in your stomach being "tied up in knots," Irritable Bowel Syndrome (severe abdominal pain, bloating, constipation or diarrhea), migraine headaches, lower back pain, skin problems or other physical discomforts.

When you feel stress, you need to identify its cause and come up with a plan of how to handle it. If you find yourself facing a work overload, for example, try to distribute your workload over a period of time, scheduling it at a pace you can handle. Do a form of whole-body relaxation exercise where you lie flat on your back and tighten and relax all your muscles, serially, from your head to your toes. For more information about relaxation exercises, check with your doctor or your counselor, or see the American Medical Association Family Medical Guide (Random House, 1987, p.19). Even if you are at work, when you feel stress you can tell yourself to relax, breathe slowly, move slowly, and carry on. Every time you look at a clock, that is a sign of tension; remember to tell yourself to relax.

At home, try taking a hot bath instead of a shower, sitting outdoors, taking a walk or another form of physical exercise.

Action/reflection cycle

Even in the midst of war, the generals get together to plan strategy for the next battle. Single motherhood is not unlike war, it sometimes feels, and there seems so little time to do anything but rush around getting things done. But there is great value in taking time out to reflect on what you are doing, how you are interacting with others, and how you could do it better next time.

An action/reflection cycle, part of an educational method called Training for Transformation, has been used effectively by educator Anne Hope to teach literacy in both South Africa and the United States (Anne Hope and Sally Timmel, *Training for Transformation: A Handbook for Community Workers*, Mambo Press, Gweru, Zimbabwe, 1973). It can be used by single mothers as well to grab control of their own lives and move forward. It is an active process. You plan time for reflection. You do this, ideally, with a support group, but you can also be helped by a supportive friend in the same way. Whatever your current problem is,

STOP:	Get together with your group/friend.
LOOK:	"What is the problem? What happened?"
THINK:	"How can I do it better next time?" Get new information at this point, if you need it.
PLAN:	What you are going to do next.
ACT:	Leave your reflection session and implement your plan.

For example, your boss comes in and dumps a project on your desk at 4:45 and says you need to finish it before you leave. You look at it and know you won't get away before 5:30. Meanwhile, the children are waiting for you, and you are waiting to get free from work for the evening. You do the work. You get together with your reflection group/friend and state the problem: Your boss repeatedly asks you to stay overtime to finish last-minute projects for him or her. Normally, you gulp and say OK. How can you count on leaving at 5:00? You look for options, you brainstorm all the possibilities you can think of to change the situation, such as 1) tell the boss you are sick; 2) tell the boss your day-care center is going to charge you a late fee; 3) tell the boss you are willing to work overtime twice a month, or whatever, but not on a regular basis, and get him or her to agree to that; 4) check with your boss around noon to see if he or she anticipates any afternoon rush projects, then try to get them early enough to finish by 5:00. Of all the options, you pick number 4 to try next time. That's your action plan. You implement that the next workday. If it works, you have solved your problem. If not, you try another option. Keep trying options until something, or a combination of things, works.

The trick is to make time to reflect so that you can think, plan and act.

Fear

Some time after you and your partner split, a feeling of fear may settle on you. Anything can trigger it—a movie, a story someone tells you, an unfamiliar sound. And that feeling of fear can mushroom until you are overwhelmed with it. You curl up in bed; you hug yourself and rock yourself back and forth; driving the car, you pull over to the side of the road and go through a terrifying panic attack.

Whatever form this feeling of fear takes, it is a real feeling, a clue that something inside you needs some attention. In order to get rid of the fear, you have to name it. You can get out a piece of paper and write down all your fears on it. **Though everyone's fear list would be different, one woman's list looked like this:**

◇ Loneliness
◇ Never having enough money to do more than get by
◇ Something happening to the kids
◇ Growing old alone
◇ Illness
◇ Losing the house
◇ Somebody breaking into the house
◇ Rape

It is important to remember that fear is an emotion. Your head can help dispel the fear. You look at your list and start reflecting, or thinking about, each item. You lump together loneliness and growing old alone, for example. Your insurance against those is friends. Count your friends. If you don't have enough to suit you, recruit more so that you will not be lonely and you will not grow old alone. A man may or may not appear, but friends are always available for you. Other ways of reflecting on your list: getting sick—get exercise, eat right and have adequate insurance; money—think ahead to a time when you will be ready to look for another job that pays more or gives you opportunity for advancement; rape—practice rape prevention, know what procedures to follow if it does happen.

Every potential problem has practical solutions. While we can't always prevent tragedies, we can take some preventive measures and have some plans in place in case they do happen. Life goes on. People survive low points and overcome difficulties. Our friends and our heads are two of our best life tools.

Defining your needs and goals

Mothers often operate on other people's agendas. That is, when someone tells a mother, "I need something," she says "What is it, and how soon do you need it?" and she will do it even if it means she will have to drop what she wanted to do "just this once." When you add up all the just-this-onces, you get a picture of the woman meeting other people's needs to the almost total neglect of some of her own.

One woman's needs list included
♦ Some time by myself every day
♦ Art and music in my life
♦ Time to be with friends
♦ An exercise program
♦ Sleeping in late once a week

Her goals were
♦ To have my master's degree in five years
♦ To buy a condo in seven years
♦ To get one song recorded (she wrote songs as a hobby)
♦ To get the kids through college
♦ To find a man

In order to meet her own needs and achieve her own goals, she had to know what they were. So she wrote them down. Then she had to learn to say no and to ask for help.

Learning to say "No"

We all can look in a mirror and say no to our own reflection with no problem. It's when we are faced with the choice between no and yes when we are looking into the faces of our children, our family, our friends, our bosses and even total strangers that we can have tremendous difficulty choosing to say no. We want to say yes. We want to be liked. We want to help the other person, to make life easier, better, for them. When it's better for them, we feel good. We have worked our little miracle.

"I have other plans" is a nice way of saying no. And the world will not disintegrate. Your plans may be that you want to kick off your shoes and read the Sunday newspaper. Saying "I have other plans" can be easier to present than "I want to read the Sunday newspaper." But you don't have to have a reason, just a phrase with which to say no.

A general statement is handy in many situations, and prevents the other person from trying to convince you that his or her need is more important than yours. **Other handy turn-downs:**

> ◇ *I need to be at home/be alone/go out that night/rest right now/ cook dinner (or whatever—state your need clearly and repeat it if necessary).*
> ◇ *I'm already booked solid that day.*
> ◇ *I can't commit to that kind of a responsibility at this time.*
> ◇ *I have to pick up my kids in fifteen minutes.*
> ◇ *I don't give out my phone number.*
> ◇ *I can't receive calls at work.*
> ◇ *No, thank you.*
> ◇ *I can't possibly afford that (this always ends the request).*
> ◇ *I'm not interested.*

No one will set limits for you. Only you know what those limits need to be, and only you can tell other people when enough is enough. Not everyone is going to be gracious when you say no, but that's their problem. When you meet your own needs first, you will be better able to carry through with what you agree to do for other people. This doesn't mean you can't sacrifice your own needs from time to time for the benefit of someone else. But consider it a rare and precious gift. As a daily way of operating, sacrificing your own needs drags you down slowly and keeps you from being the healthiest person you can be.

And the other people to whom you say no? They find other ways to get their needs met. A child who wants you to drive him across town to play with a friend, for example, can talk with the friend on the telephone and then find another friend to play with or activity to do that does not require you to provide transportation that day. Schedule a trip to the friend's house at a future time when it fits in with your plan. Tell a parent from your child's preschool who wants you to telephone six other parents about a school program that she caught you on a booked-solid evening.

Often it's not that the people aren't worth it or the causes aren't worthy, but your needs and pacing yourself are worthy, too. Whatever time and energy you have left over after your basic needs are met become your discretionary fund with which to say yes to others.

Asking for and accepting help

In our society, the view is that the intact family takes care of its own; otherwise, the family has somehow failed and is subject to shame. A single mother as sole pillar of her family is unable to handle every need and crisis that comes along by herself. If she becomes ill to the point that she cannot care for the children, she needs "outside" help. If her self-image is superwoman ("I'll do it all, come hell or high water"), then, even when she knows she needs help, she may be unable to ask for it.

But we don't need to be in a compact unit. We don't need to be isolated from the world. If we have a support group, or supportive friends, those people are a resource to call on for any emergency.

When I was in college, I would go over to my grandmother's house to rest and relax away from the campus scene. Grandma would hug me, feed me, love me and let me go. Cokes were in the refrigerator, cookies in the cookie jar. It was perfect. But at the end of each visit she would hand me a five-dollar bill at the door. I would always protest, though I always needed cash. One day, she told me that I must take the money, saying it was part of her passing on the help that had been given to her. She told me that a time would come when she would need my help, and that she hoped I would give it. She said there would be other people, all through my life, for whom I could do something, and there would also be times when I would need to take from other people, family and otherwise.

Asking for help outside your family and accepting that help graciously allows someone else to give. And it feels good for them to give. You don't have to wait until you are down and out to ask for things. What are your needs? Do you need a hug? Ask for one, and you'll get it. Do you need to hear a joke? Have some fun? Find a sitter while you do spring cleaning? If you don't ask, no one will know what your needs are. Translate them from feelings inside you into real words that real people can hear. When you ask, give people a clear option, such as, "I need someone to keep the kids while I do some spring cleaning. If you have the time and energy, let me know. But it's OK to say no, because I have other people I can ask. What do you think?" That gives them an easy out, and you don't feel you are imposing on them.

Your children are included here. "I need some privacy" is something children over five will understand. One mother drew a rough picture of herself sleeping in a bed and wrote, "Nap time for Mama." When she needed a nap or some time alone during the day, she would tape the picture to the outside of her bedroom door, and the children left her alone. It takes some energy to ask children to do things for you, but shouldering responsibility is good for their self-esteem. It takes courage to ask someone outside the family. Fundamentally, the single mother needs to enlarge her definition of "family" to include non-relatives but supportive people.

Crisis times

You are never alone. For those times when you feel all alone, when there is a death in the family, when you lose a job—you can wipe away the tears long enough to find a phone number and call someone. Many towns have crisis call phone numbers with volunteers ready to listen to you and to provide you with sound advice and reliable resource people to go to, if you need them. Your local police department would know the number. **For telephone assistance with parenting problems, see page 300.** And one of your best resources is friends. In addition to contacting people, if you are a praying person, a crisis time is a great time to pray.

Journal writing

One way to get in touch with your feelings, express anger, work yourself out of a blue mood and improve your self-esteem is through writing a journal. When you put pen to paper and let whatever is on your mind come flowing out, you find out a lot about yourself. You can clarify your thinking. You can come to decisions. Any old notebook will do to record your thoughts and feelings. A few paragraphs a day, dated, are plenty. Even once a week will work for you, though it's easier to keep at it if you try for once a day.

After the passage of time, you can look back through your entries, and you will be surprised how vividly you recall events you had forgotten. You will also see the progress you have made in your personal journey during a period of challenge and growth.

Caution: do not let your ex-partner find your journal and take it to court, which has happened in one case. And put it away where your children cannot find it and read it.

Counselors

A plumber speaks: "I went to a counselor when I was married to my first wife when we were having some problems, and by the time he got through with us, we were in the biggest mess you ever saw. I've done that once, and that's the last time I'll do it."

A research assistant speaks: "After I left my husband, I started seeing my counselor. I could tell her anything, and she helped me figure out some things. I was so confused. She even talked on the phone to my ex-husband when he wouldn't listen to a thing I said, but he listened to her!"

There are all kinds of people in the world and all kinds of counselors. There are a number of different theories of counseling, too. **So when you look for a counselor for yourself or the children,**

- ◆ Ask for recommendations from friends, health care professionals you may know, etc.
- ◆ Find someone whose personality you and your child like. You can interview a potential counselor over the phone.

And after the first session, you should know if you and your child can communicate well with the counselor. If not, change counselors. Why throw your money away?

♦ Ask what the counseling procedure will involve and how each session will be conducted. Will the counselor give advice, "just listen," use confrontation or what?

♦ How long does the counselor anticipate the sessions will continue, based on your stated need. Some counselors will say, "As long as you feel the need." Others might say, "Let's do eight weeks and then take a look at the situation." Short-term therapy—six to eight weeks—is more often covered by insurance.

♦ What are the counselor's credentials—a Ph.D.? A master's degree? In what subject? At what institution? (Note: A degree does not necessarily mean the person is the best counselor for you. A few very good counselors have no psychology degrees at all. But insurance companies will not pay for counselors without certain degrees; check with your company's policy.)

Paying attention to spirituality

Every human culture includes spirituality in the public and private lives of its people. Spirituality addresses the hunger of the heart to be filled with something beyond self, to communicate with something larger than humankind, to experience the divine in ourselves, in others, and in all of creation.

Becoming a single mother is a transition time full of losses and new challenges which offers a chance to reevaluate everything. There is a natural turning inward. This creates a positive opportunity to contact our spiritual nature, a deepening awareness of the divine within ourselves. There is a transcendence of our own inability to see deeply because we are normally too involved with the routines of life, so that separation brings a shock to our awareness, an entrance to spirituality, a new way of seeing. This gift of deepened awareness leads us to a sense of connectedness with the divine within ourselves, between ourselves and others, and among all created things.

There is a common bond. Soldiers living through days of life and death struggle, prisoners of concentration camps, parents with terminally ill children, and other victims of tragic circumstances speak eloquently about the meaning in their lives provided by a belief in something larger than humankind. It can be the greatest source of strength, everpresent, limitless, and bonding us with the rest of humanity in a community of the divine.

How does one cultivate spiritual experience? It may include worshipping with others in a church or synagogue setting. Allegiance to an organized religion is a way of sharing a personal credo and life values with a community of like-minded people, though spirituality is a fuller experience and a more powerful resource than simply going to church. And for many people, spirituality may exclude public worship altogether. More than one person uses the earliest waking hour to read, meditate and pray as a way of preparing themselves spiritually for the day. Bill Barnes, a minister and community organizer, calls this his hour of income.

Experiencing nature, music, art and even play can be ways of focusing on the connection between the human and the divine. Any activity which focuses our minds and our spirits on the expressive wonder of creation is a spiritual communion, and it strengthens our lives.

Ritual

Ritual is a powerful tool for us to express our feelings and our needs in community as we mark milestones in our lives. Weddings and funerals are rituals. Divorce is not a ritual; it is a legal process. There is currently no widely practiced ceremony recognizing divorce. However, women are creating their own rituals to take care of the gaps where society provides none. For example, on the anniversary of her former marriage, one newly divorced woman had a freedom party surrounded by friends who gave her the love and attention she needed.

Another woman invited her friends and supportive others to a Celebration of a New Beginning following her divorce. People sat in a circle and talked about what the woman had meant in their lives, or how they had made transitions to their own new beginnings. It was a time of intimate sharing complete with singing, prayer and Holy Communion.

A third woman who left her partner and moved back to her home town had a "House Blessing" event which was both a party and a worship experience where people shared their hopes for the woman as she began a new phase of life in a new apartment home, and their thanksgiving that they could renew their friendship with her.

Just as people design their own wedding ceremonies, people can design ceremonies for whatever is important to them, an event that they want to share with a community of friends. It can include words, music, dance, food, whatever best expresses the event. It is one way to turn around potentially sad and self-defeating times, such as the remarriage of your former partner to another woman, into meaningful and memorable times. Ritual can include markers in the lives of your children, as well, such as the symbolic passing into adulthood, much like a bar mitzvah, or a separation ceremony when a son or daughter goes off to college.

Exercise

Low-intensity, aerobic exercise for 45 minutes or more releases tranquilizers equated with morphine. These are endorphins, naturally produced chemicals, and they work to counteract depression. To maintain physical health, exercise three times per week. To improve your physical and mental health, exercise six or more times per week.

Women who have trouble sticking with an exercise program might consider identifying an exercise partner to help with discipline and to make the experience a social one as well.

Your personality matches some sports better than others, according to an article by James Gavin, Ph.D., in *Psychology Today*, ("Your Brand of Sweat," March 1989, pp. 50-57). And the better the match, the more likely you will stay with your exercise program. The article rates 13 different sports—tennis, aerobics, yoga, etc.—for the traits of sociability, spontaneity, discipline, aggressiveness, competitiveness, mental focus and risk-taking. You can score yourself and find a sport which fits you best.

If you are going to begin a new exercise program, it's always a good idea to see your doctor for advice on recommended rates of increased activity.

Nutrition

Caffeine. Large amounts cause an anxiety response, jitters, nervousness, depression. The amount varies with the individual; if you take in more than your body is used to, the negative effects surface. Caffeine also keeps you awake, one reason why offices usually have supplies of coffee, tea, chocolate, and certain brands of soft drinks—all high in caffeine. People who have migraine headaches should keep their caffeine intake the same each day, weekdays and weekends, since varying the intake can contribute to a migraine.

B Vitamins. B vitamin deficiency contributes to depression. Caffeine, alcohol, sugar and stress all cause you to lose B vitamins. Anything that tends to cause you to urinate sends B vitamins out of your body with the fluid loss. This includes exercise. A good high-complex carbohydrate diet should provide you with enough B vitamin for good health.

Recent studies at the University of California at Berkeley show that using C or B-vitamin supplements can have a deleterious effect on you. It's better to get B vitamins from broccoli, kale, romaine lettuce, whole grains, brown rice, and oat bran. You can get C vitamins, a beneficial companion to B vitamins in your body, in canteloupe, apricots and citrus fruit.

Chocolate. This has a physiological tranquilizing effect. Unfortunately, it also has caffeine, sugar and lots of calories.

Too much protein, fat, sugar and salt. That is the title of a chapter in *Jane Brody's Good Food Book: Living the High Carbohydrate Way* (W. W. Norton, 1985). And that about sums up the all-American diet. Fast food is fat food. But when time is short and the kids are hungry, if you fry up a meal in a hurry, or stop by the local burger window, life goes on. If you do it, enjoy it. Still, we all need to remember that our bodies are one of a kind, and the better we treat them the longer they will last. Many physical and emotional problems are affected for better or worse by the fuel we throw into our tanks. And, of course, our children are learning their dietary habits from us.

Eating habits. Single mothers can too easily neglect meals for themselves. They get dinner for the children, such as soup and sandwiches, and then they look around for something for themselves. Or they go with the soup and sandwich, but there is too little satisfaction with the presentation of food. They can find themselves snacking for satisfaction. Or snacking because they have no love relationship.

Many women who weigh more than recommended for their age and height skip breakfast, eat a light lunch, eat a full dinner and snack in the evening. Since we are least active at night, the extra food in the evening turns into unwanted weight. Shifting to eating breakfast, a full lunch, a light dinner and no evening snacks can reduce weight.

The relationship between volume of food intake and exercise affects your weight, as everyone knows. The best summation of weight loss theory I have heard is simply to eat less, exercise more. A possible improvement on that formula is eat right, exercise more.

The regular misuse and abuse of yourself does not do you or your family a favor. Make yourself a priority.

Alcoholism

Johns Hopkins University Hospital, Baltimore, Maryland, asks the following questions of patients who suspect they may be alcoholic:

1. Do you lose time from work due to drinking?
2. Is drinking making your home life unhappy?
3. Do you drink because you are shy with other people?
4. Is drinking affecting your reputation?
5. Have you ever felt remorse after drinking?
6. Have you gotten into financial difficulties as a result of drinking?
7. Does your drinking make you careless of your family's welfare?
8. Has your ambition decreased since drinking?
9. Do you crave a drink at a definite time daily?
10. Do you want a drink the next morning?
11. Does drinking cause you to have difficulty in sleeping?
12. Has your efficiency decreased since drinking?
13. Is drinking jeopardizing your job or business?
14. Do you drink to escape from worries or trouble?
15. Do you drink alone?
16. Have you ever had a complete loss of memory as a result of drinking?
17. Has your physician ever treated you for drinking?
18. Do you drink to build up your self-confidence?
19. Have you ever been to a hospital or institution on account of drinking?

Score:

> one YES—a definite warning that you may be alcoholic.
> two YESes—chances are that you are an alcoholic.
> three or more YESes—you are definitely alcoholic, and you should seek help immediately.

If you are not ready for Alcoholics Anonymous, which deals with alcoholism and other drug abuse, call up a drug and alcohol treatment center in your area and ask for over-the-phone counseling about what your next step should be.

Substance abuse is a crutch to use when you can't handle life without it. Ask Betty Ford, ask Kitty Dukakis—both of whom are recovering alcoholics. The first step is to admit you have a problem. The next step is to find out what your options are. You don't have to commit to anything, but it's good to know what's available for you on that day when you decide to throw away your crutch in order to realize a better, healthier tomorrow.

The Serenity Prayer, said at the close of every AA meeting and other 12-step programs is as follows: "God grant me the strength to accept the things I can't change, the courage to change the things I can, and the wisdom to know the difference."

AIDS

It has all been said before, but single mothers need to recite it like the rosary: protect yourself from AIDS.

One day 13-year-old Lauren overheard her mother talking with a friend about death. After a while, Lauren broke in and said calmly but firmly, "Just don't die before we grow up." Theoretically, since Lauren's brother Jake was ten, the mother had about six years to practice safe sex before she could start playing around with risky sexual encounters. That would leave her a minimum of two years in which to die of AIDS, at which point Jake would be 18 and grown.

Morbid though that scenario is, it points out the heavy-duty responsibility which single mothers shoulder, every day, to protect and raise their children until they are grown. **For safe sex,** the National Women's Health Network in Washington, D.C. recommends that you

- ♦ Always use both a condom and the spermicide nonoxynol 9. It is in contraceptive foams, jellies, and creams and kills the AIDS virus on contact.
- ♦ Use a latex condom for vaginal and oral sex. The AIDS virus cannot get through a latex condom when it is used properly and does not break. Be sure your partner is wearing the condom before penetration.
- ♦ Never have anal intercourse. Condoms are more likely to break, and the delicate rectal tissue is more likely to tear, increasing your risk of infection.

◆ Unless you know your sex partner is not infected, don't allow his semen, urine, feces, or blood to enter your body.

◆ Do not use intravenous drugs. If you do, never use a needle someone else has used.

◆ Your risk increases with each additional partner. Ask questions about past sexual history and drug use. If your partner has used intravenous drugs or had a sexually transmitted disease, that person is at higher risk of carrying the AIDS virus.

◆ Take every precaution against this deadly disease. Your life is much too precious to risk.

Other sexually transmitted diseases (STD)

The more sexual partners you have, the more you increase your chances of one of them having an STD, all of which are caused by various bacteria and viruses. Latex condoms protect you from some, but not all, STDs. Some common STDs are syphilis, gonorrhea, NGU (nongonococcal urethritis), chlamydia, herpes, trichomonas and venereal warts. Of these diseases, some are a nuisance but not permanently damaging; others can cause serious and even life-threatening problems. Some are easy to detect; others have few detectable symptoms. Like cancer, the longer an STD goes untreated, the more dangerous it is to you.

The American Social Health Association lists the earliest signs of STDs occurring "on or near parts of the body used in sexual activity. These include the penis, vagina, anus, mouth or throat, depending on how one engages in sex. These early symptoms almost always will be one or some combination of sores, discharge, pain, swelling, and itching."

If you suspect you or your partner might be infected, you should see a doctor immediately. Public health clinics often are much more familiar with STDs than your family doctor who may see one case of gonorrhea in five years. Consider going to a facility which deals frequently with the range of STDs. You will be treated with complete confidentiality, but be sure to ask about that before hand. The laws regarding AIDS are changing rapidly, so it's best to ask. Wherever you go, make clear to the medical staff that you want to be checked for STDs; there are examination procedures and tests specifically for them.

If you need help in finding out where to go, you can call the toll-free VD/STD National Hotline, 1-800-227-8922.

Breast exams

Breast cancer is second only to lung cancer as a threat to women. Your chances of getting it increase with age. The American Cancer Society recommends the monthly breast self-examination by women 20 years and older. For women 35 to 39, a baseline mammogram (a low-dose x-ray examination) is recommended, as well. Women 40 to 49 should have a mammogram every one to two years, and annually after that.

Pap smears

A Pap smear is a dry slide of a sample of cervical mucus which goes under a microscope for examination. It exposes abnormal cells for detection of cervical cancer and some but not all sexually transmitted diseases—for example, not syphilis or gonorrhea. The American Cancer Society recommends that a woman have an annual Pap test and pelvic examination. After three or more consecutive annual examinations with normal results, the Pap test may be performed less frequently with her doctor's approval. However, if a woman remains sexually active, she should strongly consider an annual Pap test and exam.

Healthy body/healthy mind

Reading this book is one good indication that you are still growing through reading. Keep a paperback in your purse for those occasions when you have to wait at the dentist's office or in line at the bank. Books and magazines in the bathroom and at your bedside are wonderful temptations. New ideas, new information and critical thinking activities can be energizing and personally fulfilling. And it makes you a more interesting and attractive person to others. But few will suggest that you should exercise your intellect. You will have to make it a priority for yourself.

Turn off the TV one night a week and do alternate activities. Listen to music. Write letters. Play a board game with the children. Read the newspaper for the news, and note local lectures and art exhibits to attend. It is too easy to let whole months and even years go by without challenging your brain, occupied as it is with work, keeping the household going and needing to relax.

Shakespeare wrote in *The Tempest*, "O brave new world that has such people in't." The world we live in—the seven continents and the seven seas—beats Disneyland any day in opportunities for excitement, adventure and enrichment. Even within one town the possibilities are countless. Go, see, do, enjoy. Do yourself a favor and make time to explore your mother Earth.

CHAPTER 10:   Working

"What am I going to do with the
        rest of my life?"
Who are you?
The master resume
Look at the possibilities
Plunge in somewhere and then upgrade
The minimum wage trap
Wanted: secretary
Two fallacies
Money versus meaning
Going back to school
Job searches
Creating your own opportunities
Resume
Sample resume
Interview
You don't have to say yes
Taking risks
Wanting to stay home with the kids
Part-time work: a stepping stone
Dealing with emotions of separation
Sexual harassment
Working two jobs
The working single mother as victim
Jumping ship too soon
Time for a new job?
Loyalty

"What am I going to do with the rest of my life?"

A woman who has never worked outside the home may have just made the decision to leave her partner (or he has just announced he is leaving her). Or a single mother who has a job is all too aware it doesn't pay enough to support herself, or the boss is on her back or the hours are too long. The list of possible horrors goes on. The burning thought in her mind is, "I need a job." One woman I know was stuck in the same boring position, with the same company at basically the same salary, for three years. She felt she would like to make a change, but she couldn't decide what her next move should be. If you don't know which move to make, stay where you are— until you can figure out your best move.

Making good career choices is vital to the single mother. An ideal plan for her is to find a job which suits her personality and her talents, one which provides a comfortable living for her family. And she would want to accomplish this with a minimum of stumbling around in the slush of the newspaper's classified ads. If you make wise choices initially, you are less likely to want to change jobs frequently. And "job hopping" does not look good on a resume. In order to make good career choices, you need to understand who you are and then analyze your aspirations, your resources, your family responsibilities and the mechanics of the working world.

Who are you?

Surveys show that women who are happiest with their jobs are those who like what they are doing; money alone does not provide job satisfaction. Most single mothers spend about eight hours a day sleeping, eight hours working outside the home and eight hours with family, friends, TV, errands or whatever. That means that if you are a typical single mother, you spend half your waking hours five days a week at work. That's about 2,000 hours a year in which to be either happy or sad about your life situation.

Nancy Ransom, director of the Vanderbilt University women's center, gave the following advice to her three children, and I have thought about it many times:

**Find out what you like to do,
then find out how you can make money doing it.**

In order to find out what you like to do, you have to know who you are. What is your personality? What are your talents? What are the tasks in life that give you satisfaction? If you do not clearly know the answer to these questions, the best investment you can make is in career counseling. It will probably cost you time and money, but beg and borrow to get it, because it can pay you personal and financial dividends for the rest of your life.

There are many counselors, tests and books that are available to help you with career development. Inquire about career counseling at the YWCA in your town, the public library (which will have many books on career planning), the personnel office of your current employer, the counseling office at a university in town. Often a career planning process involves self-reflection, taking standardized tests to assess your interests and abilities, and counseling. It can be a tremendous help in determining which direction you want to move.

The master resume

At this point, you may want to make up a resume, or summary, of all your work experience to date. Include everything, even babysitting in high school. Don't worry about dates. Just fill in everything, chronologically, in four categories: 1) Education; 2) Paid Work Experience; 3) Volunteer and Community Work; and 4) Personal Hobbies and Interests.

Even if you already have a resume, this master resume will give you the fullest view of your assets, and you can draw from this resource to pull together specialized resumes tailored to specific job opportunities. Always keep the master resume in your files.

Look at the possibilities

Once you have determined what your abilities and interests are and what kinds of jobs require those abilities and interests, you can identify those which appeal most to you. Let's say you would like to do research. You can look at your master resume and identify which jobs/interests relate to research. Let's say, further, that you are trained as a nurse. You don't like working with patients who quickly come and go, and rotating hospital shifts do not lend themselves to easy child care arrangements. Your master resume lists a summer job as a research assistant for a psychological study at your university, and you loved that job. However, you can't afford to go back to school for a Ph.D., which would allow you to become a college professor and do research. One solution would be to do medical research with a doctor at a medical school. Both your nursing training and your summer research experience would be pluses. There is a sense in which you must look at your experience critically and creatively to see how it can work for you in patching together an attractive resume for a specific job—the first step to getting that job. While some people can do this on their own, others need a career counselor to advise them. Both methods can work well.

Plunge in somewhere and then upgrade

Some women find themselves in a sudden crisis situation in which they realize, "I've got to have a job . . . any job." One way to get an immediate job is to work for a temporary employment agency. In most cases, that means typing, but not always. Call an agency (under Employment in the Yellow Pages) and ask them what kinds of jobs and how much money they can offer you. The agency finds jobs to keep you busy. You can register with more than one agency so that you will be able to work full time if you need to.

Often these jobs just barely keep you off food stamps (which is unfortunate, since food stamps expand your monthly food budget), but they can lead to a permanent position with a company which likes how you perform, even if you are short on experience and references. If the company offers to hire you, usually you have to work for the temporary agency for three months before they will release you to the new employer; then you get the higher salary and benefits. Two problems with temporary work are that you get no benefits and you have no time to interview for new jobs.

Let's say you are now a secretary for a multi-department company. You do your job well, but you know you will want to make a transition to something else as soon as possible. Analyze your new company. There may be a department within the company that you would like to move to which would better use your abilities and interests.

Get to know the people in the target department. They will tell you about the necessary job tasks and what the department atmosphere is like. Each department has its own personality, and while yours may be tolerant or even nurturing, another department in the same company may be tough on everyone. Management usually sets the mood. The better you know people in the target department, assuming you develop good personal relations with them, the easier it will be for you to break in, and they will tell you when an opening is coming up.

If you are employed but want to change employers, make sure you are improving your job situation in one of the following:

1. **Job description**—you are getting closer to the job which will allow you to use your talents and interests to the fullest;
2. **Pay**—it usually takes a 10 percent increase in pay to offset the benefits you lose in changing companies;
3. **Environment**—your new employer will not be the slave-master you want to leave behind (This takes careful investigation about things like employee turnover and the reputation of your prospective supervisor).

Whatever change you make, you should be upgrading your job situation in an important way. No job need be your dead end.

The minimum wage trap

A mother of two children who is working at a job which pays minimum wage is living below the federally defined poverty line. She is eligible for food stamps. At $3.35 per hour, forty hours per week, she makes $536 per month. In 1988, 4.7 million workers earned minimum wage.

One simple economic principle is that the lower your income, the less you can buy. So you have to start making choices. Do I need a car to get to work, or can I do without one? Can I get along without a telephone in my home? And there are other less than pleasant decisions. With child care added to living expenses, a single mother working for minimum wage does not fare well. In addition, many minimum wage jobs do not offer the employee health and dental insurance, life insurance, paid vacations or retirement plans. We're talking about fast food employees, dishwashers, baggers at grocery stores—"the working poor."

Some women who earn more than minimum wage at their full-time job will work minimum wage for a second job to help pay bills. Because of the low wage, it is a poor use of your time and energy.

Wanted: secretary

Have you ever heard someone say, "I'm just a secretary"? That is a woman who is not happy with her working image. Either she needs to change her job to suit her image, or she needs to change her idea of what a secretary is.

The catch-all description "secretary" is one of the broadest job classifications. More women work in this classification than in any other. It is relatively easy to get a job as a secretary if you can type. At the entry level, the job will probably not pay well. The pay ceiling for secretaries is also lower than many other white-collar jobs. However, if you have good clerical skills, being a secretary may be just your ticket. Clerical skills are one of the basic skill categories. About one-half of all women—and men—could find job satisfaction within that broad field.

There are many kinds of secretarial jobs open, including the foreign service and other glamorous opportunities. And you can aspire to become a Certified Professional Secretary, a challenging process which requires considerable skills and carries with it much respect. Salary varies tremendously, however, since this is determined by the individual employer.

The unfortunate second-class connotation that "secretary" carries in our society can work against some women. One older woman I know who had worked for years as a secretary in the same company was offered the position of company cashier. The salary was better, and the greater prestige appealed to her. She accepted. Her new job included controlling all the payroll for the office and factory workers, making monthly, quarterly and annual tax reports and doing other complicated accounting procedures. She found it very stressful and bemoaned the day she had said yes, longing for her old secretarial position which better suited her interests. Finally she retired early to just get out of a bad situation.

While working as a secretary can be a launching pad to bigger and better things for you, make sure you are not moving to bigger but worse things. Again, you need to know who you are and check out the lay of the land ahead before you make a move.

Two fallacies

1. *"If you work hard, you'll get ahead."* This is not necessarily true. You can work hard and well in your job and not get credit for it in either job title status or increased salary. If you are not making forward progress in your company, and you want to do so, talk with your supervisor. If he or she will not develop a growth plan with you, think about a move.

2. *"You can't get something for nothing."* This can also be untrue. People get free rides all the time. A supervisor sometimes has an eye on one employee and promotes that employee when job performance alone would not merit it, even above another employee with more skill and experience.

Make things easy on yourself. If you can identify a mentor who has the power to promote you in the company, pay attention to that relationship. In looking for a job, investigate the workload reputation of the employer. Take pride in what you do, and in doing your best, but also it is OK, and even advisable, to take advantage of anything that can make life easier for you as long as it's not illegal or unethical. You might as well work for an easy boss as a slaver. You need to be able to set a pace that is comfortable for you.

Money versus meaning

Diane was trained in a field she did not enjoy but which paid a living wage. For two years following her divorce she had been working at an interesting part-time job while her children were young, but she needed a full-time one to "keep it all going" financially. Not having found a career she enjoyed, she said that she felt she was "evading developmental milestones. I feel like I'm in a pressure cooker. There is no time to pay my dues [retooling in school or working at entry level positions]. The credentials I've accumulated are part of a lifelong effort to please other people. What do I want to do? How can I be me?"

Diane faced the difficult choice of using her earned degree to make good money in a job she did not enjoy or earning too little money at a low-level job in a field she did enjoy. She lived in a cramped, old apartment with the children. She thought ahead to college tuition for them. In the end, she chose to work in a good paying job for which she had been trained, hoping to be able to move within the institution, in time, to a job which suited her better.

Going back to school

Lorraine was 26 years old, going through a divorce, and had a three-year-old daughter. She and her husband were selling their house, and Lorraine planned to find an apartment near her work or on a bus line so that she could sell her car and live on her income as a secretary for a city real estate banking firm. Her husband had not paid child support during the separation.

Lorraine's employer offered her a sizable raise whenever she would be able to complete night courses in business management and accounting. The tuition plus child care and transportation costs forced her to moonlight at home, typing reports on weekends. She was a straight A student. She got up at 5:00 a.m. each weekday to have two hours to study. Her daughter complained that "Mama is always too tired to play with me."

The problem that single mothers like Lorraine encounter when they try to go to school to upgrade their skills is financial aid. There is a lack of stipend money or work-study options for the woman who must support her children while she goes to school. The cost of child care, transportation, books and equipment is not covered in aid money. There is a lack of financial aid for women who need to work part time and study part time. And loan regulations are overly stringent.

Getting a degree will not guarantee you a better job. But if you want to look into this option, there are library books that list financial aid opportunities for women. Many single mothers have made the time and financial sacrifice to go to school, and in changing or upgrading their career opportunities they have found greater personal satisfaction and financial rewards. A caution: if you accept financial aid, you have to pay it back. For women who exit school with $20,000 debts, it takes a while.

Job searches

Job searches are hard work and full of frustration. Anyone who has ever tried to find a job knows that. The higher the salary you need, the harder your search may be. And if you are hunting for a new job while you are already holding down a full-time job, you can soon become exhausted. But you must keep at it, sometimes for months, until you find a position that is right for you.

Job search variables:

◇ **Type of job**—Know what you want.

◇ **Salary**—Should offer you ten percent higher salary to offset the loss of vacation benefits, etc., from your current job. Like moving to a different home, moving to a different job can be expensive.

◇ **Hours**—Is there flexibility? (important for your children) Will there be overtime? If so, will you be paid for it?

◇ **Benefits**—Is there health, life and dental insurance? Tuition payment? Retirement plan and profit-sharing? Generous vacations and sick leave? Child care center? On-site, free parking?

◇ **Environment**—Corporation or small office? Hectic pace or relaxed atmosphere? Formal or casual? Dress code? Windows?

◇ **Management style**—Does your prospective new boss's match yours?

◇ **Location**—How far from home in distance? In time?

◇ **Opportunities for advancement**—Does the company promote women?

Beyond classified ads and employment agencies, a third way to find a job is through a more personal, investigative approach. If you know what position you are looking for, the location and the kind of environment you are looking for, then you can begin identifying specific companies to investigate. Your sources are family, friends, a bookstore or the public library. To take advantage of this type of search, get the paperback book, *What Color Is Your Parachute? A Practical Manual for Job-Hunters & Career-Changers*, by Richard Nelson Bolles.

Creating your own opportunities

For some people, the vision of what they would like to do simply does not exist. For example, when Karen separated from her husband, she began looking for a full time job. She had not worked since the birth of her son, ten years before. Karen was a LaLeche leader. She dreamed of working with teenage mothers, very few of whom breastfeed their babies, in a low-income prenatal clinic. She would instruct them in the health benefits of breast feeding and bonding with their babies. She decided to write a grant to get her own salary paid for, but she felt she needed to set up a relationship with a clinic first. She approached a downtown hospital women's clinic, and they were interested in her project. It turned out that they had grant money coming in soon for a somewhat different, but related, project. The clinic director hired Karen to do the project.

The idea of affiliating with someone who is doing work in the field that interests you is a good one. If you can sell your project idea, you can write your grant, possibly with the assistance of the affilitating organization, if there is one.

Getting a grant depends on the quality of your proposal, the availability of money and luck. You are competing with other people, as if applying for a job. From the time you write your proposal to the time you get your money, six to 18 months may have passed by. It takes a long time, so if you can submit the proposal in advance of the date you need the money, give it a try.

Resume

Resumes come in all forms and lengths. People who develop a resume of three pages or more are making a mistake. An employer uses resumes to screen out unlikely candidates for a position. You do not need to tell your whole life history on the resume. If you can keep it to one or two pages, you will get a better reading.

The resume should be a thumbnail sketch, an appealing introduction which is designed to get you an interview. At the interview, you can go into detail about your capabilities and describe how you can offer something special to the company. So keep the resume short.

But crystallizing yourself onto one or two pages is difficult to do well. You need to hit the high points, but be concise. You also need to be sure your spelling and grammar are flawless. To write your one- to two-page resume, go back to your master resume (page 163) and work from that. The job for which you are applying will determine what information you pull from the master resume.

Sample resume

Laura A. Swanson
115 Cannon Street
San Lorenzo, California 94580
615-555-1212

Objective
A challenging opportunity with career potential in sales,
especially trade shows, telemarketing, and specialty advertising.

Profile
Enterprising, goal-oriented individual
• Solid communication skills, including sense of humor
• Quick to grasp and develop scope of projects
• Creative—an idea person

Education
Associate of Arts, May 1984, Hayward Community College
• Business major
• Dean's list 1982, 1983, 1984

Experience
Sales representative (August 1986 - November 1988)
Bethany Michael's Cosmetics, Inc., Oakland, California
• Expanded sales markets in central California
• Broke sales goals in 1987 and 1988
• Demonstrated and sold products at regional department
  store promotions
• Reorganized and expanded retail client files for more
  efficient contacts
• Suggested and developed in-house newsletter for better
    interdepartmental communication and for morale enhancement

Executive secretary (1982 - 1986)
American Can Company, Oakland, California
• Carried out daily administrative operations for office of CEO
• Managed factory tour bookings and trained tour guides

Personal
Enjoy travel, people, gourmet cooking. Excellent health.
Native Californian. Two children.

**(Note: Bring your references to the interview rather than listing them
on resume)**

After you develop your resume, you will want to type a one-page cover letter for each prospective employer to whom you send the resume. In the cover letter you can include a few details that you did not put in the resume, ones the employer would view as advantages. After you type your resume and cover letters, have at least one friend read them for errors and general comments.

Some people pay professional resume companies to clean up their resumes (Look under "Resumes" in the Yellow Pages). The company will take the information you provide and organize it, if it needs it, format it and print copies for you. The cost for a one-page resume is around $20 and up. The result is usually slick-looking. Maybe a little too slick. Make sure you see a sample of a finished resume, and be sure you like it before you put your money down. There is nothing wrong with typing your own resume, as long as you follow a consistent format; you may well come up with a product that pleases you. A neatly formatted resume that is printed with a good ribbon on a typewriter or done on computer will present itself well to a prospective employer. If you photocopy your resume, make sure the copies are clean and sharp. Quick-print shops have quality copiers and a variety of paper selections.

Interview

People get understandably nervous about interviews. The trick is to let that extra adrenalin work for you to keep you alert and focused on your task. **A few tips:**

- ◆ Do your homework. Know the basic facts about the company to which you are applying: how long it has been in business, its history, how many people it employs, what products or services it offers. You can call the company in advance and ask them to send you information. They will appreciate your interest; it's good business. Many larger companies have brochures, annual reports and other information they can send you.
- ◆ The day before the interview, think through things you have done in the past that directly relate to this job. Write

them down. This will help you remember them in the interview.

♦ Write out a script of possible questions and answers. Practice your responses in front of a mirror, with a friend, or with a child. Do not try to memorize your answers. You want your responses to be informed but fresh.

♦ If you can visit the company unnoticed before the interview, observe what women at your job level are wearing and wear something similar but conservative. For most interviews, a simple medium-to-dark suit with a skirt, blouse and heels works well. Avoid showy jewelry, colored nylons, sexy clothes and perfume. Do not smoke.

♦ Be squeaky-clean and well-groomed in every way. Neat hair cut.

♦ Think of a friend you can telephone after the interview, and let that be a reward for you to look forward to.

♦ Take either a small purse or a slim briefcase, but not both. You may want to take a few notes, so carry note paper and pen.

♦ Before you enter the front door, pause, take about five slow, deep breaths. Relax.

♦ Go to a restroom and comb your hair.

♦ Find your interviewer. If you have to wait, do more slow breathing.

♦ Give a firm handshake, smile and introduce yourself.

♦ If there are photos in the interviewer's office, you might ask, "Are these your family?" This will break the formality and put your interviewer at ease.

♦ Questions you will be asked to answer may vary widely: "Why do you want to work for our company?" "What is your philosophy of life?" Expect anything. And be ready to answer anything. Some people like to throw you off guard to see how fast you think. There is nothing wrong with saying, "That's a good question, but I need some time to reflect on it rather than give you a superficial answer now."

- ◆ Be honest. Be sincere.
- ◆ Keep your answers brief. No more than three or four sentences, if possible. Expect about 15 minutes for the interview. You may get 30 or more, if they are interested. Watch the interviewer to determine if he or she is pressed for time or can move at a more relaxed pace.
- ◆ Remember that while the prospective employer is interviewing you, you can interview him or her in order to find out if you would be happy working for this company. Ask about whatever is important to you in management style, environment, flexible hours, opportunities for growth within the company. Often an interviewer will ask, "Do you have any questions?" This is your chance, but keep it brief. Do not ask about benefits until you talk about salary.
- ◆ Generally, the salary question will be, "What kind of a salary are you looking for?" You need to have done your homework ahead of time to know what the going range is for this level of job (the Occupational Outlook Handbook put out by the Federal Government each year will give you an idea about this. It is in the public library). But if you can postpone answering this, do so until you get closer to being offered the job. You might try, "Money is a secondary consideration at this point. Let's talk more about the job, and I'm sure we can come to an agreement about salary later on."
- ◆ Remember that your goal is to present yourself as having something unique to offer. Look within yourself and find those qualities that will translate to fresh ideas, high energy, or whatever, for the company. Again, keep your responses brief.
- ◆ Ask what the next step will be in the hiring process. You will want to know how soon to expect word from the company. If your interviewer says, "We will finish interviewing this week and will let you know something by next Wednesday" and you don't hear from him or her by

Wednesday, you can call on Friday morning and say, "I hadn't heard from you, and I'm just calling to say I'm still very interested in the position." You will get an update on the process.

♦ Write a thank-you note after the initial interview and mail it the next day.

You don't have to say yes

Judy had been trying for some time to transfer to another job within her own company, which had three divisions. She liked the company and wanted to keep the benefits she had built up over five years. But no one would hire her. A friend suggested she apply for a good middle management position in another company. Judy said she would. Then she hesitated. Her friend told her that she could take the process as far as it would go, and that if they offered her the job, she didn't have to say yes. With that, Judy made application. She was nervous going into the interview. When it was over, she called her friend on the phone and said, "I loved the interview!" The board that met with her must have been impressed, because they offered her the job, and she accepted.

If you have questions about a job, the interview is the place to ask them. On the basis of what you hear, you can decide yes or no. Keep your options open.

Taking risks

Life does not often offer sure things. Marriage certainly isn't a sure thing. And job satisfaction isn't a sure thing. You give it your best shot. Usually it is not until women get into emotional or financial crises that they take risks. Women tend to be more conservative than men. They want to hedge their bets. Or they want a sure thing.

Sometimes that means they stay overlong in bad situations. They worry about what will happen if they make a change. Granted, change is stressful, and who needs extra stress?

The "trapeze bar" experience, outlined by Paul Tournier in his book *A Place for You* (Harper & Row, 1968), is a leap of faith. You throw yourself into the process, go as far as you can, then let go. There is a mid-air breathlessness, an anxiety effect, when you let go of one bar and grab onto another. You have to believe you are going to connect.

Then there is a limiting way of behaving called "the brick wall that isn't there." People build imaginary brick walls in front of themselves which they then are unable to get around. Brick walls that aren't there. Who needs them? We build them to avoid having to face some unpalatable truth—that we are doing a lousy job in our current position, and so we need to find another one; or our loyalty to an employer is misplaced; or the stress of changing to another job might be more than we can bear; or if we begin searching for a new job, maybe no one will want to hire us; or we might be too old to go back to school. Whatever that brick wall is, it inhibits our freedom of rational choice. We need to knock it down and look honestly at our choices, naming our fears but holding them in check. It is as if our emotions build the brick wall, and our minds say, "Well, as long as that wall is there, I really can't get beyond it." So it's a stalemate. And we can put ourselves through major grief enduring a bad situation that needn't be.

Wanting to stay home with the children

Especially when your children are preschoolers, you may want to stay home with them to care for them like no one else can, to watch them develop at close range daily, to introduce them to the world with you at their side. Money is the key.

Welfare is not an attractive option for most single mothers because of the poor neighborhoods and severely reduced standard of living you have to put up with. However, there are single mothers who have done and are doing a good job of raising their children on welfare checks. It is just an unending financial strain.

Living with parents is rarely a satisfactory long-term solution. But for the short term, it can be an opportunity for the single mother to save some money to put down on an apartment or to pay off some bills.

Nancy became a single mother when her boys were six months and two years old. Her ex-husband paid her $700 child support each month. She felt committed to staying home to care for her children, and she met all her expenses out of the child support money and food stamps. They lived in subsidized housing, did not travel or spend a lot of money on entertainment. But Nancy was rich in friends and led an active social life. By the time the boys were four and six and Nancy felt she was ready to go back to work, she got a research job at a local university which paid her $21,000 a year—enough to move into a duplex in a neighborhood near her friends.

Some women are able to make a living working at home. The advantages are that you have fewer office interruptions, you have flexible hours, you may have attractive tax breaks, you do not have to lose time commuting to work, you save on child care and you can be there for the children. The danger is that at home you will be your own boss. It is tempting to do housework or other errands instead of working. If you can handle self-discipline, you may be able to make some money at home, either full-time, or part-time.

Some working-at-home options include:

◊ Caring for the children of other working women (generally low pay)
◊ Typing, editing and copy-editing dissertations, resumes and manuscripts from publishing houses
◊ Writing
◊ Typesetting—some typesetting firms "farm out" jobs to women who work at home with either the firm's equipment or their own. Other women get their own equipment and solicit their own business.
◊ Tutoring
◊ Teaching music, dance or English as a second language
◊ Tailoring and dressmaking
◊ Operating retail businesses from the home, including telephone answering services
◊ Catalog sales
◊ Independent sales representative
◊ Accounting
◊ Computer software development and consulting
◊ Photography
◊ Telemarketing and market research done on the telephone

There are other options, as well. Most of these occupations require concentration for blocks of time which is difficult when you need to simultaneously supervise a child younger than four years old. However, the women who manage this say it is worth the effort to be able to stay home with their children. If you are enterprising and have a skill to offer, you can look into starting your own business out of your home. This is a major financial risk, and to avoid failure you can start small by moonlighting at home. When the home business builds up to a point where it can support you, you can give up your outside job with greater confidence.

If you are interested in starting a home business, the Federal Government's Small Business Bureau can help you with licensing and small loans. Their SCORE program (Service Core of Retired Executives) matches you with a seasoned business person for free consultation.

Part-time work: a stepping stone

Part-time work can function to your benefit in several ways:

♦ If you have not worked in a while, it can allow you to enter the work force at a slower pace before you move into full-time work. You can often use volunteer experience to get a part-time job.
♦ It can give you a steady income while you are building up your part-time business at home.
♦ It can allow you to be home with the children more—a plus for children of any age.

Dealing with emotions of separation

Separation and divorce, like death, provoke some of the strongest human emotions. You find yourself arriving at work feeling like your nerves are exposed and raw. You are under a lot of stress, and you may cry easily. If your co-workers understand that you are going through tough times personally—and everyone these days understands divorce—they will understand why you might be more easily upset. It is important that you talk with your supervisor about your separation, saying that you know that it is normal for you to be under stress, that you will make every effort to continue your workload as usual, that you know this phase will pass, that you would appreciate his or her continuing support through the process, and that you welcome feedback at any time.

Sexual harassment

Sexual harassment is illegal. It violates Title VII of the Civil Rights Act of 1964, which states

> Unwelcome sexual advances, requests for sexual favors, and other verbal or physical conduct of a sexual nature constitute sexual harassment when: 1) submission to such conduct is made either explicitly or implicitly a term or condition of an individual's employment; 2) submission to or rejection of such conduct by an individual is used as the basis for employment decisions affecting that individual; 3) such conduct has the purpose or effect of unreasonably interfering with an individual's work performance or creating an intimidating, hostile or offensive working environment.

Examples of sexual harassment include

◇ Verbal harassment or abuse of a sexual nature ("I was discussing my work in a public setting when a professor asked if I had freckles all over my body.")
◇ Subtle pressure for sexual activity
◇ Sexist remarks about a person's clothing, body or sexual activities
◇ Unwanted touching, patting, or pinching
◇ Leering or ogling at a person's body
◇ Brushing against another's body
◇ Demanding sexual favors accompanied by implied or overt threats concerning one's job, grades, promotion, pay, letters of recommendation
◇ Physical assault
◇ Inappropriate display of sexually suggestive or pornographic materials

---

Women constitute 97.1 percent of the reported cases of sexual harassment (for men, it's 2.9 percent). Single mothers are prime targets, being less able to pick up and move on if they need to due to financial and family constraints.

No woman should tolerate sexual harassment. Her work will suffer, her self esteem will drop and the unhealthy atmosphere created by sexual harassment will affect everyone. But what can you do?

Do's & Don'ts of Sexual Harassment

◇ Do stare the harasser in the eye.
◇ Do use a direct and honest approach.
◇ Do deal with the situation immediately so it won't continue.
◇ Do say "No!" emphatically to the harasser.
◇ Do keep detailed records of each incident.
◇ Do demand respect.
◇ Do report the incident immediately.
◇ Do ask for help!
◆ Don't smile at the harasser.
◆ Don't look away from the harasser.
◆ Don't let someone lean on you or get too close. Stand up and move away.
◆ Don't worry about the harasser's ego; worry about your self-respect.
◆ Don't think that if you ignore the problem it will go away.
◆ Don't let anyone ask you questions of a sexual nature, especially in an interview.

(*"Sexual Harassment: Vanderbilt University Guide for Faculty, Staff and Students,"* Margaret Cuninggim Women's Center, Nashville, TN.)

Working two jobs

If you have to work more than 40 hours a week to keep yourself financially afloat, you need to find a job which pays you more or decrease your consumer appetite.

Working a second job, or working overtime regularly while you have custody of children is difficult for those children. Child care is OK for an eight-hour workday, but no one can replace Mom when it comes to mothering. No one has your child's interests at heart more than you do, and good or bad, mistakes or not, you need to interact with each child as much as possible and on a regular basis for him or her to feel secure.

When Purdue University professor A. Charlene Sullivan surveyed 600 married couples who either moonlighted or worked overtime regularly, she found that these couples were depressed about their budgets. **As compared to couples who did not moonlight, these superworkers:**

◇ Were having more trouble repaying their debts
◇ Felt more strongly that they were too deeply in debt
◇ Felt a greater need to borrow to keep up their lifestyle
◇ Were more likely to have no extra money at the end of the month
◇ Were less likely to pay off their credit cards in full every month
◇ Thought that credit cards did more harm than good.

Single mothers sometimes find themselves in the same leaky financial boat, killing themselves to pay their bills and never getting ahead. They get into compromising positions and have to rely not infrequently on family or friends to bail them out. These are women who make over $17,000 a year in Nashville (double that amount for California and New York City) plus child support, whose homes are charming and whose cars are new, but whose finances are a mess. This is only to say that a second job is not necessarily an answer. It may be a symptom of an inability to set realistic financial limits on yourself.

The working single mother as victim

Carol was a single mother with two children. She and Sharon, who was married, were secretaries in the same department. Their two bosses quit within one month of each other, leaving Carol and Sharon to run the department. The president of the company called them in and said they would have increased responsibilities until new management was hired. They got immediate title promotions. If they did a good job, they would get salary increases after three months.

They both assumed much of the work of their former bosses (who had made three times their salaries, and they made plans to move up the ladder together. The president's evaluations of their first month's work were highly complimentary. Then Carol went out of town on business for a week. While she was gone, Sharon began talking with the president of the company about Carol's alleged "poor performance." By the time Carol returned, the president's secretary was avoiding her, and the president seemed noncommittal. On Carol's next business trip, she returned to find that she had been demoted to secretary at her original salary, while Sharon had gotten a $7,000 raise and a second title hike. No one would ask Carol to lunch. She was isolated and miserable. She had gone the extra mile for the company and her reward, she felt, was a stab in the back by her former best friend at work. Carol hung onto her job, her self-esteem slowly sinking, for another four months. She could not afford to quit because she had no husband and, therefore, no financial backup. When another company offered her a better job, she took it gratefully.

Whenever there are people in vulnerable positions, there are people who will take advantage of them. Single mothers are vulnerable. They cannot easily put their jobs on the line by confronting someone with power who figuratively stomps on them. They feel they cannot defend themselves when bosses complain about their taking time off to be with sick children. They feel they cannot argue about unpaid overtime when someone appears at quitting time and asks, "Do me a favor, will you? Type up this report before you leave. I need it by 8 a.m."

Single mothers will remain victims as long as they remain in low-paying, powerless positions, living on tight budgets with children at home whom they must protect. And the price is too often silence in the face of injustice at the workplace.

Jumping ship too soon

A woman might hate her job because it is boring, too demanding, involves too much overtime, pays too little money, offers terrible working conditions—or whatever. She is nervous, tense, bursting to move on. She fights to control her emotions. One day she reaches the breaking point, walks into the boss's office, drops a letter of resignation in the boss's IN box, and thinks, "Well, at last I've done it." With some nervousness, she returns to her desk to await the inevitable meeting with the boss. In two weeks she's gone. But to what? Temporary secretarial work does not come close to paying her former salary, but she thinks she can get by on it until she finds another, better-paying job.

This avenue for the single mother is Russian roulette. There are many people vying for the same jobs as the single mother. Some of them do not have children and, therefore, look a little more attractive. The job search and interview process is so time-consuming and laced with luck that no one—no one—who is not independently wealthy should leave her job without another job to go to or a school situation with a guaranteed income that will pay her bills.

Long before you reach the breaking point at your job, listen to your head. When you begin to feel real dissatisfaction, take a look around and make an assessment.

Time for a new job?

Whether because of office politics or boredom or claustrophobia, one morning you may pop open your eyes and have that sinking feeling, "Oh, no, I have to drag myself to work today." And you realize that lately you have been having that feeling every morning.

Possible trouble signs are
◊ You got a lower raise than others the last time around
◊ You received a lukewarm job evaluation
◊ Your ideas and requests are dismissed
◊ You are cut off from office gossip or socializing
◊ You are depressed at work
◊ You are regularly stressed and feel you cannot handle your job load
◊ You feel trapped or at a dead end with nowhere to go in your career

An unhappy job situation can become overwhelmingly depressing and stressful. You need to change the way things operate at work— or start looking for a new job.

The best thing you can do is confront the situation, whatever it is. Do not drift. Talk with your supervisor. Find out how he or she can help you become more challenged and define and solve problems with co-workers. Discuss the supervisor's own problems regarding your performance and otherwise problem solve together. If your supervisor says, "That's the job. Take it or leave it," or "If you aren't satisfied here, you may need to make a change," your worst fears may be true, your worst obstacles insurmountable in this situation. In that case, it is better to leave before you become entrenched in mediocrity or are fired.

Loyalty

Your priorities must be taking care of your children and yourself. Where company loyalty is concerned, keep it business only. If you have to leave an employer after years of service or after only three weeks, do it. You are not indispensable to your employer (there are a lot of people reading the want ads who would love to do your job and would do it well). And you are probably making a lot less than the supervisor to whom you might feel some obligation. Supervisors often leave their own positions without a backward glance if they get attractive offers elsewhere. It's just good business. When you quit your job, give two weeks' notice, even if you are leaving a bad situation and would like to get revenge, or don't think you can hang on for two more weeks. You owe it to yourself to finish in good form.

Always keep your strongest loyalties at home, your strongest commitments at home. That's where your greatest investment will bring you the greatest return.

CHAPTER 11: Finances

Living within your means

Knowing how you spend

Insurance

Establishing credit

Credit crunch

Chapter 13 bankruptcy

Taxes: filing jointly with your ex

Claiming dependents

Head of household

Filing statuses

Earned Income Credit

Tax forms

Tax helpers

A home of your own

The down payment

Shopping for mortgage money

Retirement

Making your money grow

Financial advisors

College funds

Ready-cash funds

If it's hard for you to save

Wills

Cultivating feeling rich

Wolves prowl in my head
hungry for me
watching me at the bank
at the grocery store
at the gas station.

There must be no mistake.
I have been careful.
I have stretched taut my desires,
my wishes for marmalade
and sometimes for bread.
Still it is not enough.

Tomorrow is a living standard away.
Today the phone bill is due.
The mortgage is due.
Gas, electricity, water.
The hedge needs clipping.
My nails need clipping,
My mind needs ironing
to get out the humpbacks of the wolves
who howl and wait.

Living within your means

Joel Grey and Liza Minelli sang "Money makes the world go 'round" in the smash musical "Cabaret." Money certainly makes life easier when you manage it so that you have enough each month to pay the bills and then play a little, and when you have made provisions for emergency situations. You may or may not be good at managing money. Lawyers, CPAs, investment brokers and others have made oodles of money helping other people manage theirs. This chapter will cover some of the basics of money management, a tool which can dramatically affect the quality of life for you and your children.

One thing many single mothers have to do is lower their cost of living when they begin to live on their own salary. At that point you make some decisions about what is important to you and the children, and how you can hold onto most of that when it costs money. You ask yourself, "What provides quality in our lives? How can we maintain that with our budget?" Instead of thinking consumption, you think conservation, making do, recycling, being creative with resources, sharing resources and skills with other people.

You may have big-ticket plans of buying a car, buying a home, going to school, taking a trip to another country, saving for the children's college educations. So you keep today's expenditures lower than you would like, coping with today while planning for tomorrow.

Knowing how you spend

Keeping a record of your expenses for a three-month period can tell you how you spend your money. An easy way to do that is to pay for purchases with checks, when possible, and keep receipts faithfully for every cash purchase. At the end of the three months, you divide every expenditure into two categories: Basic Needs and

Optional Purchases. Rent, food, utilities, transportation to work and school, medical expenses, clothing, and repayment of credit purchases are basic needs. You may have additional basic needs, but many other purchases we make are optional: a new bathmat and other household items, gifts for family and friends, entertainment and travel, hobby items.

You group your expenses into categories—utilities, entertainment, etc.—and add up the totals for each category for three months. Divide each category by three, and you will have the average of how much you spent each month for that category. Clothes, for example: you spent

$ 60 in June
$180 in July (sales)
$ 0 in August
$240 total, divided by 3 months = $80 per month average for clothes

If you want to cut down on your monthly expenses, take a look at all the basic needs items. Rent is usually the biggest item. One possibility is to move to less expensive housing. Or food and clothing may be areas in which you can cut costs. Credit payments are one category you want to work conscientiously to reduce month by month, until you can clear your credit bills to zero at the end of each month. But you may not want to reduce most of your basic needs items. Add up the total amount of money needed in an average month for your basic needs. Subtract that from your salary and other income, and that is the amount of money you have left over for optional purchases. For example, a single mother's financial report looks like this:

$1,500 salary and child support
$1,100 basic needs
$ 400 leftover for optional purchases

Every month in which she spends more than $400 on optional purchases, she goes over her budget and borrows, in one way or another, from another month. This "borrowed money" will have to be paid back, to herself, in future months, leaving her with less optional purchase funds for those months. For every month in which she spends less than $400 on optional purchases, she is under budget and can apply that money to pay off credit, save for big-ticket items, or whatever.

The advantage of living on a budget is that you can understand where your money is going and make informed choices about how you use it for short and long-range planning.

Insurance

A newspaper carried a tragic story of a nine-year-old boy, son of a single mother, who was walking on the side of the road when he was hit and killed by a drunk driver. The article said, "Funeral expenses for Carter will be paid by Big Brothers . . . . 'I didn't have any insurance because I couldn't afford it,' the mother said. 'It took every penny I had just to keep a roof over his head and clothing on his back.'"

Though it is a struggle for many single mothers to stretch their income to meet the bills, because we have children we are responsible to plan for the care of ourselves and those children in case of emergencies. The questions you need to ask yourself are,

What will happen if I die? If I am disabled? If I have health problems? Where will the money come from?

Life insurance is cheap for adults under 35 years old. "Term" insurance is like renting your insurance by the month. It is pure death protection, and it is the least expensive life insurance. If you get group term life insurance at work, that's a cost benefit to you, but when you leave work, you leave your insurance.

Disability income insurance is offered by many employers. If you are disabled, it will pay you a percentage each month (about 60 to 75 percent) of your working wage at the time you left work. It is inexpensive, about $30 per month.

AFDC and Social Security benefits are available to you, in case of disability, but to survive on that income alone would probably severely reduce your current standard of living. However, if you become disabled, you should know that there are many support programs available to women on AFDC, programs that are seldom used because women don't know to ask about them. Social workers, tax lawyers, the mayor's office—many resource people know about these support programs.

Health insurance can be either Cadillac or Honda. Your employer may pay all or part of this. With health insurance, the higher the deductible, the cheaper the monthly insurance premium will be. What you may need most is catastrophic coverage for liver transplants and auto accidents and other regrettable but possible big-ticket items.

Some states offer health insurance plans for people who have been turned down for insurance by other companies as poor health risks. The premiums are higher, but you are insured. People who have AIDS, for example, can get this kind of state-subsidized insurance (this is for people who earn too much money to qualify for Medicaid). Check with your state department of Commerce and Insurance (or whoever in your state regulates insurance).

Auto insurance is a must so you don't lose your privilege to drive. Your license can be confiscated if you don't have insurance. "Minimum limits" payments enable you to pay in twelve monthly installments, with a slight fee for processing the payments. Your insurance costs will depend on your accident record and your car's model and year.

Other kinds of insurance you need are homeowner's or renter's insurance, for property and household goods, and dental insurance, which is becoming a more common employment benefit. When you are looking for a job, remember that insurance benefits from your employer can add over two thousand dollars per year to your salary.

Establishing credit

If you do not have credit in your own name at the time of your divorce, you can begin by opening a savings account at your bank. Even if you put in the minimum amount to open the account, you are establishing credit. Next, find a locally-owned store in your area—a bookstore or a dress shop, for example—which will set up a credit account for you. Charge something and keep your bills paid on time.

When you make application for a major bank credit card, you will offer information about your personal life and your financial situation. If you have paid all your bills on time for at least six months (this includes, ideally, your local store credit card), you may or may not get the card. The bank will give your application to a credit officer to review and make a judgment based on how the officer interprets the information you have given. If credit is denied, call the bank and find out why. Reapply when you have straightened out the problem, or apply to a different bank.

It's easier to get almost any gas credit card. Some have to be paid in full each month (Chevron), but others do not (AMOCO). If you don't have a major credit card, you must have something to cover car repairs and tires so you can keep rolling down the road. Save your gas card for these one-time large cash outlays, but use cash to buy gas.

Some people collect enough credit cards to play poker with, but once you have one major credit card you can charge yourself into bankruptcy court—which, of course, you want to avoid. Keeping your cards to a minimum makes it easier to keep track of them in your purse, makes for fewer monthly bills and gives you fewer phone numbers to call to cancel all those cards in case your purse is lost or stolen.

Credit crunch

Denise kept buying things on credit until she could not pay the bills when they came due. One by one, the credit companies canceled her credit, and some things were repossessed. Denise was 19. She married, and her husband, a successful plumber, spent 13 stormy years with her struggling to bail her out of one financial problem after another. During a period when Denise and her husband were separated, Denise's house and car were nearly repossessed. She spent $600 on new clothes for a three-day training program she attended. She gave her parents new dining room furniture which she could not pay for, and she harangued the Small Business Administration until they loaned her $20,000 for a business that went defunct within a year. In each of these cases, Denise's husband paid for purchases he did not agree to in order to avoid financial disaster.

Credit can be a handy way for you to loan yourself money, but if you can't pay back one credit loan before you find yourself charging more, you may soon find yourself owing over $2,000 to credit companies, with a monthly repayment expense of over $100 and interest charges of 18 percent or more—a bad use of your money.

Time magazine printed an interesting article by Anastasia Toufexis on compulsive shoppers in the December 26, 1988 issue. The article profiled people who buy things—sometimes useless things like clothes that don't fit—out of an uncontrollable need which overrides financial considerations. Like overeaters or alcoholics, they can't help themselves. It's a sickness, the root cause of which may be low self-esteem, according to the article, and these people need help to change their buying habits.

The woman who finds she is unable to pay back her charges on a monthly basis might consider not carrying her charge cards in her purse to avoid impulse buying. If that doesn't work, she can cut them up and throw them away, one by one, until she reaches a point where she can manage what she has. Then she can build back her card collection, if she chooses, slowly and with caution.

You can pay off all your 18-percent-plus charge accounts by taking out one large loan (called a debt consolidation loan) at 10 to 12 percent interest. Once your charge accounts are back to zero, it is tempting to charge against them again, but then you would have the debt consolidation loan and your new charge bills to pay, magnifying your problem. Putting away or cutting up your credit cards can help you resist the temptation to charge.

If you are more than 60 days overdue on a credit bill, the creditor will report you to the Credit Bureau, which will record this blot on your financial reputation and will provide information on your credit record to anyone who pays for it. The creditor, or a collection agency, will write you letters and then start calling you on the phone, which is both annoying and embarrassing. This prompts some parents to ask their children to lie about their whereabouts. If you know you can't pay your bill, do not avoid the creditor. Write a letter explaining your circumstances and suggesting a repayment plan which you can afford. Many people do this. The company will probably be receptive to any suggestion, because they want to collect their money eventually. When you and the company agree on a repayment plan, ask them to write to the Credit Bureau to take your defaulted payment off your record and to send you a copy of the letter. If you don't get the letter, call the company and restate your request until you get your letter.

Chapter 13 bankruptcy

Filing for bankruptcy is an option if you cannot meet your credit commitments. This happens to many people through no fault of their own when they incur unexpected medical bills, lose their job, lose their support, etc. Chapter 13 bankruptcy is a tool to use to get back on your feet financially without losing everything you own, as long as you have a fixed income—a job, alimony or money from a renter. Here's how it works:

You hire a lawyer (find one who has experience with bankruptcy law) who files a petition for you. You meet with all your creditors and your lawyer in the courthouse hallway. You specify what your basic monthly expenses are to take care of your family and how much money you will need to meet them. You will pay what is left over from your fixed income to your creditors. You and they negotiate the value of your property (i.e., car, clothing, furniture) and the principal and interest you can pay the creditors. You get to keep your goods, but you can't use credit, without the court's permission, for the duration of your repayment plan, usually three to five years. Often the deal is struck in the hallway, and then you all go and present the plan to a Chapter 13 trustee of the court. Only if one or more creditor objects to the plan do you have to go before a judge, and usually this does not happen, because no one wants to pay the additional lawyer's fees.

There is a filing fee, $90 at the time of this writing, which can be incorporated into the repayment plan along with your lawyer's fee. So you need no up-front money to go through the Chapter 13 bankruptcy process.

The disadvantages of bankruptcy are that it goes on your permanent credit record, which will discourage some creditors from giving you money in the future, and there is a social stigma against it.

If your paychecks are being garnisheed to pay debts or you are threatened with foreclosure on your house or repossession of your car, you may want to get advice from a lawyer regarding bankruptcy and other options.

Taxes: filing jointly with your ex

You cannot file jointly with your ex-husband for the tax year during which you were divorced. You can file jointly if you are separated but not yet divorced, however, and it may well be advantageous for you to do so, because joint filing brings the highest return on your money. If your ex-partner makes considerably more money than you do, then you may be better off having the option to file alone. You can use that as a bargaining chip. Let's say that if you file alone, you would get $300 back on your taxes. If you filed jointly, your husband would have to pay $700 less on his taxes. The difference between your $300 and his $700 is $400. The two of you can split that for $200 apiece. Your ex-husband gives you $300 plus $200, or $500 to file jointly. He keeps his extra $200 and you both come out ahead.

Claiming dependents

If you and your ex-partner have a high-low income split, the higher wage earner could claim the children for a bigger tax benefit and share the overage with the other earner. For example, if you would get $50 for your child and your ex-partner would get $100, you could let him claim the child and the two of you would split the $50 "profit." You would both win financially.

Head of household

This is a filing status. It means you are the main financial support in the family which includes at least one dependent. A child is your dependent if you provide more than half of the care for that child, or if the divorce decree states the child is your dependent.

Filing statuses

The amount of tax break you get on your income depends on what category you declare yourself to be on the tax forms:

Married, but filing separately—the worst tax break
Single—better
Head of household—better
Married, filing jointly—best tax break

Earned Income Credit

If you have one or more children living with you and you make less than $18,576 (1988 figure), you are eligible for up to $874 back, even if you were not due a refund originally. Child support is not taxable annual income, so if your child support puts you over the $18,576 mark, you may still be eligible. To qualify for Earned Income Credit you must file as 1) head of household or 2) qualifying widow (if your spouse died within the last two years). Complete qualifications are in the instructions that come with your tax form 1040A or 1040 long form.

Tax forms

Federal tax forms are available at most post offices, banks, U.S. courthouses, and public libraries. To know which form you need, look up the telephone number of IRS (Internal Revenue Service) Forms. Call that number and ask them to send you the primer called "Your Federal Individual Income Tax." It explains which forms you need and helps you know what questions to ask the IRS or whoever figures your taxes. After the first year you file taxes in your own name, the IRS will mail tax forms to your home address. If you move, you have to request the forms again.

State tax forms are available from the Revenue Department of your state government. Call and ask them to send you forms. Once you have filed a return, they will send one every year until you move.

If you work for an employer who withholds tax from your paycheck, you file taxes only once a year. If your wages are not withheld for taxes, you need to file both federal and state taxes quarterly. **For tax forms and publications, call 1-800-424-3676.**

Child support is not taxable income. Property settlements are not taxable income. Alimony, however, is taxable income. If you know anyone who is facing divorce, encourage her to get tax advice from a CPA or tax lawyer before settlement of property. A family law attorney may not consult a financial expert, and your friend may be the loser. The way you design your divorce decree determines how much the government will take in taxes.

Child care credits are not deductions and are based on a percentage of your AGI (adjusted gross income). Such credits are changing yearly, since child care is a hot item on the national agenda nowadays, so one question you should always ask whoever helps you with your taxes is how you can get the most benefit from child care expenses.

Tax helpers

The IRS will help individuals fill out their personal tax forms at local IRS offices. You can just walk in and ask, or you may be able to make an appointment, depending on how busy they are. The assistance is free. Call ahead for the office hours and to make sure you can get help on the day and at the hour you want it.

There is a national program set up for low-income people to get help filing out their personal taxes. It is called VITA (Volunteer Income Tax Assistance). The volunteers are trained in basic tax law by the IRS. They can prepare simple tax returns, basic forms and attached schedules such as itemized deduction schedules or capital gains schedules. The VITA sites are scattered into communities at libraries and other convenient locations. They are open nights and weekends for the benefit of working people. You do not have to answer such qualifying questions as how much money you make per year. If you feel you need this kind of free help, call 1-800-424-1040 or your local IRS office. If you want to hire a professional to help you, your options include the following:

H & R Block is purely a tax form filing service. These people are good historians, that is, you bring them the information, and they will put it on your form in the proper manner. They do not give advice.

PA (Public Accountant). This person is a licensed service provider. He or she is also a historian and, although able to give elementary tax advice, is more expensive than H & R Block. In looking for a PA, find someone who has a lot of experience. That is the biggest factor for this and the following categories of experts.

CPA (Certified Public Accountant). He or she is viewed as an expert at tax filing and giving tax advice. A CPA is more expensive than a PA. Unless you have a complex financial portfolio, you probably do not need a CPA.

Tax attorney. Probably the most expensive service provider; you pay by the hour. He or she gives purely tax advice and also plays a warrior role in advocating for a client at the time of a divorce, for example. A tax attorney can also help structure your finances to avoid death taxes charged against your estate if you should die. A tax attorney is familiar with wills, trusts, insurance and other matters which relate to preserving your resources while you are alive and in the event of your death.

A home of your own

This is a dream that many women think is unattainable until five, maybe ten years down the road. Or maybe never. Usually the cost of the house and the down payment seem prohibitive. But some homes are much cheaper than others, and you might be surprised to hear that it is possible to buy a home for as little as $1,200 down in some locations.

Owning your own home, if you have a fixed mortgage (which means the interest rate stays constant for the duration of the loan), gives you a sense of security. Real estate agents will tell you that women, more often than men, tend to be emotionally tied to their homes for stability, security, a sense of family, of belonging. Children, too, seem to settle down when they have their own room in their own home.

Consider Sam and Lulu, two young children whose mother had just bought their first home, who jumped out of the car and ran all over the yard and the house proclaiming, "And this is our tree! And this is our backyard! And these are our very own stairs! Can we slide down them on the sleeping bag? And this is my bedroom." Since leaving their father, they had lived in a succession of apartments and houses—all owned by someone else. Now, they felt, they had finally stopped wandering.

Buying a home is attractive as a retirement plan. You can probably pay it off by retirement time, and meanwhile, with a fixed mortgage, your monthly payment does not go up. Regarding paying money toward rent, as realtors say, you're either buying your own home or someone else's. And your mortgage interest is tax deductible. In about five years, you start making money on your house because it appreciates in value. Of course, once you buy one home, you can move to another and simply transfer your down payment to the new house. But each time you move, your mortgage payment will probably go up because of appreciation on all homes. Staying in one place can save you money every month.

Your state may have low-cost mortgage money available to you as a single wage earner. Check with your state and local housing authorities. In the states where such funds exist, these mortgages are several percentage points below standard loans. For example, if the current interest rate were 11 percent fixed (a rate which does not fluctuate with the economy), the state interest rate might be around nine percent fixed, possibly lower, depending on the house you buy. You would be looking for houses priced at the low end of the market. At 11 percent interest on a 30-year $50,000 mortgage (after the down payment), your monthly payment would be $476.16. At nine percent interest on the same mortgage, your monthly payment would be $402.31.

There are wonderful, inexpensive homes in older neighborhoods, neighborhoods which also are organized with community centers, crime watch programs, a neighborhood organization and active parent groups at the schools. More important than the average price of the homes in a neighborhood is the quality of community life. A well-organized community is probably a stable, neighborly and safe community. Duplexes are good possibilities, since you can live in one half and rent out the other for income which can pay your mortgage. Lease-purchase deals are available, though if the house is being sold by the owner without an agent, it may be more expensive than the market value. You would have to check this out yourself or, for a small fee or gratis, an agent friend may do this for you.

Once you have checked with your state or local housing authority for low-cost loans, you should look for a real estate agent who has been selling homes in your desired area for at least five years. Ask for references from your friends. There are agents who specialize in moderately priced housing and enjoy working with low and moderate income families to secure homes for them. The seller pays your realtor's commission, so the realtor's services are free to you, the buyer. The realtor should know about the quality of neighborhoods, be able to guide you to mortgage money that will work for you, and work with the mortgage company to see you through the deal.

When you are looking for an older home, which will cost less per square foot than a new home, you can pay about $100-$200 to have the house inspected for sound condition by a third party. Do not trust appraisers to do the job, for some simply cruise by the outside and price the house by the neighborhood average and the "curbside appeal" if they are swamped with work that day. Ask your realtor to recommend someone who will do a good job for you.

The money will be well spent. You can think of it as a kind of insurance against moving into a structural disaster which you have to pay to repair or unload on someone else at considerable cost to you.

The down payment

While owning a home is not everyone's dream, if you want one, you have to come up with a down payment. Sometimes you can purchase new condominiums without a down payment, but the monthly mortgage payment is usually too expensive for low and middle-income wage earners with a single paycheck. So the down payment is the obstacle that you might not be able to get around.

In planning for your down payment, put off buying a new car. That can come later. This is a car-fixated society, but a dependable used car can serve your needs. And a $300 car payment often prevents you from buying a house, since that $300 could go a long way toward your monthly mortgage payment. Do not take out any large, long-term loan. Having to list it among your fixed expenses could deny you approval on a mortgage loan. And if you owe $2,000 to credit, don't pay off the credit card; instead, save that money for the down payment.

The buyer has to pay closing costs on the house, which can amount to $2,000-plus. Usually the buyer pays this at the time of closing, but the buyer and seller can agree to add the closing costs to the mortgage, to be paid off over time, and the seller pays at the time of closing, saving the buyer $2,000-plus in up-front money.

You cannot legally borrow money for a down payment. But you can get a large gift of money from your parents. If you do not sign a contract, this "gift" can actually be a loan, interest-free or not. One woman's father gave her a large down payment for a condo, which left her with a $500 monthly mortgage. He told her that no matter what happened to him, he wanted her to have a place to live that she could afford. Gifts can also come from a friend, your employer or any group. You write a letter to the giver acknowledging the gift legally, and keep a copy for yourself. Whether you repay that gift at a later time is up to you and the giver. Some people who have good relationships with their bosses have asked for and received down-payment money. Others have received funds from their church community. You know your resources, and while it takes courage to ask for money, it can get you into your own home.

More and more companies are setting up 401K plans for their employees. These allow the employee to arrange a payroll deduction from each paycheck for a tax-free savings account. The employer matches 50 cents on the dollar, or dollar for dollar; the rates vary from company to company. This money remains in the account until you leave the job, at which point you pay taxes or roll over the money to an IRA, except for a "hardship withdrawal" for 1) major medical expenses, 2) education for you and your dependents and 3) the purchase of a residence. You might be able to borrow money against your own account and repay it within five years.

One woman had a yard sale and netted over $400 toward her down payment. Two young brothers who had been saving for a trip to Florida were asked, "Would you rather go to Florida or have bedrooms of your own in a house of our own?" It was no contest; the boys "jumped their jars," according to the real estate agent, and came up with $142, which they proudly carried to the bank to deposit in the family mortgage account.

Shopping for mortgage money

For about $35, you can get a credit check for a pre-application of mortgage money with a bank, or other lending institution. Your credit needs to be good, though it needn't be extensive. The lender will approve you for a loan of, say, $70,000, or another amount which they decide. Then you know what your house price limit is, and you start looking. Another option is to find a house, first, and then try to find a mortgage lender. In this case, you wait out the credit check and hope that you have not chosen a house that is too expensive, i.e., that you cannot qualify for a loan that will cover what's necessary for this particular purchase.

Some mortgage terms you should know include:

◇ **Adjustable rate loans** are those with interest rates which will
fluctuate with changes in the economy. You need to make sure
there is an interest rate ceiling for your loan at no more than
six percent over the rate at the time you assumed the loan.

◇ **Fixed-rate loans** have the same interest rate for the duration of
the loan.

◇ **FHA (Federal Housing Administration) loans** require as little
as five percent down payment. The loan insures the lender,
and was designed to let people with steady incomes, but not a
lot of cash, into the housing market. The borrower has to meet
credit and income guidelines, and the house needs to pass a
stringent appraisal.

◇ **VA (Veterans Administration) loans** are available to military
veterans. No down payment is required. Credit, income and
appraisal standards are similar to FHA.

◇ **Conventional loans** are available through banks and mortgage
companies. The amount of down payment, the length of the
loan, and other requirements are set by the lender and can
fluctuate widely.

You should shop around for mortgage money just as you
would for cars or for a refrigerator. Some lenders are more liberal
in their underwriting policies than others. Some will give you a
larger loan limit than others. Your realtor will be able to give you
advice on where to look for money, as in "See Jim Taylor at Domin-
ion Bank. He'll help you out."

If you think you can afford a larger mortgage than the lender
will allow you based on your income alone, you can have an affluent relative or friend co-sign the loan for you. Then you both are
legally responsible for keeping up the payments, and the house will
be in both your names, but you can pay the mortage yourself.

Retirement?

You'd better be planning for retirement now, because these
days people work only 50 percent of their lifespan. Living 30 years
beyond your date of retirement is not an unrealistic expectation, and

you want to have some financial flexibility during those years. Who looks forward to 30 years of poverty? And the poverty class is, increasingly, single mothers, their children, and retired citizens. There are more women than men living below the poverty line.

Elsie N. wrote the following for her local newspaper:

"I am 78 and live alone. My pitiful little 'fixed income' is $243 a month . . . . In 1987 my check was increased by one dollar. In January of this year I would have gotten an increase of $10.90 but Medicare went up $6.90. So I got a $4 raise. That $4 won't buy a loaf of bread a week . . . try buying food, paying electric bills, heat bills and insurance on $243 a month, in addition to all the extra, unexpected bills like doctor bills, etc., and then you will know what 'fixed income' and 'growing old' means."

The younger you are when you start saving, the more you will have at retirement.

Making your money grow

Retirement planning is a three-legged stool:
1. **Social Security benefits,**
2. **pension benefits from work,** and
3. **personal savings.** In the area of personal savings you have the most opportunity to create financial growth.

The 401K plan (see page 203) gives you a high percentage of growth on your money, and anyone who has access to this plan should use it. Since the money is deducted from your paycheck, you never miss it once you begin the plan. And it adds up fast. If you pay in $5 per week, and your company matches that, you get $40 per month, or $480 per year. You can increase your matched deduction up to about 5 percent of your salary. Some plans allow you to contribute more unmatched funds as well.

Some companies have **profit sharing plans**. If the company annual profit is $50,000, you get your cut according to your salary as a percentage of the whole salary pool. The money is kept in an account for you by the employer. With profit sharing, long-term employment works to your advantage.

Saving money at your bank for retirement is a poor idea, because the interest rate is often lower than inflation.

Securities—bonds, stocks, Certificate of Deposits (CDs), and real estate—are available as investments. Financial advisors suggest that you diversify your assets so that if one hits a slump, the others will carry along your overall financial plan.

Financial advisors

When you have a small amount of money to save or invest ($1,000-$5,000) you might want to create a personal banking relationship with the branch manager of your bank or with a bank officer. Explain your personal and financial situation and ask for advice. "I need to be aware of my options. What can you offer me?" He or she will probably be happy to explain the range of investment options which the bank offers and will be able to describe other investment options, as well. The advice is free, as are some of the investment options—no broker is needed. Banks also have both discount and full-range brokerage services for stocks, bonds, mutual funds and CDs. Explore their services.

66 *If you need a broker, always get recommendations.* **99**

If and when you need a broker, look for a woman. Women brokers are growing in numbers, and they have had to fight for every advance in a previously all-male club. They understand what it's like to make it on your own. They are going to be more sensitive to single motherhood; some are single mothers themselves. But as always, get recommendations. Ask your banker. Check with the National Association for Professional Saleswomen and other women's networking organizations represented in your town (the YWCA can help find these). Even at the beginning stages, if you choose to educate yourself about your investment options, you will make more informed choices.

College funds

The amount of money you need from your pocket to send your child to college may be zero to $20,000 per year or more, depending on scholarships, contribution by the father, loan resources, whether the school is state or private and other variables. Two important factors are 1) how much you are able to offer and 2) how much you are willing to offer. And the related question is this: How much responsibility do you think your child should assume in paying for his or her own college education? There are no right or wrong answers to these questions. It's a matter of choice based on values and goals. Each family needs to draw up its own plan.

There is a treasure trove of literature in bookstores and libraries which deals with financial resources, selecting a college, and making the transition from home to college. One survey book is *The College Guide for Parents*, by Charles J. Shields, published by The College Board, 1988. This book, and others, provides information on college loans, scholarships, work opportunities, expectations, and other priceless information as you and your children prepare for higher education.

Many colleges and universities offers tuition discounts to an employee's children after she has worked there a certain period of time, and can mean thousands of dollars as an employee benefit.

One single mother joked when her children were five and eight, "Well, he'll play ball and she'll be damn smart, and they'll get scholarships . . ." The funny thing is, they did . . . and to Yale as well as several state schools.

The responsibility your child assumes in paying for college is not only financial. It begins by doing the hard work so that they are eligible to apply for grants and scholarships. SAT scores are often the result of sweat equity and desire for knowledge that begins in first grade.

Single mothers can help by checking homework assignments, attending school functions, and otherwise emphasizing the importance of education and presenting the option of higher education for their children throughout their school years.

Ready-cash funds

Ideally, you would build a small savings account, say $700, to have cash on hand in case you need to fly to a funeral, buy a new washing machine, pay a car repair bill, etc. To save for a vacation, you could add to that base figure monthly. But you may choose, instead, to use your credit accounts to borrow money —the spend now, pay later option.

A far more serious consideration is a savings account in the amount of three months' salary. You never know when you may lose your job, through no fault of your own, or even quit in disgust (not recommended). Jan B. was fired from a $27,000 job. Six months later, the unemployment insurance ran out, and she found a similar job which paid slightly less. Three weeks after she was hired, the company was purchased by another company, and Jan was let go. Desperate to find a job, any job, to keep her house and car, she paid her bills only because her parents were able to support her and the children. This is not an unusual story. Bankruptcy court is full of people who hit a financial snafu.

Three months' salary stashed away can be your insurance against disaster. But make your money work for you. Choose a cash-equivalent, interest-bearing account. See your banker for advice.

If it's hard for you to save

Barbara Gilder Quint, former stockbroker, author and lecturer, suggests these ways to save money:

- ◆ **Pay yourself first.** When you deposit your check, deposit your savings amount, no matter how small. Or take advantage of an automatic deduction plan offered by your employer.
- ◆ **Fool yourself.** If you get a raise, put it in the bank and continue to live on your old salary. Or split your raise and put half in the bank (remember to pay yourself first) and half in your checking account.
- ◆ **Deposit windfall money.** This includes part or all of birthday money and other gifts, tax refunds, and other such money which can go into savings.
- ◆ **Drive your car another three months.** If you are going to

trade in your car, wait three months and bank the money you would have allocated for new car payments.

♦ **Pay bills you don't owe.** Whenever you pay off a long-term credit bill, medical bill, etc., pay that monthly amount to your bank account for the next three months.

♦ **Save breakage money.** Pay your bill at the grocery store, gas station, etc., and put the change in a separate purse. At the end of the week, deposit your change into your savings account.

♦ **Do not make long distance telephone calls.** Write letters or send cards or "letter cassette tapes" instead.

♦ **Cut one routine expense** for a limited time. Skip renting videos or going out to lunch or happy hour for a week or two and put that money into the account.

♦ **Go cold turkey.** Cut every optional purchase to the bone (see page 189-91) while you budget your usual amount for them. After a couple of pay periods, you may end up with a little bundle of green which you can transfer from checking to savings.

Wills

Everyone needs one. If you don't design your own will, you get the state's will by default. The state will give 100 percent of your estate to your children, if you are not married. The court then appoints a guardian for your children, if they are minors, younger than 18. The court appoints a conservator of the estate, and in no time at all the entire estate has disappeared in legal fees, leaving your children with nothing.

More than one book is out on writing your own will. Any number of women have a hand-written will in a file drawer somewhere. In my opinion, the future of your children should not be left to the best guess of an amateur trying to wade through legal land. Saving the $150-plus fee for a tax lawyer to write up your will may end up costing your heirs hundreds of dollars, because you neglected one detail in your self-drawn will. The legal system of inheritance is a game which you have to play by the rules or you lose the game.

You will probably want a trust fund set up for your children while they are young and in case they contract a long-term illness. Your will allows you to name the trustee. You "forgive bond" in your will, and the trustee can act as you would if you were alive. In setting up trusts, many people follow the thirds rule:

◇ One-third of the inheritance at age twenty-five *(this allows for one "bad" marriage where the ex-spouse gets half of all property)*
◇ One-third at age thirty *(this allows for one generic mistake)*
◇ One-third at age thirty-five *(when the child has "settled down")*

Settlement of your property in a will is basic. Setting up a trust is more complex and will probably cost you a little more.

Shop around for a good tax lawyer. Talk to friends and relatives. Ask, "Who do you know that is honest? Who has experience? Who is a specialist? Who do you like in this business?" Call the lawyer. Ask if he or she charges to interview. If he or she does not work out, ask that lawyer for a referral. Insurance agents will know good tax lawyers, since they deal with them regularly.

As you design your will with your lawyer, provide for someone to take custody of your minor children, in case their father is unable or unwilling to take them. You may want to name a friend or relative. If custody is not specified, the children could become wards of the court and go to foster homes. When you specify custody, you have some control over who your children's caretakers will be.

Remember to read your will about once a year to make sure it still reflects your financial situation. One single mother who had remarried stumbled on her will one day and found she had given her two children everything, including the kitchen sink, in a house she no longer owned. Go back to your lawyer when you need an adjustment.

Cultivating feeling rich

You feel rich when you pay off a credit card bill. You feel rich when you find a five-dollar bill in your coat pocket. You feel rich when you see a credit on your water bill because you overpaid last month. Part of feeling rich is feeling lucky, feeling fortunate.

Then, if you feel lucky or fortunate, do you feel rich? If you can answer yes to that question, that opens up many opportunities in your life to feel rich: On Friday, your last day of work, when you look ahead to a long, sunny weekend. When you gather the first spring flowers in a bouquet on your dining room table. When you see the faces of your children returning from their father's house, their arms reaching up to give you a hug.

To the extent you can take the focus off of acquiring things and put it on developing relationships and celebrating creation, then money takes a back seat, and feeling rich is something you can feel right now.

CHAPTER 12: Personal and Home Security

Night fears

Analyzing your environment

Don't appear vulnerable

Doors

Windows

Lighting

Electronic alarm systems

While you are on vacation

"Join Hands with the Badge"
    programs

Problems related to apartment
    complexes

Miscellaneous tips

Telephone contacts

What a burglar does in your home

Game plans

Fires

Guns

Rape

"Now you know why
I read so long into the night, Mommy.
It's because I think of all kinds of things —
the house might burn down,
a robber might come,
the tree might fall on our roof —
and I keep thinking of them
and they won't go away
in the night
in the bed,
so I read, and then
I don't think of them.

"At Daddy's house I'm not afraid
because Daddy works until two in the morning
and he could smell a fire
and wake us up,
and Grandma and Grandad watch TV
until really late at night.
So I'm not afraid.

"But here there's just you.
So I read."
                    — Laura, age 7

As single mothers, we need to recognize the difference between paranoia and justifiable fear within ourselves, and use our heads to make our environments safe for our families.

Night fears

Women fear sleeping alone. And that makes a lot of sense. The 20th-century world of drug addicts supporting their habits and rapists getting their revenge and psychotics exorcising their demons is our world. Women and children have a right to live without fear and without being violated, yet 36 percent of women 12 and over in the United States in 1989 will be victims of completed violent crimes—rape, robbery and assault—in their lifetimes (U.S. Department of Justice, Bureau of Justice Statistics, Technical Report, "Lifetime Likelihood of Victimization," March 1987, Table 1). That is not a pleasant thought. And even though we may believe that most people are good-neighbor material and others would at least have the decency to leave us alone, there is a violent minority of our population that is armed and on the prowl.

> 66 The trick is to identify what you fear in living alone, and then find a solution to alleviate that fear. 99

Noises in the middle of the night can drive you crazy. One 80-year-old widow panicked after the death of her husband. Her adult children had left town after the burial, and she was alone. She could not sleep. She found a neighbor who was willing to spend the nights with her until she could get used to the idea of staying by herself in the home she loved. She never adjusted. Within a month she left town to spend the rest of her healthy years living with her various children. It was a less than ideal arrangement, but she could again sleep at night.

Fortunately, single mothers with children are younger and better able to adapt to new circumstances. One woman got herself a hamster, and when she heard noises in the middle of the night, she said to herself, "Oh, that's just Harry" (the hamster) and went back to sleep. Another woman rented a second-story apartment in an old house above a family she got to know well and who, she felt, would come to her rescue in an emergency. Another woman who worries about entering her empty house at night leaves the home of friends, telling them, "I will be home in ten minutes, and I'll call you. If I don't call in fifteen minutes, you call me. If I don't answer, call the police." She feels safe.

The trick is to identify what you fear in living alone, and then find a solution to alleviate that fear. If you have to use sleeping pills or alcohol more than once every two weeks, you need to find a healthier solution to your fear.

> ❝ Children often fear the night. Use night lights, white noise machines, teddy bears—whatever makes them feel good. ❞

You can expect your children to have their own fears. One ten-year-old boy I know is afraid to sleep in a room by himself at his mother's house. His father's house has an electronic alarm system which makes the boy feel safe. His mother's house does not, so she allows him to sleep in the same room with whomever he chooses, using for his bed a thin foam hospital mattress she has covered with bright fabric.

Children often fear the night. But as a single mother you can expect your children to feel less secure with you than they would if their dad were in the house as well. Night lights, white noise machines, teddy bears, baseball bats by their beds, a certain kind of window covering—whatever makes them feel safe will help them sleep better and wake up refreshed to give their best to a new day.

Analyzing your environment

Feeling secure is a state of mind. *Being* **secure is a matter of preparation.** The rest of this section on security deals with lifestyle and hardware. Your local hardware store clerk can probably show you samples of all the items mentioned here. Recently I walked to my own neighborhood hardware store and said I wanted to see home security devices. The clerk said, "Oh, you want a dog and a gun," and laughed. Then he took me on an amazing tour of home security hardware, all reasonably inexpensive. And when I asked for things he didn't have, he said I could look in his catalogs and order anything I wanted. That's the good news.

The bad news is, a professional burglar can get into any home he wants to. However, he would rather open a door lock quickly and quietly than blow out a hole in the wall with dynamite. The harder you make it for the burglar to get in, the sooner he will look to other homes for an easier job, and the safer you will be.

> 66 *Feeling secure is a state of mind.* ***Being*** *secure is a matter of preparation.* 99

A typical burglar wants to get into your home in about ten seconds. You want to delay him from twenty seconds to never.

Consider having a police officer come out to your home to look it over for security. The officer can tell you how effective your current security system is. He'll look at hardware, ask you about living habits and suggest improvements. Police suggestions often include both state-of-the-art security equipment and inexpensive alternatives, so you can suit your taste and budget. All you have to do is call your police department and ask. If an officer cannot do a site evaluation, you can describe your doors, windows and visibility, over the phone and still get some good advice.

Don't appear vulnerable

- ♦ Keep some mail coming to your house in a man's name.
- ♦ List only your first and middle initial in the phone directory, or take your number out of the directory.
- ♦ If you have an answering machine, do not mention your name. Say only "*We're* not able to answer the phone right now," so that you leave open the possibility that a man lives with you, and that in any case, *someone* lives with you. Or have a male friend or relative make the recording for you.

- ◆ Do not put your name on your mailbox.
- ◆ Close your blinds and curtains at night. Do not dress in a room with open blinds. This encourages Peeping Toms and rapists.
- ◆ Refer to yourself as Mrs. _____ when you call to arrange for household repairs, and when strangers enter your home, try not to divulge your marital status. Don't chat with the plumber, the carpet cleaner, the man who comes to repair your washer. They might come back uninvited. One single mother leaves articles of menswear in plain view—an old jacket in a cleaning bag, mens' socks, underwear, shaving gear in the bathroom. Her favorite: size 13 work boots, muddy and left outside her front door.

Doors

Unlocked doors and windows accounted for 45 percent of all break-ins between 1973 and 1982 (U.S. Department of Justice, Bureau of Justice Statistics, National Crime Survey Bulletin, "Household Burglary," January 1985, Table 1).

When you move into an apartment, **have all the lock tumblers changed by a locksmith.** Make sure you have permission to do this before you sign a contract. Also make sure repairs to your apartment will take place only when you are there. Avoid a large complex where a maintenance person has a key to your apartment; sometimes these people, as well as security guards, serve as "inside" contacts in burglary rings.

Your **locks should be double-cylinder, dead-bolt locks requiring a key** on both the inside and outside. Other kinds of locks are less secure since they can be opened easily with a credit card, a strip of plastic or a screwdriver. Keep a key somewhere near the door, inside, in case you have to escape a fire. You may want to leave a key with a neighbor, but do not hide one under the doormat or in the mailbox or anywhere else. Burglars will find them.

A lock story from New York City:

A woman moved into a walk-up apartment that came with four locks. She was delighted. A week after she moved in, someone broke in while she was at work and took all her electronic equipment. She added a lock and replaced the equipment. Two weeks later, another break in. She added a sixth lock and then a seventh lock to no avail. In despair she called a locksmith who asked her, "Do you lock all your locks faithfully?" "Oh, yes," she sobbed. "Well, next time, only lock four of them." She did as he suggested. The burglar could not tell which locks he was unlocking and which he was locking, and the woman was never bothered again.

Put a peephole in your door at eye level to view anyone outside the door. Old-fashioned peephole glass is only about one-quarter-inch in diameter, and while it magnifies the view, it is inferior to more modern models as large as three inches in diameter. Get a larger model, and don't open the door to anyone you don't know. Intruders often pose as salesmen, repairmen, people looking for lost dogs. Direct them to the police department, or just say, "I'm sorry, you can't come in," walk away, and *don't feel guilty* for saying "no." Then call a friend, explain what happened, describe the person. Teach your children how to use the peephole and when not to open the door.

Some exterior doors are not solid-core wood but are hollow-core, intended for interior use. These can be kicked and easily smashed. Watch out for these in inexpensive apartment complexes and wherever construction materials seem minimal, even cheap. You can tell if a door is hollow by knocking hard at its edge and then at its center.

Doors with large windows as a design feature should have metal bars over the window area.

Windows

You can **install iron bars on the outside of your windows,** and that is popular in some cities like Charleston, South Carolina, and New York City, especially on ground-level windows. They can be an attractive design feature, but they are expensive, and they can trap you inside in case of a fire.

Sash windows should have metal locks. You can buy them with keys as well as the more usual, but less safe, swivel-latch kind. If your sash windows are wooden, an alternative to the metal lock is simply to nail your windows closed with large nails where the upper and lower window wood overlaps in the right corner. Leave the nail heads sticking out just enough to be able to pull them out when you want to. In the spring and summer, if you prefer open windows, remove the nails, open the windows no more than six inches, and nail them open in that position. This is cheap and effective.

Windows covered with storm windows further discourage a burglar.

Sliding glass "patio" doors and sliding windows can be locked with wooden dowels or broomstick handles cut to the proper length and laid in the groove of the sill. A better method is to install a key lock on the metal frame itself on both the permanent and slid-from the inside in case of fire. Also consider installing a dead-bolt lock on the door at the top of the basement stairs.

If you have a **skylight** that opens, it needs a lock, too.

When you return home at night, go on a quick tour of your house to see that all the windows and doors are secure. The children or others may be unlocking them. One rapist, for example, would go to a house during the day, pry open a window lock, close the window and leave, then return at night through that window to rape. **Checking your locks takes only a minute and should be part of your routine, like checking the mail.**

Sometimes people do not lock their bathroom windows, thinking they are too small for a burglar to enter through them. Wrong. Lock yours.

Lighting

Outside lighting all through the night is recommended. If your apartment entrance is not well lit, request a change with the manager. If your house is not well lit by a streetlight, install outside lights under the eaves. You can buy an inexpensive timer or a photo-cell (about $15 to $20) that will automatically turn the lights on at dusk and off at dawn.

Inside timers are small boxes that plug into your electrical sockets. Then you plug a lamp, radio, TV, or whatever, into the timer. You set the timer to turn on and off automatically at certain times. That way, if you are away from your home when dusk falls, your timers can turn on your lights and make it appear that someone is at home. They cost about $10 and are very easy to use; a hardware store clerk can show you how in 30 seconds. Consider the variable timers which alter the on-and-off time slightly each day to confuse a burglar who might be casing your home while you are on vacation.

Electronic alarm systems

Their name is legion. You can pay thousands of dollars to a security company to provide, install and maintain your system. You can go to a store like Radio Shack and get a less expensive but effective system. Or you can forget alarm systems and still have a reasonably safe environment using the guidelines described above.

The disadvantages of electronic alarm systems are that they are usually expensive and can malfunction, causing them to go off when there is no burglar. Like the little boy who cried "wolf," an alarm which goes off by mistake loses its power as a danger signal, and neighbors learn to accept its noise as an infrequent nuisance in the neighborhood.

A properly working alarm can deter burglars and give you peace of mind. A sticker on your window announcing your alarm system can be effective, but make sure you really have an alarm system to back up the sticker. A red electronic signal moving across your door when the alarm is on is more effective. And the actual noise, if a burglar breaks in, should strike terror into his heart and alert neighbors to the danger; they, then, call the police. Some systems trigger alarms in private security company offices which then send out their own armed security guards to check out the alarm.

You can buy alarms which respond to noise, movement, pressure and breakage of some mechanism. *One tip about alarms: A loud outside alarm will alert the neighbors and the police. A screeching inside alarm will scare the pillowcase from a typical burglar and, psychologically, make him beat a hastier exit.*

To investigate what's available in your area, look in the Yellow Pages under "Security," or call your hardware store and ask where you can buy low-cost systems. They will know.

In my area, as a point of comparison, a one-room motion sensor, the least expensive electronic device at Radio Shack, sells for $59.99. A whole-house system starts at about $200, depending on the size of your house. And you have to be able to install the system yourself or pay someone to do it for you.

Once you begin looking into the world of electronic security, you can be overwhelmed with what is available and the special devices designed to prevent burglars from entering your house in a wide variety of ways. Remember that the burglar is looking for an easy job, and that even with the most sophisticated equipment, no house is guaranteed safe against burglary. Shop around before you buy. You might call up the police department again and go over your choice with an officer with whom you have previously talked.

While you are on vacation

Have neighbors pick up your mail and newspapers and put a sack of garbage in your can before each trash pickup. Leave a key with the neighbors in case of an emergency, and have them check to make sure no notes or flyers are left on your front door. (You can repay your neighbors with the same service when they go on vacation.)

Have someone cut your grass or shovel your snow. Turn down the ring on your telephone or have it temporarily disconnected, a free service now offered in some cities. Leave a bathroom or hall light burning and some draperies partly open. Put a timer on a living room lamp and on a radio that you turn up loud.

"Join Hands with the Badge" programs

Whatever they are called in your city, these programs are offered by most police departments to neighborhoods. Usually a police officer comes out and talks to a group of neighbors about crime prevention: personal security, watching out for each other, and advertising the neighborhood's anti-crime program for the benefit of potential burglars. This works best where there is a feeling of community and stability among the neighbors.

Apartment complexes can present a problem to these kinds of programs. It seems the closer people live to each other, the less they interact with their neighbors, possibly because privacy is at a premium. There is often a high turnover in apartment tenants, and people think, "Why waste time getting to know these strangers?" That mentality breeds burglars, some of whom live in complexes and break into their neighbors' units. They watch and wait.

One old woman who lived in an apartment complex saw a burglar breaking into her car. She had a gun, leaned out her second-story window and shot him in the heel. Police came and asked a crowd that had surrounded the burglar, "Who shot this man?" The old woman said, "We don't know." The apartment complex manager later called the police to come and talk to residents about security, and at that meeting the woman acknowledged her deed, to the laughter (because of her age) and cheers of the residents. The gun question aside, this incident brought residents together to take community action to reduce crime.

Problems related to apartment complexes

Every city has apartment complexes made up of five or ten or twenty large block buildings set at odd angles and identified as A through K, or some other scheme. If the police receive a call about a break-in, they may easily find the complex but have difficulty finding the apartment. That gives the burglar a little more time to get in and get out.

If you decide to live in a complex, avoid the ground-floor units which are the most vulnerable. Make an effort to get to know your neighbors. Make sure your landlord will allow you to add deadbolt locks, if they are not already there, and if you want an alarm system, make sure the lease allows it before you sign.

Miscellaneous tips

◊ Don't leave your back door open, thinking no one will poke around back.
◊ While burglars prefer first-story windows, if they see a ladder in the garage, or if a climbing tree snuggles up to your house, they may climb.
◊ If you return home to see a busted door frame or other sign of entry, *do not go in*. Go to a friend's house and call the police.
◊ Have a telephone by your bedside with the jack in your room. Install a lock on your bedroom door and use that room as a place to retreat if you or the children need it.
◊ Burglars don't like dogs. If you do, consider getting one that barks to alert you of possible intruders.
◊ Keep the shrubbery around your house or at the entrance to your apartment trimmed low to discourage burglars.
◊ Yards with privacy fences provide good screens for burglars.
◊ Have emergency numbers marked on the outside of each telephone.

Telephone contacts

People will call you up wanting all kinds of information from you about your personal life. Many of these people are harmless. However, some burglars use the telephone to identify potential victims. A typical opening is, "Ms. _____, my name is Joe Smith, and I would like to ask you just a few questions about your television viewing habits." You agree. "What program are you watching now?" This line of questioning moves on to " How many people live in your house over the age of 18? What is your occupation?" By the time you finish answering these questions, a burglar can find out that you are a single mother absent from home until 5 p.m. Monday through Friday, and you probably make enough money to have a VCR (the number one stolen item since 1987) and other valuables in your house.

Avoid answering any personal questions to strangers on the phone for any reason. Memorize a standard answer with which you are comfortable. Some suggestions are:

"We are not interested."

"I have a policy that I do not buy anything or answer questions over the telephone."

"I need to get off the phone."

These are what I call "no" statements. Do not give the caller a *reason* why you don't want a product or can't talk with him or her. Some of these people are very sophisticated and have been trained to come back at you in response to anything except "No." Do not feel sorry for the caller. You do not need to take responsibility for the caller's feelings. You have a right to privacy, and your needs come first.

What a burglar does in your home

He does not carry a tool box, ladders or ropes. Just a small screwdriver and a credit card, and with these he breaks in. He heads for the bedroom, and on his way he figures out all the exits. He grabs a pillowcase off the bed and begins to fill it with jewelry, money, guns and silver. He checks shoebags and between mattresses in the bedroom, between frozen meat in the freezer, and other common hiding places. He does this in a matter of minutes. Then he goes for the heavy electronic equipment: VCRs, TVs, stereos, radios, computers. The entire operation should take him no more than 10 to 20 minutes. If he has an accomplice, he gains entry first, then signals the driver to pull up the van (looking like an official delivery company, for example), and they start loading. If his operation is successful and he gets some good stuff, he may hit your next-door neighbor in a few days. He may even come back and try to rob you again. And the profile of the most common burglar is one who is on drugs. He's supporting his habit; it's business.

Game plans

When you are in a crisis situation, experience indicates that you will do what you have rehearsed in your mind. For example, a 70-year-old woman returned from church one day to see two young men standing on her lawn. Without a word, she passed by them onto her porch. They followed, grabbed her and began to rip off her clothes right on the porch. The next thing she remembers is seeing them fleeing from her yard. She then heard a whistle and looked down to see herself holding one that hung around her neck—a whistle she had received and used at a senior-citizen safety meeting a month before.

Many of us go through "what if" situations in our minds. It is a good idea to do the same thing with your children in a matter-of-fact way, as in, "What would you do if a strange man sitting in a car called you over to his open window, asked for directions and you clearly saw him exposing his penis to you?" This happened to an 11-year-old girl walking across a college campus toward her mother's office. Sometimes children will think these questions are funny; at other times they may say, "That's creepy," or some other response. You can put aside their fears by saying, "Well, this probably will never happen to you, but what would you do if it did? How could you get yourself out of it?" See if they can provide more than one solution.

> 66 Teach your children how to avoid trouble, what their escape options are, who their friends are in emergencies, what telephone numbers they can call. Help them form their own game plans. 99

If the game plan comes from their heads, they will more likely be able to use it instinctively if, God forbid, they need to. Then you can add information, like, "Well, what about running to Mickie's house?" Teach your children how to avoid trouble, what their escape options are, who their friends are in emergencies, what telephone numbers they can call. Help them form their own game plans.

Fires

♦ Put up smoke detectors. Some go off from kitchen smoke, so people take them down when they cook and forget to put them back up. Make sure your detectors stay up on the wall.

◆ Do not allow anyone in your house to smoke in bed.

◆ Repair or replace electrical cords which have exposed wires.

◆ Have gas appliances checked once a year by a gas company repair person. This is a free service.

◆ Do not store kerosene or gasoline in enclosed or hot spaces. Avoid storing them at all, if you can.

◆ Space heaters are fire hazards, and some homeowners insurance companies will increase your premium if you declare you own one.

◆ Discuss fire prevention with your children, including safe handling of stoves, irons, candles and fireplaces.

◆ Rehearse fire safety rules and exit routes with children.

Guns

I cannot recommend them. They are dangerous to adults and children alike. ***Accidents with guns happen at home to the very people you hope to protect.*** More homicides are committed by family members with guns than any other combination of people and weapons.

Here is what a convicted rapist has to say about guns: "The gun is in her bag. She don't know when she's gonna get jumped. She might even not have time to get to the bag. There's a lot of rapes been happening lately. I see guns as causing problems. She doesn't know when she's going to get raped. Carrying it in her purse: no problem. Put it in the drawer: no problem. No big deal. Only thing they're doing is, if he [the rapist] gets by with it, he's got a gun that he can sell and cause some other crime or somebody else to get killed."

However, the question of guns is a very personal one. If you want to get a gun (most women who have guns use .38-caliber specials because they are easy to handle), call your police department and find out where to buy one, how to register it, how to keep your children from having access to it, and then learn to operate it as safely as possible at a local gun range.

Rape

Rape is a violent crime of power and anger. Nothing is more destructive to a woman than the violation of her body. And rape is a perennial fear.

It takes two elements for a crime to be committed:

1. *Idea or intent* in the mind of the criminal, and

2. *Opportunity* to commit the crime.

Only you can remove the opportunity. Being aware of your surroundings at all times and being prepared in important ways cuts down the odds of your being raped.

When traveling alone in your car, for example, keep plenty of gas in the tank. Travel on well-lit, well-traveled streets. Keep your doors locked. Keep windows rolled up while stopped in traffic. If you need air, use the air conditioner or roll down your windows no more than two inches. If someone tries to run your car off the road, try to overtake another car and stay close behind. If someone bumps your car on a deserted street, do not stop, continue driving to a gas station or other public place. Do not stop your car to assist strangers. Call the police for them.

If your car breaks down, park on the shoulder of the road, raise the hood, get back into your car, lock doors, shut windows and put on your emergency flashers. If someone stops to help, lower your windows slightly and ask them to please call the police. Refuse all other help.

If someone tries to force his way into your car, turn on the headlights and flash them repeatedly. Sound the horn continuously or in serial blows to attract attention. If he should break the window, do not let him reach the locking latch. Jab at his hand. Do not ever get out of your car unless the attacker gets into it.

Much of the information above, "Traveling Alone in Your Car," was taken from a booklet called *Preparation for Self-Protection* prepared in 1987 by the Victim Intervention Program and the Join Hands with the Badge section of the Nashville Police Department (Crime Prevention Division, Metropolitan Police, 1625 D.B. Todd Blvd., Nashville, Tennessee 37208). Other sections in this same booklet are titled Parking Your Car, Returning to Your Parked Car, Walking Alone, At Home Alone, Discouraging Obscene Callers, If Attacked, What to Do If You Are Raped, and Carrying A Weapon. This booklet alone is ten pages long, all of it worthwhile reading.

The scope of this book will not allow an adequate treatment of rape prevention and response. However, **all city police departments offer solid information,** similar to the above, on the subject. Women's centers, the YWCA and the public library are other good sources for rape information, which is usually free. A rape crisis center may exist in your town, and you should know about it and what services it offers.

Rape is such an important topic that *every woman owes it to herself to call a resource and get information on it*. Call your police department first. The police should have useful booklets on rape, the names, addresses and phone numbers of all the local agencies you would need to contact in case you or a friend is raped and information on rape prevention and self-protection workshops in your town.

Many women learn and enjoy self-protection skills, such as karate. Rape prevention workshops usually illustrate simple physical moves you can make to throw your attacker off balance and allow you time to escape. Investigating these resources now may help prevent a tragedy.

Do not hesitate to pass on rape prevention information to your daughters and sons as well. It is in their best interests for you to prepare them as you prepare yourself.

CHAPTER 13:   Fixing Things Around the House

It's so nice to have a man around the house

Marguerite's ex-husband was a little clumsy with a hammer and saw, but he did most of the basic fix-it work around their house—carpentry, electricity, plumbing, painting. For difficult jobs they called in professionals.

After she and her husband separated, Marguerite and her two children moved into an old house with friends. Her upstairs bathroom shower head did not deliver the water massage she was used to in her former home. She was frustrated; she knew what needed to be fixed, but her fix-it man was gone. With some hesitation, she went to her local hardware store, bought a massage shower head, asked the clerk how to install it, borrowed a wrench from a friend and did the work herself. The actual job took her about 30 minutes. She felt a tremendous sense of accomplishment and power.

When your fix-it man is gone, your choices are to live with the problem, learn how to do the job yourself or get someone else to do it for you.

Basic tools

Depending on who you are and where you live, basic tools can vary from a telephone (to call for help) to a tool box the size of a refrigerator. The wonderful part of living in apartments and condos is that much of the building maintenance is done by the management. However, management may be slow to move on your job, management may be unwilling to fix anything or you may own your own home, which means that you are the management. But even in a well-maintained apartment complex, you need to hang pictures, tighten screws, connect VCR and TV equipment and do other basic work to maintain your own equipment and space. For these small jobs, it's nice to have a

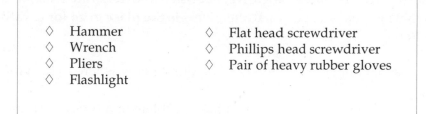

- ◇ Hammer
- ◇ Wrench
- ◇ Pliers
- ◇ Flashlight
- ◇ Flat head screwdriver
- ◇ Phillips head screwdriver
- ◇ Pair of heavy rubber gloves

A gold mine: your local hardware store

Barbara was at a friend's house down the street when her two sons called her and said, "Mom, come home quick! You know that outside faucet thing that you put the hose on? Well, it was bent over and we tried to straighten it, and now . . . well . . . there's water spraying up all over the place."

It was Saturday. Barbara ran home, thinking fast all the way. How do you get a plumber on Saturday? Look in the Yellow Pages? She saw the little river of water already trickling down the gutter as she ran. When she approached the house, she saw that the boys had put a trash can lid over the broken spigot to keep the water off the house. Barbara calmed the boys, went into the house, sat down by the phone, and said, "What am I going to do?" Her Uncle George, a real handyman, lived 60 miles away, and this was an emergency. Who do you call in an emergency? Who knows how to fix things? The hardware store. They would know what to do. She called. The clerk said she needed to shut off the water at the main valve by the street. She could try it with a wrench, or they had a tool for $6 that was made for that purpose. She bought the tool, shut off the water and called Uncle George who came out and fixed the spigot later in the day. She watched him do it and got a brief lesson in plumbing.

The men at the hardware store helped Barbara replace leaky washers, install a timer switch on the light in her living room, fix her leaky toilet and many other things.

If you need a fan or a set of picture hangers, you can buy them cheaply at a discount store like Wal-Mart. But **your local hardware** store—which is more expensive, but where the clerks are ready and willing to give you personal attention—**is the place to go (or to call) when**

- ◆ You have an emergency and don't know where to turn for help
- ◆ You need advice about a fix-it problem or a type of product
- ◆ You want to buy and install something that you've never done before

Especially if you own your own home, your local hardware store can become as valuable to you as your family physician. Inexpensive how-to books on home repairs are available at hardware stores, too, and if you can follow a recipe in a cookbook, you can follow most fix-it directions. If a job is clearly beyond you, the book will help you know the right questions to ask the hardware store clerks or professional workers.

When it makes sense to get help
◇ Know thyself.
◇ If you are not good with your hands, get help.
◇ If you don't have the time to spend half a day or more on a job, get help.
◇ If you don't like getting up to your elbows in tools and dust and goo, get help.
◇ If fix-it work frustrates you and you are facing a big job, get help.

Hiring a professional

One day I asked Helga, whose hair was always perfect, how she kept it that way. "The secret," she said, "is my hairdresser. She always cuts my hair just right. Maintaining it is easy once you have a good cut." I asked her how she found her hairdresser. "I saw a woman whose hair I really liked. I walked up to her and asked her who her hairdresser was. She told me, and I've been going to that hairdresser ever since."

You can do the same with professional fix-it people. Find a friend or neighbor whose home you admire, and ask that person for a recommendation for a painter, for example. People who set high standards of maintenance for their homes—especially professional people who have more money than time—often have a complete set of reference names of reliable fix-it people. Ask people at work. Ask relatives, ask your local hardware store (they often post business cards on a bulletin board, cards of customers with whose work they are familiar). Ask a real estate agent you know. They are in the business of selling homes, and often they dabble in real estate purchases for rental or quick fix-ups and resale. People are usually flattered to be asked for advice from you. Try to get at least three names to call, so that you can compare prices and other aspects of the job.

Caution: Check out a prospective worker thoroughly. If you get the name of a carpenter, for example, from a friend, call up the carpenter and ask for the names and phone numbers of two other people for whom he or she has done work. You will want to know

◇ Was the quality of the job excellent?
◇ Did the carpenter work in a timely fashion?
◇ Did the carpenter damage any of the client's property?
◇ Did the carpenter clean up his or her mess after each work session?
◇ Did the carpenter charge the price that was quoted or were there cost increases?
◇ Would the client hire the carpenter again?

Do not hesitate to call perfect strangers to ask these questions. Introduce yourself on the phone. "Mr. Jones, you don't know me, but Mr. Smith gave me your number. I need a carpenter to help me with kitchen cabinets. Do you have time to tell me a little about Mr. Smith? Did he do a good job for you?"

The sad story of Beth's painter:
Beth formerly worked with a man who said he painted houses. Beth called up her former boss and asked her if she thought the man

would do a good job painting three rooms in Beth's house. The boss gave a glowing recommendation of the employee. Beth hired him. He and his fellow worker set up their equipment, and Beth and the children left the house to spend the day with a friend. When they returned that night, Beth found paint splattered all over her furniture, rugs and hardwood floors because the men had not used drop cloths properly. Some of the trim was painted cleanly, and other trim had "holidays," or missed spots, and the paint had slopped over onto windows, floors and walls. Beth learned that the badly-painted trim had been done by the assistant. The lead painter had said he would sand and wash surfaces where necessary before painting, but he had not done this. With one room finished and two rooms partially painted, Beth dismissed the painters. There were bad feelings on both sides. Beth called her former boss, who felt responsible for the situation. She had given the painter a good recommendation based only on what he had told her; he had never actually done any painting for her. Three months later, Beth was still removing paint spots from odds and ends. She painted the unfinished rooms herself.

It pays in time and money to check references and ask specific questions about the quality of the work. When you call, some people will even invite you to see their finished job, and if they do, take them up on it. For large jobs, seeing a work sample is a must, so do ask if and when that's convenient.

Trading skills

If you can't afford to hire someone and don't want to do a job yourself, you can ask someone else to do it for you. Relatives, friends, neighbors, work associates—anyone is a possibility.

Make them an offer they can't refuse. Find out what their needs and pleasures are, and see if you can supply something of value to them. Like food. Send Uncle George home with a hug and a loaf of cranberry bread. For a handyman neighbor, contract to babysit with his children for a certain number of hours for free, so that he and his wife can go out on the town. Cook a dinner for someone, sew a tablecloth or otherwise do a little decorating, mow the lawn, wash and wax the car. If you know how to do taxes, offer that; if you know how to write a resume, offer that. If you are a good music critic, offer to put together a 90-minute party tape. Everyone has something they would like help with. Ask them and see if you can provide that help in exchange for fix-it work.

When you approach someone for the first time to set up a barter deal, start small, a job that takes no more than two hours, for example. If both of you are satisfied with the arrangment, you can continue to work together in this way, increasing the size of the barter deals as necessary and convenient.

Be aware that when you contract to exchange services with another person, you are accepting whatever quality the other person can provide, just as if you were paying money for the service. Check out the quality of the person's work ahead of time. You can say, point blank, "Will you do a good job for me?" and smile, smile, smile. You can ask to see a work sample. Since many bartering arrangements are between friends or aquaintances, there is an element of friendship tied in with the deal. State up front that "We both need to realize that this is strictly business. Right? And, oh, by the way, can we still be friends?" A little humor never hurts. Because friendship is an element in the deal, you have an added incentive to prevent disaster. Starting small provides some insurance for the friendship, so that in case of unfortunate results you can forgive and forget and get on with the friendship. There is a risk.

And there is a plus. Working with a friend can further cement the friendship. It's nice to be able to trust the person who is working on your property, and he or she will probably have a personal incentive to do a nice job for you.

Some neighborhood associations form talent pools where people sign up to barter their skills with other neighbors, and there are tool pools as well. Basically, the more people you know, the greater your resources for bartering talents, tools and time. In this way, you can save money while you meet your fix-it needs.

CHAPTER 14:   Managing Space and Time

Letting go of perfection

Rachel's four children had gone to her ex-husband's house for a holiday. She spent her first day alone cleaning up her house. "My house is always a wreck," she said. "Max [the youngest, age five] is the worst. And it's so frustrating. I can never get ahead. I keep my laundry down in the basement, and some of it never comes back up. The kids go downstairs to find clean clothes for school. I've heard of other mothers who live out of their laundry rooms. And I don't know where I'd put the clothes if I brought them all up. We don't have enough room in our apartment. There is one closet upstairs and one downstairs. That's it. The children don't know where to put things, because there isn't enough storage space. I have to be very creative in finding little niches for things. Does it ever get better?"

> 66 Somewhere between total chaos and total perfection lies a place of peaceful compromise where all the parties can agree— *Well, this will do for now.* 99

The answer is, yes. Her son Sam, age 13, had already started doing his own laundry. Her daughter Kate, age 11, had done a load once or twice. The older the children get, the more responsible they can be for their own things and the more helpful they can be in many ways.

Long ago, Rachel had given up on trying to keep a perfect house, but she thought that other single mothers probably did. Actually, single mothers consistently bemoan their constant battle against "stuff" littering the floors, tables, countertops—wherever there is a horizontal surface in the home, in the car, in the yard. Rachel's problem was compounded by the fact that she and her four children lived in a one-bedroom apartment. With two children in the only bedroom, two in bunkbeds in the dining room and Rachel on the couch in the living room, they were crowded.

Whenever there are children in a home, there will be "stuff" to clean up, because children get very involved in their toys, books, food, music; and your home is their home, too. They seem never to mind that littered, lived-in look in every room in the house, at least not enough to volunteer to do something about it. But most mothers prefer a neat, clean environment.

Everybody has to compromise. The children need to help clean up, even though that may not be on their agenda. And the mother needs to let go of her neatness standards to a certain extent in order to keep from constantly crowing, "Clean it up!" Somewhere between total chaos and total perfection lies a place of peaceful compromise where all the parties can agree, "Well, this will do for now." The mother usually sets the standard to work toward, and the children usually test that standard from time to time, at which point the mother has to reaffirm the standard.

Getting the children to help

From toddlerhood on, children can help around the house. A toddler can put a toy on a shelf. A five-year-old can take the dishes out of the dishwasher and put them on the countertop for you to put away. An eight-year-old can wash the dishes. A 14-year-old can do just about anything that you can do.

No thinking mother wants to overburden her children with housework and adult responsibilities. On the other hand, U.S. children may lead the world in the little they do to assist their families. As mothers, we often err in requiring too little of our children. Regular chores are a good way for children to learn responsibility. What a disservice it would be for a mother to settle her grown son or daughter in his or her first apartment without that young adult's knowing how to cook, clean, shop for supplies and otherwise manage household affairs in the new apartment. So childhood is a time of gradually shouldering increasing responsibilities as preparation for competent adulthood.

The difficult part is that a single mother has to get the troops to do their work without any reinforcement from a partner who might say, "You heard your mother. Do as she asks." In the short run, it is often easier just to do the job yourself. You'll get no complaint from the children if you do. But in the long run, assigning your children responsibilities and making sure they follow through with them will make the children feel good about themselves. It will keep the house neater and will free you to use your time in other valuable ways.

To get your children to help around the house, use any technique that works—short of arguing, screaming or slapping.

◇ A simple request: "Please take out the garbage."
◇ Appeal to their sense of family: "You are a part of this family; you enjoy the benefits of family life, and you are expected to contribute to the maintenance of our home."
◇ Bribe them: "If you wash the dishes for me, I'll rub your back." The problem with this technique is that the children may ask you the next time, "If I do this for you, what will you do for me?" (Answer: "Feed and clothe you.") Use this sparingly.
◇ Use a kitchen timer to help children work on delayed tasks. For example, if you go to the store for a loaf of bread, set the timer for five minutes, at which time you want the children to turn off the TV.
◇ Make sure the child knows what is expected. For example, if you say, "Clean up the living room," does that include putting away things, vacuuming, and dusting, or just putting away things?
◇ Set up an inspection: "Let me know when you finish so that I can inspect your job." When you inspect, point out improvements you think need to be made, if any, and set up a final inspection.
◇ Establish consequences: if they fail to do their jobs, ask them a second time and give them an additional job to do.
◇ Praise their work: "You did a great job on the car. It means a lot to us all. Thanks."

Managing the mess

Some ideas that mothers have used successfully to try to maintain civility in their homes while their children are young are

◇ When the whole house is a mess, clean up one room (the bathroom is a good choice, since it is small). Continue room by room through the house if you've got the time and energy. But even one clean room can lift your spirits.

◇ Keep your own room neat and pretty. Use that as a refuge from the madding crowd, or

◇ Let your own room be a mess, the one place in your life where you don't have to put out an unwanted effort.

◇ Enlist the children to help you clean up the communal rooms in the house after dinner and before children settle down to do homework, watch TV, read or do other quiet activities. That way, when the children go to bed, the house will be fairly neat for the night.

◇ Yell (as in "Announcement! Announcement!") "OK, everybody clean up the living room and dining room. Go!" This is a ritual one mother used whenever she felt overwhelmed with the mess. Everyone in earshot got up and pitched in to straighten up the rooms. It only took five minutes with everyone working, it was generally fun, and it promoted a feeling of family.

◇ As soon as the children learn to read, make lists for each child's work for Saturday, for example. After breakfast (or cartoons, or whatever), each child goes immediately to work on his or her list. The children scratch off the chores one by one until they are done. Then they can play. The lists allows the mother to avoid assigning jobs verbally and getting verbal complaints back. The children complain to the list!

◇ Assign routine daily chores—kitchen clean-up, feeding the dog— to family members on a rotating basis. For example, Sam washes the dishes on Monday, Wednesday and Friday. Jill washes them on Tuesday, Thursday and Saturday. Mom washes them on Sunday. Everyone must begin washing before 7 p.m. If children older than ten forget, warn them once. The next time, assign a work consequence. Once you train them to be responsible for managing their own time on their day with that chore, you will *not* have to say, "Sam, isn't this your day to do the dishes? It's almost seven o'clock!" It makes your job easier, and it makes the children more responsible, a plus for them.

◇ When the children are doing housework, let them crank up the radio or otherwise work to the beat of their favorite music. The faster the beat, the better for your young workers; it's energizing and uplifting. If you can work *with* your children and find some fast music that you *all* enjoy, it can be a lot of fun.

A few words from the children

Child: *"But Joey (a friend) doesn't have to fold clothes."*
Mother: *"Joey doesn't live in this house. He has his rules, you have yours."*

Child: *"Dad never asks me to fold clothes."*
Mother: *"Dad has his rules, I have mine. We are both trying to help you grow up to be a responsible adult."*

Child: *"I'll do it later, my favorite TV program is coming on."*
Mother: *"Do it now, please." Or, "OK, we'll make a contract. What time can you have it done by?"*

Once the child commits to a specific time, hold him or her to it. If the task doesn't get done, give a work consequence. Contracting with a child in this way puts more responsibility on you to monitor the job, but it allows the child some flexibility and provides some experience in learning to manage his or her own time.

Child: *"I don't know how to mop the floor."*
Mother: *"Let me teach you right now."*

Child: *"You always ask me to do more work than Sherry. How come she gets to go play?"*
Mother: *"I love you, and I'm not going to ask you to do anything unreasonable. I am trying to be fair about workloads, but you must remember that in the end, I am the judge."*

Getting rid of things

One way to encourage neatness is to **provide ample storage space** in convenient locations for everything you own. If you need a chest of drawers in your living room to keep board games, magazines or whatever, then put one in the living room. Do whatever works.

Space limitations spawn problems for which single mothers have found interesting solutions. For example, Faith keeps her exercise bicycle in her living room, since there was a bare corner where it just fit. The children and their friends use it frequently, and adult guests often climb on the seat to give the wheels a spin. The bicycle has turned out to be a conversation piece.

Not everything in Faith's house gets as much attention as the bicycle, however. There are over 15 grocery sacks full of papers that she has moved from one house to another at least twice before, papers she has not looked at in years because she hasn't had time. Recently she went through about ten boxes full of household goods, many old toys and children's clothes, and much of that she gave away. She now faces the 15 sacks, intending to reduce her inventory to a fraction of that. Soon she will have gained more room and less clutter—a big improvement in a small house.

Getting rid of clutter, by selling it, giving or throwing it away, automatically gives your house a neater appearance. With children strewing their belongings around the house in the normal course of their activities, every effort toward an uncluttered look is its own reward.

Managing time

"Time ain't on my side" just may be the single mother's theme song. There are some management techniques which can help, but in the end, you need to recognize that

◇ You are finite
◇ You are doing the best you can
◇ It is OK to look up to the sky and yell, "Give me a break" and
◇ It is OK to take that break.

We were goin' down some street —
three of us in the car,
me knowin' we were late . . . again.
And we'd probably slip behind all day,
all overflowing Saturday.

With my foot layin' heavy on the gas
and my eye jerking between road and speedometer
I was tryin' to whiz through the city
but escape a ticket.
Jonathan said, "I'm glad I've got my seat belt on.
Do you have yours on, Mommy?
We might get into an accident."
I said, "I've got mine on, too.
But don't worry, we're not goin' to
get into an accident."
"How do you know?" said Laura.
"'Cause I don't have time to get into an accident today, honey."
Laura giggled.
"Oh, Mommy, you're so funny," she said.

Cooking. By all means, let the children help you. They can set the table and help with small tasks in assembling the meal. Starting at about age four, children can do "Get me" work, as in "Get me the milk and butter from the refrigerator," or "Get me a big pan from the cabinet."

Even small children enjoy breaking eggs, stirring together ingredients, forming dough into balls and other muscle functions in cooking. They can shuck corn, snap beans and tear lettuce.

Small tasks done by the children are a big help. And if you and the children are in the kitchen together, it gives you an opportunity to talk about your day. In order to make this pleasurable, sibling fights, running children and loud noises must stay out of the kitchen.

Teenagers can cook an occasional meal for the family, perhaps once a week. If you let them choose the meal, they will probably come up with pizza, nachos, hamburgers or some other fast food delight. That's fine; just ask them to add a green salad and milk. Fleshing out the menu with your teenager can be an opportunity to teach nutrition in an unstructured way. If your teenager asks for help from a younger brother or sister and you agree, tell the teenager it's OK as long as you don't hear any complaints from the younger child. This will cue the teenager to practice management techniques which emphasize encouragement rather than bullying the younger child. Meanwhile, you can go into the living room, prop up your feet and bask in a few minutes of freedom.

Children can and will eat all day long. To avoid dirty dishes in the sink and dirty plates, sticky wrappers and open boxes all over the house at night, one single mother would declare "Kitchen is closed!" after she had washed the last load of dishes in the evening. After that, children could drink milk or water but could not eat food. Another family lived by the "Use it or lose it if you don't wash it" rule—snacking privileges were discontinued unless everyone cleaned up all traces of food, dishes and related garbage.

Fast food. Working mothers buy far more prepared foods at the grocery store than housewives. Most single mothers work outside the home, and their daily fare is often fast food or prepared foods—macaroni and cheese mixes, spaghetti sauce in a jar, fish sticks, prepared meat pies, prepared pizzas, hot dogs and pork 'n beans in a can, canned or frozen vegetables, a piece of toast and voila! One more meal on the table.

Fresh vegetables and cooking from scratch may taste better than fixing prepared foods, but no single mother need feel guilty about relying heavily on prepared foods. There is only one Julia Child, and she gets paid for cooking. For the rest of us, whatever works is probably OK. After all, the problem most U.S. citizens have is overeating, not undereating.

There are a few simple guidelines to remember which are the same ones your children learn in school and from their dentist for good nutrition.

> **Good Nutrition Guidelines**
> ◊ The five food groups are
> **vegetables**
> **grains**
> **fruit**
> **meat and poultry**
> **dairy**
> ◊ Try to serve your child some of each over the course of the day.
> ◊ Milk builds strong teeth and bones. Serve milk with meals.
> ◊ Eight glasses of water each day is recommended. Few people do this, but encourage your children to drink water. This works well when they are watching TV or doing other quiet-time activities.
> ◊ Go easy on the sweets and fried foods.

"To Do" Lists. A number of time management experts recommend that you

1. Write down all the things you need to do on a given day.
2. Prioritize them according to their importance to you.
3. Do them, one at a time, until your time runs out.
4. Move leftover tasks to the next day's list.

How you prioritize your tasks is important. Edwin C. Bliss, author of *Getting Things Done* (Charles Scribner's Sons, 1976), suggests that action can be broken down into five categories:

1. **Important and Urgent** (Such as changing a wet diaper—you can't really put this off to another day);
2. **Important but not Urgent** (An annual medical checkup—it's important, but you could postpone it forever, since no one is breathing down your neck about it);
3. **Urgent but not Important** (You have to attend a lecture on financial planning with your sister—she asked you to go with her, and it had been so long since you and she did something together that you said yes, though you'd rather just talk with her);

4. **Busy Work** (Reorganizing the bookshelves when you should be paying bills and balancing your checkbook. There is a hint of avoidance in getting sidetracked this way); and

5. **Wasted Time** (Whenever you feel you would have been better off spending your time doing something else).

Bliss believes that people tend to allocate too much time to things in categories three and four, and not enough time to things in category two. He suggests setting priorities according to *importance*, not urgency.

Don't expect to get more than about six things on your list done in a day. If you do more, that's great, but concentrate on those most important first six tasks.

At the end of the day, reflect back on the day and pick out five things you did that you are proud of. They don't have to be on your list. A victory at work, a kindness to a stranger, a quiet time of sharing with one of the children—anything counts. It is good to remember that while your time seems so short, you are doing valuable things in your place in this world and that your life counts.

Learn to say "No". If someone asks you to assist with a Brownie troop, canvass your block for the Heart Fund, sign up for two hours to register voters for the next election—and these are all worthy causes—think seriously about saying no. If you say yes because you believe strongly in the cause and are eager to promote it with your time, that is fine. But if you feel a twinge of pain when the request comes, if you ask yourself the knee-jerk question, "How will I find the time?"—then say no. One good rule to follow is, "When in doubt, say no."

> 66 One good rule to follow is— *When in doubt, say no.* 99

Granted, if everyone took that attitude, our worthy volunteer causes and systems would die. But people go through phases in their lives, and as the phases change, demands on people's time change. **A single mother frequently has little time to do anything but attend to her job, her children and herself.** When her children become teenagers, she will have more free time, and when they leave home, more time still. Then time can be devoted to discretionary work for causes and family and friends without overburdening her or causing her to default on her primary responsibilities.

Simplify your life. Find ways to cut down on the number of errands you run, the number of bills you have to pay each month, the number of loads of laundry you do or trips you make to the grocery store each week, the number of personal phone calls you make or day-care centers you take your children to each day. Wherever you can save yourself time and extra steps during the day, you will be saving energy. The philosophy that "less is more" means that by cutting down on material consumption and by simplifying our overly complex lives, we can live more satisfying lives.

Slow down. Take 5- to 15-minute breaks during the day. If you've been sitting, get up and walk. If you've been working physically, sit down and prop up your feet. Change your pace and your activity. Stare out the window, read a magazine, close your eyes and feel. Breathe deeply, drink water, do whatever relaxes you and refreshes you. It will help you to keep going with greater energy through the end of your day.

> 66 *Life is short. Childhood is shorter, so enjoy the kids.* 99

Think "relax." You can go to the store in a frenzy, or you can go to the store in a more leisurely way without taking any longer to do the task. Your mental attitude can help you approach life in a calmer, more peaceful manner.

Relaxing is a learned skill. These days, the pressure is on us to accomplish big things at work and at home. We are pressured to be superworkers. For what? Life is short. Childhood is shorter, so enjoy the kids. "Waste" a little time with them. Look around you. Enjoy the air, the sky, the glint of sun on a building, the refreshing drizzle of rain.

Schedule some leisure time into your week, with or without the children. Because it is important but not urgent, scheduling it helps you to carry it out. Plan something low-key, like listening to music or taking a walk. Look forward to that time. Think about it during your busy times, when you feel stretched taut. And when the time comes, put on your most comfortable clothes and shoes—or go barefoot!—and enjoy.

CHAPTER 15: Updating Your Social Life

Everyone's gone to the moon

The importance of connecting
with friends

So where do you find friends?

Men as friends only

"While I'm out on the town,
what about the kids?"

Socializing with the children

The art of celebration

The newness terrified me.
Still I floated on, rejoicing
by myself

and with others.
My children came riding on me weightlessly
laughing and gathering up my edges.
And the firm broad faces of friends
(seeking re-election) on billboards
hung on stars in the sky by night.
I gathered them to me.
They animated and we danced
like popcorn blossoming.

Everyone's gone to the moon

It's Saturday night. You are all alone. Well, the kids are there, but it sure would be nice to have a friend to talk to. Chances are the friends you and your partner had as a couple are not around anymore. After the separation they may fall away from you for at least five reasons:

- People who related to your ex-partner more than to you will probably feel like they need to "take his side" and will not make an effort to see you.
- Many couples have difficulty making the transition. They feel you and your ex-partner have failed, and they're afraid that marital failure may be catching. Their own fear, together with the sadness and sorrow they may feel for you, makes them uncomfortable.
- Other couples may see you as a direct threat to the stability of their own relationship. Especially to women, you have become a "radioactive" single, someone on the loose looking for a partner, and they don't want that partner to be theirs.
- In a social situation with couples, you as the odd number may be the odd one out.
- Or *you* may not care to continue the relationship.

In addition, you may change the places you frequent after you separate from your partner. Because you are making all the decisions for your own life now, you may decide to go to a different gas station, grocery store or place of worship. You may move. You may change jobs. You may drop the old health club and join a new one. And all these changes in where you spend your time and money mean you see different people in the course of a week.

For all these reasons, some or most of your friends will surely change. And that can be good.

The importance of connecting with friends

Your need to be with friends is a universal need. James S. House, sociologist at the University of Michigan, concluded in a study called "Social Relationships and Health" that loneliness can kill you. "The data indicates that social isolation is as significant to mortality rates as smoking, high blood pressure, high cholesterol, obesity and lack of physical exercise," according to House.

A good social network of friends takes the pressure off you to find a man. When you are lonely, it is too easy to establish a quick romantic relationship with a man who does not really meet your needs. Nutrition experts caution us never to shop for food when we are hungry. Likewise, we should never shop for a man when we are starved for friendship. A man is not necessary to living a full and satisfying social life. In seeking new relationships, the first step for a single mother is to establish some solid friendships with people who are not romantic possibilities. Just friends, men and women, people with whom you can let your hair down and know they will not be judging you for a beauty contest or any other contest. They just like to be with you.

> ❝ One of the most important insurance plans a single mother can secure is a strong network of friends to stay with her through thick and thin. ❞

Like finding a new job, making new friends requires effort. And with the frantic pace that single mothers sustain as they juggle job, children, housework and arrangements, the energy for establishing new relationships is scarce. But one of the most important insurance plans a single mother can secure is a strong network of friends to stay with her through thick and thin. One friend will call up when you are sick and offer to go to the grocery store for you, a second friend will take care of your children in an emergency situation, a third friend you can call on when you feel depressed or angry, one to whom you can vent those feeling without fear of rejection. You'll want several friends with whom to share good news and to celebrate, to have fun, to share your children.

A strong network of friends can act as your main support
in lieu of your partner.

So where do you find friends?

They are all around you. Single mothers, like their cast-off
partners, find themselves reaching out to people, sometimes those
they didn't have time for before the split. Since you are not invest-
ing your emotional energy in building a relationship with your ex-
partner, you can invest it in people you brush up against daily.

The people at work may become more important to you, and
you may find yourself saying more often, "Let's go out for lunch
today." Lunch is OK, but beware of going out regularly with co-
workers in the evenings and on weekends. It is often wise to build
your network of friends with people away from your workplace. In
this way, you have non-co-workers with whom to complain about
work, when you need to do that. Within your network of friends
you'll be sharing intimate disclosures, and you never know when a
co-worker will use such information against you in the political
games that infest workplaces just as cockroaches infest kitchens.
Most people will not turn on you, but are you willing to take that
chance? Also, getting away from co-workers means you are getting
away from work concerns. Sometimes, after-hours shop talk can be
tedious, so give yourself a break. When you associate socially with
people who work in other places and in other occupations, you have
a little variety in life and a rest from the constant presence of your
work scene.

As you pursue your own interests, you will find people with
whom you have much in common.

Likely places to find new friends are clubs and organizations.
If you like to cook, there may be a gourmet club in your town; check
at a gourmet shop. If you like athletics, there are sports teams and

running clubs; check at the local YMCA. If you like to read, there are book clubs; check at the public library. If you are interested in politics, choose your favorite issue, such as Central America; contact a political science professor or a Latin American Studies professor at a local college or university to find a group working on that issue. If you have a home computer, you might want to find out about computer clubs; check with a computer store. Business and Professional Women (BPW) and organizations related more specifically to your job can be located by calling the YWCA or the Chamber of Commerce. If you ask around enough, you will find some appealing groups to participate in.

Hundreds of volunteer organizations are waiting for you to get involved. The Red Cross, the American Cancer Society and other health organizations, the League of Women Voters, your child's parent-teacher organization, your neighborhood homeowner's association or your apartment complex's tenants association. Check with the mayor's office or the public library for service options, or look in the Yellow Pages under Social Service Organizations or Human Services Organizations.

Taking a class in an adult education program or college is a good plan, if you have the money for tuition of $35 and up. Art classes are available at many community centers and museums. Music, drama, sewing, professional development courses—look around, and you will surely come up with interesting personal development options.

Singles groups established for social purposes usually include elements of both friendship and romance as a part of their operation.

Men as friends only

A male prisoner who had been locked up for two years on a drug charge was released for his first eight-hour furlough. His fiancée drove him to her house. He said later, "I walked in the door and I felt the carpet under my feet, I saw soft little pillows here and there, and it was . . . it was . . . it just SMELLED like Woman."

You can get starved like that for the opposite sex, even if you don't want to be romantically linked.

For a lot of reasons, it is nice to have a man for a friend only. He can be married to someone else or not, as long as everyone understands the boundaries and approves of the friendship. Men tend to be rough, direct, assertive, if not aggressive, and they are often risk-takers. They look different and yes, they do smell different than women. A single mother can long for simply being around a man and yet not want a romantic relationship. A man as a friend can satisfy that need for connecting with the other half of humanity.

Often, married men form friendship attachments with women other than their wives and talk with this "other woman" about finances, sex, job difficulties, problems with their wives—things that they can't or don't share with their wives because they feel they have too much on the line in the relationship with them, too much emotion and too much at risk. So these men find other women to talk with. That's one kind of friendship, a sort of talking friendship. But if the wife knows about the relationship, she picks up vibrations that may make her wary of it. She may easily become jealous and feel threatened. More often than not, the man chooses this other woman carefully, someone who does not intersect with his home life at all: a co-worker or a club member.

Be on guard with the husbands of your friends. Once your separation announcement is public knowledge, perfectly docile men with whom you and your partner related socially can come on to you sexually. You just have to make clear your limits. Use humor when possible to deflect the advance but save the friendship. "Down, boy," works well.

Another kind of friendship is with a man, usually unmarried, with whom you can pal around in the sunshine when you want a date to a function, when you want to go on an outing, or when you want an adult companion for a night of VCR movies and popcorn at home with the kids; someone in the "brother" category.

When you find a man whose company you enjoy, you can be very honest with him and say, "Look, I like you. How about going out to dinner (or lunch, which is less threatening) as friends? You pay for yours, I'll pay for mine." Your offer to pay your own way is one indication that you do not have romance in mind. A straightforward approach is refreshing. What if he says no? You smile and say, "OK. Maybe some other time. The ball is in your court." And let it go. If he says yes, then you take that first step.

One woman approached a newly divorced man with just such an up-front suggestion: "I want to be your friend. I'm not interested in a romantic relationship with you at all, but I like you, and you will probably need a lot of support right now. I would welcome a new friend, but remember it has to be just that: friendship." And she meant it. They took walks together, ate lunches together, talked over their lives, and it remained a good friendship even after each remarried.

"While I'm out on the town, what about the kids?"

Even if you have an infant in diapers, you need a social life all your own; everyone does. And it is a mistake to sacrifice that completely because you have a child or two to care for. If they were older and looking back on things, they would probably say, "Gosh, Mom, I wish you had been able to go out more when we were kids." *And children should not be an excuse to hide in the house and avoid a social life.*

In fact, it is to your children's advantage that you do socialize, for if you do not, you can become resentful of being "tied down" at home, resulting in heightened tension with them. Be glad to go, have fun and be glad to come back, refreshed. Your children will probably help you decide what to wear, will love seeing you "dress up."

Socializing with the children

In parts of our society, children are taboo, such as in bars, most workplaces, adults-only parties, clubs and meetings, adult education classrooms, and so on. However, in people's homes and in many public settings—parks, museums, restaurants, movie theaters—children are welcome. If you find another single mother whose children are about the same age as your own, the children can romp around together while the mothers share an adult conversation. In addition to other single mothers, any adult whom you consider a friend is a candidate for integrating into your family life.

Here are some ideas for socializing, as a family, with friends:

◇ Have a pot luck dinner at your house with one or more friends.
◇ Host a TV party on special occasions—like Super Bowl Sunday or election nights or the Academy Awards presentations. Serve popcorn and soft drinks.
◇ Have an invite-a-friend event, either an outing or an at-home affair, for which each family member can invite one special friend. This could even be a sleep-over party with a lazy Saturday morning breakfast (in this case, your friend should be female). This has the flavor of relatives coming to visit.
◇ Select an inexpensive but good all-in-one-pot food, like vegetable stew or chili, and target one day a month—the first Saturday, for example—to invite a new person over to your house for a meal and conversation. This could also be planned for a small group of people.

Much entertaining in our society involves food. If you keep the food simple, and let everyone serve themselves, you'll be freer to concentrate on the conversation and other details of the evening. Also, planning to serve a simple meal which you prepare regularly reduces your stress level in getting ready for company. Keep everything as casual as you like. If you enjoy candles and cloth napkins, great; paper plates and napkins are equally satisfactory. Do whatever makes you comfortable and sets you up to enjoy the evening. Your guests will pick up those vibrations.

Everyone appreciates an invitation to a meal, and you get to share another adult's world view, cares, concerns and humor for a short while. The advantage of targeting one day a month is that you program sharing your home life with others into your cycle of living.

> *On special family occasions like Thanksgiving, especially if you are unable to be with members of your own family, by all means invite someone or some family to share that occasion with you. Create your own extended family.*

Foreign students love invitations from American families on traditional occasions, and they are often wonderful with children, in part because they miss their own brothers and sisters. If you can't go to a foreign country, let the country come to you! Colleges often have lists of undergraduate and graduate students who would like to participate, and you can choose what country and sex you would like. Probably the best idea is to invite a foreign student and an American friend (or family), as well, for the first time.

Explore the great outdoors with friends and children: a walk around a lake, a trip to a park, whatever. Even if your house is a mess by your standards, the great outdoors is always in shape to receive and enrich visitors.

Not only do you benefit from social contact with other adults, but your children benefit. They, too, are exposed to new ideas, new jokes, new ways of doing things, new people who show them attention. And building a social life with your children bonds you together more as a family. You are sharing the same friends, having common experiences and building common memories. One day one of your children will say, "Hey, Mom, remember that lady who spilled her hot coffee all over the table and it fell through the crack onto the cat, and the cat screeched and took off into . . ."

A word about other adults and your children: those who see the beauty in your children get repeat invitations. You should keep those who are obviously uncomfortable or unaffirming around your children away from them. Children quickly pick up on how people feel about them, and who wants to feel like a nuisance? Fortunately, there are many people who will certainly appreciate your children for the beautiful and interesting people they are.

The art of celebration

Some people are good at this. They light candles with dinner. They always find fresh flowers or greens to decorate their homes. They consider a phone call from you to be a gift in their day. They delight in your children's accomplishments—a good report card, participation on a sports team, a clever comment, a helpful gesture. These celebrators consider making it through a week of work to be reason enough to get together for laughs on Friday night. They understand that simply doing your job conscientiously is a tremendous accomplishment, one to be proud of. If you can find someone like this (or more than one person) in your circle of friends, recognize that person and take lessons. Make every effort to develop your own ability to celebrate life. Step back from your problems enough to point out the good things happening in your life and in the lives of your friends, and then celebrate those good things. There is something very good about the life process itself, and for that we can be thankful and celebrate. Even in the darkest pit, you can light a candle.

CHAPTER 16:   Romance

"Will I ever trust a man again?"

Dating can be a drag

Sex and the single mother

Date rape

Looking for love in all the wrong
  places

Singles groups

Classified personal ads

Computer-match-for-fee companies

Quality relationships

Co-dependent relationships

Levels of commitment

Making excuses for having children

Revealing a sexual relationship
  to the children

Your man and your children

Living together

Kids' reactions

Blended family blues

Prenuptial agreements

I am a mountain.
I waited for you.
You have climbed me.
You have put your flag in me.
I wear your colors, your smell.
My rock will not fail you.
My soil will flower for you in spring.
Your body is so warm on me
where you stand there is no snow.

"Will I ever trust a man again?"

Jeanna's husband had affairs with more than one woman while he and Jeanna were married. One day he left for work and said he would not be coming home that night. He left Jeanna for another woman whom he eventually married. And that story is not even news, because it happens all the time. Jeanna was stunned.

So was Louise, when her husband left her for another woman. Louise was attractive, intelligent, educated and sociable. She would be judged a good catch, if we were talking fish in the sea. But when her husband walked out, her self-esteem took a dive. She began wondering what was wrong with her, and she stopped trusting men. She was so hurt by her husband that for over a year she couldn't face another relationship with a man. At the same time, however, she was looking around at men judging them against her yardstick of the ideal man, although she didn't want even an ideal man anywhere near her.

You feel vulnerable, as a newly single mother, you feel whipped. And with men, you feel like a pimply-faced adolescent on review at a school party ("Will anyone ask me to dance?"). Your confidence as a woman—whether he left you or you left him—is damaged. Even if you left your ex-partner, the pain you felt in that relationship hurt badly enough for you to need to heal before approaching a man—a potential hazard for you—again

Dating can be a drag

June had been separated from her ex-husband for seven months. One evening, the phone rang. "Hi," the voice said, "I'm Lionel. I met you at the [organization] meeting a couple of months ago."

"Right. I remember who you are. How are you doing?" said June.

"Fine. Listen, I just wanted to call and ask you to dinner next Saturday night."

Plunk.

Going through June's head like lightning was *But I'm married. Well, no, I'm not married anymore.* I guess there's no reason why I couldn't go out. Is this a date? There's no reason why I should say no that I can think of, I mean, I guess it's OK for me to go out to dinner with another man. And what June said to Lionel was, "OK, I guess that would be all right."

That was not exactly a warm or sophisticated response, but June was caught off-guard. Though she had been looking at men everywhere for months, she never thought anyone would call to ask her out. Her self-image was still that of a 35-year-old wife and mother. Now she was faced with a situation which challenged the leftover image of herself as wife. She clearly was not a wife anymore. She was a date.

June's first date was hardly a misty-eyed romantic whirl. She met Lionel at an Italian restaurant. He ordered in Italian. They ate a meal which Lionel pronounced "excellent" and June thought was good spaghetti. Afterward, they both drove to June's house. Lionel asked himself in (the children were gone). They sat on the sofa for a while, and June found it an effort to make conversation with him. He told her a little about his wife's leaving him and how devastated he was. Then, out of the blue, he grabbed her and began to French-kiss her. It was awful, to hear June talk about it. They were both embarrassed, and she walked Lionel to the door. That was their first and last date.

June brushed her teeth.

It was sad, in a way (in spite of the good spaghetti), but that evening served to change June's perception of herself and restore some of her confidence as an attractive woman. Part of the continuing job of a single mother is to let go of old definitions and see yourself with new eyes—the reality, the possibilities, the strengths of the new you.

June never did date again. Instead, a friendship she had with another man developed into the stuff that makes marriages, and in two more years she made the transition from single mother to wife in a blended family.

Sex and the single mother

Everyone likes to be touched. It can be both comforting and exciting to have a man hold you, stroke you, moan and groan because you and your body turn him on. Meanwhile, you are doing the same thing. The complete sexual act between a man and a woman is powerful. It can be either ecstasy or shattering, depending on how you feel about it. For now we will talk about sex that is healthy, satisfying and fun.

What do you do when your man is gone? You can 1) satisfy yourself, 2) find a sexual replacement or 3) do without.

Some women enjoy masturbation a great deal, and for them, self-stimulation is a perfectly acceptable sexual experience, if we go back to our assumption that sex is healthy, satisfying and fun.

Other women prefer not to practice sexual stimulation in any form, and the choice not to have sex is perfectly acceptable.

Probably the most important and reasonable sexual right of every woman is to control her own body, so that whatever she chooses to do with it—as long as it doesn't hurt anyone else—is OK.

Single mothers who choose to be sexually active with men abound. (From here on when I speak of sex, I mean sexual intercourse between a woman and a man.) Societal pressure on single women, whether mothers or not, has switched from strongly discouraging sex and socially punishing single women for sex acts to strongly pressuring them to have sex. This means that in former days it was more difficult for a woman to say yes; now, however, it is more difficult for a woman to say no. The dominant view of college men is that if a man pays for a date, the woman is obliged to have sex with him, and the national trend in sexual attitudes has been going in that direction for years. If he pays, she puts out. And there is the story of the man who approached an over-35-year-old single woman at a bar with an offer of sex. She said no. He said, "You better take it while you can get it, baby. I may be your last chance."

Unfortunately, single mothers needing sex and men in their

lives can fall for that—or any—line. But who's to judge? Women will do what they need to do in order to get by. If a single mother can feel good about herself in however she chooses to use her body, she should go with that. If she does not feel good about it, if she feels frustrated or out of control or inadequate or "dirty" or any other negative feeling, she should stop to reflect on what she is doing and why it is causing those negative feelings. If she can't improve the situation by herself or with the counsel of friends, she should seek professional counseling for either emotional guidance or sexual therapy. Both are absolutely confidential.

A last word about sex: protect yourself from AIDS for the sake of the children and others who love you and depend on you (see page 156).

Date rape

One unfortunate fact of contemporary dating is the prevalence of date rape, which has become more common than AIDS and equally unwelcome. Date rape is sexual assault against a woman by someone she knows. Let's say a woman is out on a date with a friend of her brother. They both enjoy the evening. He brings her home and stops in for a drink. He begins to rub her shoulders, then he kisses her and it moves on from there. At some point, she says no, but he does not stop. She begins to resist him physically. He comes on stronger, pins her down, penetrates her, climaxes and, soon after, leaves. She is stunned.

Later, she says, "I told him no, but he didn't stop." He says, "She said no, but she didn't mean it. She had been coming on to me all evening." The truth is, it was not her fault; she was raped. That he was a friend of her brother does not make it less a crime. It is a serious crime.

The woman should go to a friend's house or call a rape crisis center. She should not shower or change clothes, no matter how much she wants to. She should go to a hospital to be examined for evidence of rape and for treatment of any injuries. She should then seek counseling, ideally from a rape crisis center, to help her decide whether to press criminal charges against the man and to deal with the long-term emotional injuries from the experience.

If you mean no when you say it, and a man continues to escalate the sexual experience, you may reinforce your no with a statement like, "**Date rape and other physical violence against me is a crime punishable by time in prison.** Neither of us wants to go through court. Good night." You can bet he will be angry, but he may stop. You must remember that your body is your own to give or not, to stand up for or not, as you choose.

Looking for love in all the wrong places

A bar is not necessarily a wrong place to look for a man, but a woman needs to be careful she does not end up with a substance abuser or a habitual cruiser. She needs to know how to say no firmly and to accept that because it is a bar, some men will size her up as a piece of meat instead of a person with a head and a heart, too.

Married men are definitely bad news. When you think of it, once you give your heart to a married man, you lose the game. He may leave you and go back to his wife, or to another woman, and break your heart. That could be the best scenario. He might maintain the relationship with you for years, with or without promising to leave his wife; and while you long to have him all to yourself in the sunshine, it is his wife who attends public functions with him and who gets all the legal privileges of her status—which she should, since she has to put up with him. On holidays he's with his family. And as long as you stay with him, his attitude can so easily be "Why change? Why rock the boat?" The harder you push, the uglier things get, and he may brush you off like dandruff, keeping his wife and their life.

And what are you left with?

In another scenario, he may leave his wife for you, in which case you will have played your part in dissolving a family that was together in some form before you came along. Then, some of his financial resources and his time will be siphoned off to his former wife and children.

In the end, it is poor form and a poor risk to get involved with a married man. But it can happen so easily. A friendship with a married man can turn into something more. Or you can become involved with a married man who may or may not tell you that, "Yes, I'm married, but my wife just doesn't understand me." One option for a woman who is becoming involved with a married man, or who is being hotly courted by a married man, is to say, "Look, I am not interested in you. Whatever problems you have with your wife, well, you need to settle them with her. Good luck to both of you." If his marriage does end, then you can approach him with a good conscience and begin a relationship with him in the open, a relationship you both can be proud of.

Singles groups

Singles groups established for social purposes exist in many towns. Some are sponsored by churches or synagogues; of those, some have a religious emphasis and some do not. Other singles groups are independent of any affiliation. To find what is available in your area, you can check with your Chamber of Commerce, a marriage couselor, other single people and your local newspaper (they do stories on singles from time to time and keep files on them).

Each singles group has its own personality, just as each office has its own personality. Once you have a list, you can track down a member by phone and inquire about the group, asking when and where it meets, what the average ages of the women and the men are, if children are involved in the program, what a typical meeting is like. Then you simply have to take a deep breath, go to a meeting and check it out yourself.

The Vanderbilt Single Mother's Group did this in Nashville. Three women volunteered to attend three different singles groups. Two of the women returned with positive reports, but the third woman came back to say that she didn't get a good feeling about the group from her initial phone conversation. Later, at the meeting, she found "old men in plaid suits" and a "sleazy" atmosphere. One man had picked up her two-year-old daughter and held onto her in a way which sent off alarm bells in the mother. She snatched her daughter away from the man (who offered to come fix up her house. Where did she live? Maybe she could do a little sewing for him...), and she left the meeting early. It was the wrong group for her.

Classified personal ads

The history of classified personal ads in the U.S. began when Colonial American men placed ads in newspapers in England for wives.

Reading today's classified ads, or personals, can be entertaining. In placing them, some people are looking for a personal relationship; others are looking for sex without the complication of an emotional relationship.

If you like to take big risks, you can either answer or place an ad yourself. Remember, though, that there are crazy people out there reading the ads, too. Nancy Evins, a hypnotherapist-counselor who has much experience working the classifieds, says you want to avoid having some man stand outside your window screaming, "I'm going to kill you! I'm going to kill you!"—which actually happened to her once through an ad experience.

The larger risk, by far, is in answering an ad. Because you have to give your phone number or an address by which the placer of the ad can contact you, you cannot easily control his access to you.

The safer approach is for you to place the ad listing a post office box drawer for written responses. Then you can maintain your anonymity, read the responses at your leisure and choose which ones you want to respond to. In writing your ad, mention the age, height, and general professional background of the man you would like to meet. Beyond that, whatever your values and interests are, mention those: meeting of the minds, creativity, sensuality, whatever. The mention of religion puts men off, probably because they fear meeting a rigid, frigid fundamentalist (stereotypes die hard). Humor and originality are popular in ads (and in people, as well).

When a man responds to your ad, check him out. You can call him on the phone, but do not give out your phone number. You can write to him, but keep your post office drawer for a while to maintain your anonymity. If he still sounds interesting after a few interactions by phone or letter, meet him at a very public, neutral place (for lunch or some other safe encounter), then leave separately. Proceed very slowly with revealing your home address or where you work to him.

Do not trust men to tell you the truth. One man said he was divorced. The woman checked with the city clerk's office for a record of the divorce; there was none. Soon after, his wife called and said, "How did you like the dozen roses my husband gave you and charged to my account?" When a man is reluctant to give you his home phone number or says, "The people at the office don't know we are divorced," or some other fishy story, be very suspect, and, as always, check it out. Call his home; what do you have to lose?

Another man was dating a woman he met through an ad. She was bored and placed another ad. This same man answered the new ad while he was still dating the woman. So while you are playing your games, he is playing his games.

Much of the safety in working the classifieds is in checking out stories to see who is and is not married, who is and is not as he presents himself. Good and lasting matches have been made in this way. But the wise woman who is willing to risk is also willing to protect herself while she checks out her prospects.

Computer-match-for-fee companies

These companies may or may not make an effort to screen their applicants. Many of the same rules for working the classified personal ads apply to match-for-fee companies. Try to protect your anonymity until you get to know your blind date and have time to check him out yourself.

Computer match companies can charge $200 or more for the filing and membership fee. Though they are not cheap, you will know that the men who list with the company have enough money in their pockets to pay the same fee.

However, as one woman says about income, "So what? Their income is hardly the issue; they could be relatively affluent weirdos, rapists or axe murderers." With men, you have to take risks and expose your own vulnerability in order to form relationships. And most men are within the range of normal. But three important words to keep in mind are *caution, caution, caution.*

Quality relationships

One dear old lady from a wealthy Boston family was well loved and well educated, but she had never married. Apparently she was very beautiful and had several serious suitors, but she refused them all. She felt, "The right man just never came around." She has lived a long, interesting and satisfying life with many friends.

Then there is Zsa Zsa Gabor, who has so far been married eight times, and she still may be looking for the right man.

Most of us settle for less than perfection, but the degree to which we have to compromise puts a strain on the relationship. Each person has to make that difficult judgment, "Is this enough for me?"

One way to look at a man is "If you miss one bus, another will come along soon." If you need to end the relationship, or if he ends it, there are other men whom you will meet later on who will be just as interesting, charming, funny, or whatever as the one you need to say goodbye to. The catch is that you don't know if the next man will come along in a month or three years.

Another way to look at a man is "A bird in the hand is worth two in the bush." If you've got a man in your life, at least he's better than none. If that were true, if any man were better than none at all, women would not leave their men at the rate they do. We need quality relationships in our lives. Our children need quality relationships. These can be built with many people, male and female, but we have to be patient, give it time, accept false starts philosophically and keep our standards high. People stay in our lives longer that way.

Co-dependent relationships

Co-dependency is a fairly new concept in psychology, and some counselors, therapists, and social workers take a dim view of it. But a surprising number of single mothers who have read about it tend to say, "That's me!"

Co-dependent people, both men and women, have not completed developing their own identities. Normally, this happens in late adolescence, a gradual pulling away from parents and other authorities and becoming an autonomous person. A co-dependent woman's view of who she is comes from others. She is dependent on others' view of herself, and feels a sense of personal worth only when others tell her she is real and worthy.

Co-dependent people often come from families with alcoholism or other chemical dependency, families where there is physical or sexual abuse, families which are religiously fundamentalistic, with rigid rules and dogmatic, tight control and families with psychological problems—families which are not healthy.

Characteristics of a co-dependent person:
◇ The need to control
◇ The inability to trust others
◇ The inability to identify and understand her own feelings
◇ Being over- or under-responsible
◇ Thinking in terms of all or none; extremes
◇ High tolerance of inappropriate behavior from loved ones and of pain and suffering in herself
◇ Low self-esteem
◇ Ungrieved losses (deaths of relationships, unfulfilled dreams)
◇ Fear of abandonment
◇ Difficulty in resolving conflict
◇ Difficulty in giving and receiving love
◇ Unrealistic expectations of being always strong, good and happy
◇ Being dishonest, saying she feels one thing when she really feels something else

---

Robert Subby, in his book called *Lost in the Shuffle*, says that in a co-dependent person,"**The need for love, acceptance, approval, and recognition becomes the transcendent value.**"

(Health Communications, Inc., Deerfield Beach, Florida, 1987, p. 24).

The feelings and needs of the self, then, may need to be re-pressed in order to maintain co-dependent values. Suddenly, the co-dependent person can find herself sacrificing too much of herself to maintain a working relationship with parents or husband or lover or boss—whomever.

When you look at the list of core issues above, you can see that many, perhaps half, of those issues appear naturally in the early stages of single motherhood, including low self-esteem and un-grieved losses. Therefore, even though a woman may have achieved autonomy in late adolescence, the process of becoming a single mother may cause her to lose that solid foundation temporarily. Now she needs to re-establish her autonomy, without her part-ner, as a process of pulling away from that partner and that former life.

A woman with co-dependent tendencies needs to be very care-ful about the romantic relationships she develops to be sure they allow her to grow stronger in her own sense of self, her ability to stand up for herself, and her ability to set limits on the behavior and demands of others when these conflict with her own needs. Sup-port groups for co-dependent people exist in many cities. Ask a mental health agency or counselor for a reference.

Levels of commitment

Angel had two children, ages ten and seven when she met Charlie, who was ten years older than she but lots of fun. They soon became involved sexually, and they found that they enjoyed each other whether relaxing at home, on vacation or visiting with his or her family members. He helped her, she helped him. In short, they became good friends. Charlie was good with Angel's children, and they loved him. They began to ask Angel when Charlie would become their stepdad. When Angel would say, "I love you," Char-lie would say, "Oh, I'm just an old guy." Sometimes he would tell Angel she could do better than him, since he was such a stay-at-home type, and that he felt he was standing in her way. When she protested, "What? I don't want to go out and party every night. I enjoy staying home, too," Charlie would become further upset and leave the house.

For a while, Angel couldn't figure out what was going on. Then she realized that he wanted to leave. Whenever things got too good between them, he would cut and run. When they finally talked about future plans, Charlie said that he had already raised his children (who were in their early twenties), and he didn't want to take responsibility for two more, even as much as he liked Angel's two. Moreover, he felt he couldn't ask her to wait until the children grew up to look at marriage. What he did not say, but which Angel suspects was implied by his behavior, was that he did not want to take her on as a financial responsibility.

It makes a lot of sense to get nervous about spending a lot of time and money on three more people. Doing it on a day-by-day basis is different than committing your future to that responsibility. To Charlie's credit, he was able to both understand his own reluctance and deal fairly honestly with Angel about it. For a while, Angel hoped that in time, Charlie would change his mind. A year later, there was no change. At that point Angel decided to stay with Charlie until someone wonderful and willing came along. So far, no one has bested Charlie in Angel's heart. And they do have a commitment, but it does not include till death do us part.

Almost anything can come between a man and a ring: his job, his ex-wife—whatever he values more than a possible life-companion will cause him to put the brakes on commitment. Probably the two biggest blocks are children and financial liability.

It is interesting that men these days consider women who earn high salaries attractive. A woman's financial prestige may have replaced her social prestige as a more valuable asset.

However, while Charlie exercises his right to remain "free," he fixes things around Angel's condo and gives generously to her and the children in time and money. That's the level of giving with which he is comfortable.

Another couple, Lia and Mark, lived together unmarried. They originally contracted to live together for one year and then assess their next move. At the end of that year, they decided to continue the arrangement for one more year. At the end of that year, Lia was ready for marriage, but Mark was not. Lia moved out because, as she put it, "I've got to get on with my life, and I want someone I can count on to grow old with." Six weeks later, Mark came knocking on Lia's door, suggesting they live together again. Lia said, "You know my conditions." He nodded his head yes. He never could bring himself to say the "M" word. But at the marriage ceremony, it was Lia who burst out crying and took about five hard minutes to say, "I do."

Every couple explores the limits of their abilities to commit. Either they find mutually agreeable boundaries, or they move on, separately.

Making excuses for having children

"It's like people see me as handicapped," Charlotte said. "The minute I tell a man I have a child, I can see in his eyes that he has lost interest. Some day, I hope, society will look at a single mother and her children as OK—because we are. It just makes me angry."

A single mother meeting new people is in a baseball game of sorts, playing with two strikes. Strike one comes when she says, "I'm divorced." The assumption is that she has "failed" in her relationship with the father of her children, so she is a poor risk and "used" merchandise. Strike two comes when she says, "I have a child." The assumption is that her child is a liability—maybe not to her, but to whomever she is meeting. So she's got one strike left. If she is independently wealthy, she hits a home run. Otherwise, she swings the bat and runs like hell and hopes she's got enough of what she needs to make it to first base in the first encounter.

"My child is very independent."
"My child is a good kid. No problems from him."
"My child is bright and plays the flute beautifully."

All these statements may be true, but can be spoken by a single mother in defense of her child's worth as a human being in an adult-oriented society which does not set much value on children.

Sometimes you might ask yourself, "Will anyone ever love my kids? If people can't see your children as being worth some time and attention, if your children don't like certain people you bring around, trust the children's instincts and don't bring those people around. If the person is a man, find another man or expect to suffer personally from an untenable relationship between him and your children.

Revealing a sexual relationship to the children

I don't know of any single mother who has sat her children down and said, "I must tell you that James and I are now sexually active." Teenagers would react in any number of ways, depending on how they felt about James, but they all would be at least slightly embarrassed. Younger children might wonder just exactly what you meant by that but might not want to ask for more information. Preschoolers might ask, "What's for dinner?"

But all children except infants know that Mom is getting close to James in some way. And it may be threatening to them. Many children cling to the hope that their biological parents will reunite, so having another man on the scene with Mom, even though they may like him, can make them insecure about their own future. Two children I know run to the family photo albums and engross themselves in family history whenever they sense a shift in the family makeup.

Consider a question like "Are you and James going to get married?" or an appeal like "I wish James would stop taking you out every Saturday night. We used to have fun here, just the two of us." These present opportunities for you to clarify just what your relationship is with James by replying to the children's questions and comments straightforwardly, such as, "We may marry some day, but we have no plans right now," or "I know I go out with him most Saturdays, but I want to be with him. Maybe we can talk about doing something together—the three of us."

> The burning question in a child's mind is, *"How is this relationship going to affect me?"* That's the question you need to answer.

It is reassuring to a child to know that his or her life is going to remain stable. The home, school, friends, parents—all these will remain as before, at least for now. And if a change should occur, you will talk it over with the child before you make any decision about anything.

If a child should press you for sexual information, which probably won't happen, you can say, "I like/love James. I like to touch him. He likes to touch me. That's part of being an adult. It all happens very naturally as a part of our close friendship with each other." That's all the child keeds to know about you and James specifically.

But everyone has his or her own style. A "James" I know left his house and told his two pre-teen children, "I'm going over to Dede's house. I'll be back around ten o'clock." "What are you going to do over there?" his son asked. "We're going to make love," the father tossed over his shoulder. His daughter's eyes bugged out; she turned to her brother and grinned. The boy covered his mouth, scrunched his head into his shoulders and giggled.

If you have exposed your children to good sex education for their age levels, they will know what you are talking about, and knowing what's going on will ease their concern.

Your man and your children

You don't have to introduce your children to every man you go out with. Some women make a point of keeping the men they date casually from knowing their children in order to protect the children, thereby avoiding potential hassles. At some point in the development of a relationship, however, you will bring the man and the children together.

You must feel your children are safe with any new man. He must not abuse them emotionally, physically or sexually. You want the same response from the man that you would want from a good father: he should enjoy them, play with them, talk and listen to them. But most often, men are much more interested in you than in your children. Still, you need to be able to trust the man not to harm your children. The number of "boyfriends," live-in partners and stepfathers who abuse the children of their women is frightening. And the number of women who know about the abuse and let it happen is equally frightening.

If you start getting serious about a man, you must look closely at the quality and the potential quality of his relationship with your children. You want someone who likes the children. You will want someone who will interact positively with the children and who considers them part of his relationship with you. A woman who has to keep her man and her children apart in order to keep peace is a woman in trouble. She constantly has to choose whom to pay attention to and whom to neglect. A great line in the movie "The Breakfast Club" occurs when one teenage boy asks a teenage girl what her parents do to her that is so terrible. Her response: "They ignore me."

Does your man say hello to the children when he comes over and goodbye when he leaves? Does he ask them how their day is going or what's happening in their lives? If you left them together in a room, would they have a conversation? With little children, would the man talk to them and help them play with a toy? Would he reach out to pick up and soothe a crying baby?

These are solid clues about how willing a man is to get involved with your children as real people. How willing is he to invest in them a little? Keep your eyes wide open. If a man does not invest in little ways, he will not invest in big ways later on. Time does not change that quality, it only intensifies it.

Try to avoid having a man stay overnight in your bed while the children are at home. Avoid hanging on each other or engaging in foreplay in front of the children. A casual kiss and a hug are OK, but more than that may make the children uncomfortable. **One rule to follow is "If you can do it in front of your parents, you can do it in front of your children."**

Living together

Sandra and Ed had gone on a wonderful nine-day vacation together without children. When they returned, he went to his house, she to hers. He didn't call for a few days. When he did, it was for a casual conversation, and he closed with, "Well, I'll talk to you later. Bye."

"When?" thought Sandra. It was almost a week until the next phone call. Sandra was confused and very distressed. They had been so close on the vacation, and now Ed seemed distant. Sandra told Ed she was upset. They met for lunch.

"I don't understand. What do you want?" asked Ed.

"I want to move in with you," she said, which was a surprise to her the minute it came out of her mouth.

"I don't think I can do that," he said. "I have other [women] friends who wouldn't understand. They've been good to me. What would I tell them?"

"I don't care what you tell them. This is not a threat; it's just what I need for my sanity: Either I move in with you, or I need you out of my life. Don't call me again. "

"Ever?"

"Ever."

Ed looked at his plate. His face turned red and seemed to swell. Finally he said, "Well, you bring your kids over on Sunday, and let's talk about arrangements."

As it turned out, theirs was a live-in relationship that led to marriage, but it could have gone the opposite way, which Sandra would have accepted. She had gone too far in the relationship to be content with casual dating.

Living together has the advantage of being an arrangement for today, one you don't have to commit to for the rest of your life. Many couples think of it as a trial marriage. But there are big differences between living together and marriage. Your relatives will probably not accept your live-in partner as a member of the family; to them, he will remain your date. Further, depending on their religious or moral beliefs, they may not sanction the arrangement. At income tax time, you must file separately, since you do not qualify for the cheaper joint tax status of married couples. If he should die, you do not arrange the funeral and sit with the family, nor do you inherit any part of his estate, unless he has written you into his will.

Beyond family, legal and financial concerns, there is a different feeling when you are married—a feeling of being yoked, of your belonging to someone and his belonging to you, a certain settledness. But you are not making your own decisions as independently as you were before. Once you are married, you and your husband must jointly agree on most aspects of your lives together—including how to raise the children and how much money to spend on them. You give up some freedom for some security. And after you do, you may miss that freedom, that autonomy, and wonder if you moved too soon, thinking, "If only I had known."

Kids' reactions

Recent research by psychologist Marla Beth Isaacs and sociologist George Leon of the Philadelphia Child Guidance Clinic shows that children of divorce exhibit behavioral problems and manage social competence—their own friendships—in the following order (all 87 subject mothers had custody):

1. **Mother not seriously romantically involved—** *children fared best*
2. **Mother seriously involved with a man—***slightly worse*
3. **Mother remarried—***worse than number 2 above*
4. **Mother living with a man but unmarried—** *worst adjustment*

Isaacs and Leon suggest that for children whose mother is living with a man to whom she is not married, the children feel insecure about the mother's and their own relationship with the man. Their biological father may object to the relationship. And the children, especially teens, may feel awkward about morals.

The researchers do not feel the mother should either move out or rush into marriage for the sake of the children. She needs to form her own life-partner relationship in her own time with the man of her choice. And if she moves too quickly in any direction because of the children, she may resent their "intrusion" in her relationship.

There are times when the mother's needs and the children's needs may conflict. These are times of hard choices as we all search for a better life for both ourselves and our children.

Blended family blues

It is a mistake to marry for social, legal or financial reasons, or to recruit a father for your children. The quality of the relationship has to come first. If it is not there to begin with, you are taking a big risk in trying to build it after the marriage. And if you have been married before, you know how wrenching divorce is, like death.

Above all else, you need realistic expectations about blending two pre-formed families into one through a second marriage. There are some myths about such marriages that need to be exposed:

> *Myth 1:* There will be instant family love, that cozy family feeling.
> *Myth 2:* It will be like a first (biological) family.
> *Myth 3:* You, the stepmother, will make up for the defects of the biological mother.

The two families blending into one have two separate histories. Because the blended family is born from loss, the loss of the first families, each family member in the new family is faced with giving up the past. This does not mean erasing it from your memory bank, but understanding that you can never go back to it—a particularly difficult process for those children who fervently wish their first families were back together. In the creation of the second family there is a sense of loss of the first. Everyone asks, "Who am I? Where am I going?" And everyone goes through a grief process again.

Your second husband is not going to be the same as your first husband, for better and for worse. Generally, you go into a first marriage with high hopes of living forever with a man you love, heart and soul; you are young and full of dreams and romance. With the second husband, he is, well, second; the newness is not there. A certain innocence and purity and exploring the virgin land of marriage is not there, since it's your second visit to the country. You are older, more practical, more cautious, less idealistic. And all that is OK. You might argue that this is your first second marriage, and you would be right. It's just a different road. I don't know any remarried woman who wouldn't have preferred to have found her prince charming the first time around, but there are no perfect princes.

And there are no perfect princesses.

Whether it is your first marriage or your second or your eighth, is your man someone whose weaknesses you can accept and even smile about and whose strengths are important to you? Are his values your own? Can you trust his behavior and motives? Can you talk with him easily? Does he like and accept you for who you are? Is he someone who feels like family, a supportive friend who will stick with you?

If you can answer such questions with a yes, consider yourself fortunate, for these are facets of a jewel of a man. To the extent you can recognize that and celebrate it, you are maximizing your circumstances. A wise woman named Barbara Gupta says, "Whatever circumstances I find myself in, I learn to like them." You can carry that too far, but that kind of positive attitude will help you through some very rough periods in trying to blend two families.

There are blended families who are very happy together. But not many are happy without a lot of hard, ceaseless work, especially in the early years. One estimate is that it takes five to seven years for a blended family to truly feel like family together. It takes a lot of time to build up trust and loyalty among stepchildren and between stepchildren and stepparents. It takes time to build common family memories. It takes time for children to believe that a stepparent is not here today, gone tomorrow.

And children can resent the whole new arrangement. Ten-year-old Dorothy, for example, was alone in a room with her new stepmother fixing Christmas decorations. Dorothy said, "Well, you are here this Christmas. Miki was here last Christmas. I wonder who will be here next Christmas?" Was she expressing some insecurity about the temporary status of the women in her life? Was she throwing a jab at her new stepmother? Telling her to get lost? Implying she'd be discarded, too? Maybe all of the above? Girls can be jealous of stepmothers and stepsisters, and stepmothers can be jealous of stepdaughters. Boys can be jealous of stepfathers and stepbrothers, and stepfathers can be jealous of stepsons. Competition, one-upmanship, turf battles—all this can go on, day after day. There will be problems with children, you can count on it, even if the children are wildly enthusiastic about the marriage. After the honeymoon, problems set in. There simply is no blood tie that binds to make everyone believe that the new family is a sure thing. There are ties to ex-partners and other biological parents which conflict with building a sense of family. There is resentment of lack of freedom and space by both adults and children. And unconditional love is not there, perhaps for the first five years. After that, there is a chance.

One woman could not stand her stepdaughter. There was just something about that girl that irritated her. She decided she would look for something in the girl that she liked. When she noticed that the girl always set the table with great care and precision, she praised her to the skies for it and began to watch the stepdaughter more closely. Before long, she found something else that she liked about the girl, and after a while was able to accept certain things that irritated her. Finally, she welcomed the girl into her heart.

Beyond liking the children, if the two parents do not agree on how to raise them, that's a recipe for disaster. If one parent takes up for his or her child against the stepparent in front of the child, say goodbye to any sense of control of the child by the stepparent. That child will never again do anything the stepparent says unless the child's parent is there to say, yes, do it this time. And if the stepparent cannot control a child in his or her own home, say goodbye to any hope of a peaceful family life. So communication becomes all-important. You need to become adept at conflict resolution, or talking through your problems to the satisfaction of all parents and children. You can expect strong feelings to be stronger in a blended family.

From the children's point of view, they don't belong anywhere. That they are thrust into this new family may not be their choice, and even if it is, they feel as if they are on the outside looking in. It takes a long time for the strangeness to wear away. Beginning your blending process by including the children early on, in the planning stages, is a good practice. Some couples plan a marriage ceremony with the children to include them in a part of it. Some go on a honeymoon as a family (and have another brief honeymoon for parents only). Some go house shopping as a family.

Blending two families is further complicated because nothing stands still. You can't count on your family structure remaining stable. The divorce decree may give custody to the mother, but many children have gone back to live with Dad for one reason or another when they become teenagers. In many such situations, stepmothers have had to make fast and unwelcome adjustments which they never anticipated, considered or agreed to when they married. Even adult children can come home again to live after college, between jobs, in case of illness. The complications are staggering.

If this seems a grim picture of blended families, it should, for they can become more tangled than day-old spaghetti. They can also work well, in the long run, and bring much happiness to family members, but as long as children live in the home, a blended family is more at risk than a biological one.

The following elements encourage positive blending and promote a sense of family:

◇ A quality relationship between the parents
◇ A common understanding on how to raise the children
◇ 100 percent support of each other in front of the children
◇ A basic liking of all the children
◇ An expectation that there will be difficult times
◇ A commitment to making the family work

Resources for parents in a blended family are counselors, family meetings, consciously practicing good parenting skills, spending time with the children, providing time out or privacy for both children and adults when they need it, family vacations and books and articles on blended families or other family concerns.

Prenuptial agreements

Before marrying for the second time, consider asking a tax lawyer to draft a prenuptial agreement for property settlement. It is natural and logical for you to want your assets to revert to you in the unfortunate circumstance of another divorce. At the same time, you can draft a will that enables you to arrange your estate for the benefit of your children if you should die. Marriage brings with it certain legal rights for the spouse. You may love and trust your new husband-to-be, but you should know the law and your options before making such an important and irreversible move. No one gets married expecting to divorce. Every marriage is a risk, and you want to cover all your bases.

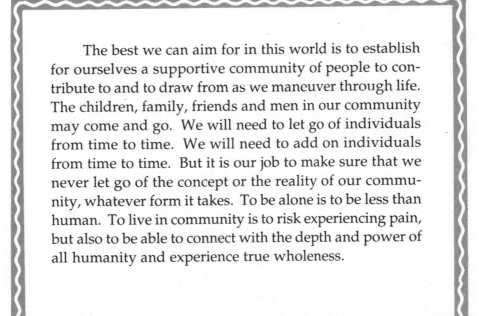

The best we can aim for in this world is to establish for ourselves a supportive community of people to contribute to and to draw from as we maneuver through life. The children, family, friends and men in our community may come and go. We will need to let go of individuals from time to time. We will need to add on individuals from time to time. But it is our job to make sure that we never let go of the concept or the reality of our community, whatever form it takes. To be alone is to be less than human. To live in community is to risk experiencing pain, but also to be able to connect with the depth and power of all humanity and experience true wholeness.

APPENDIX A
Starting Your Own Single Mothers Group

Much of the information in this section relates to the structure of the Vanderbilt University Single Mothers Group which operated during 1986 and 1987. It was organized by the Margaret Cuninggim Women's Center and sponsored jointly with the Vanderbilt Child Care Center. Its genesis, its structure, its purposes and its activities were tailored for one group of women in one city. However, it can serve as a point of reference for developing other single mothers groups.

Divorce adjustment groups

Many towns offer periodic courses, groups, seminars and lectures on the theme of adjusting to divorce. Some of these offerings are structured to include children of divorce. Almost all are available to both men and women. And while quality and content vary, almost all can provide the single mother with

♦ Information about local resources
♦ What to expect from divorce as a life circumstance
♦ Other people in the same boat with whom to share experiences.

You can find out about such groups by calling your local mental health association, the YWCA, a counselor, social service organizations or a clergy member. Announcements of such events are often made in newspapers and posted on library bulletin boards.

If you can't find something that suits your needs in your town, you can suggest to the resources above that they create a way to address divorce adjustment.

For single mothers only

A group open to single mothers only is different from a group which includes men in the following ways:

♦ The structure automatically puts women in control of the group, promoting a feeling of empowerment and increased self-esteem.
♦ There is no male-female sex interest, allowing women a time out from feeling pressure to dress, make up or behave in response to the presence of men.

♦ There is no male-female sex interest to upset a woman who needs time out from involvement with all men. She is healing her wounds and can count on an all-female support group to be a place of refuge.
♦ Women feel freer to say *anything* in an all-female group, to talk about sexual subjects as well as personal intense anger and deep pain associated with their ex-partner. Such comments as "*All* men are _____" surface inthe group, often as an expression of humor to relieve personal tension.

Starting your own group

Your town may already have a single mothers group. Unfortunately, there is no national clearing house for single mothers groups. They are far less common than male-female divorce adjustment groups. Family counseling centers sometimes structure all-male or all-female support groups under the guidance of a counselor, but you have to pay an hourly fee to participate. This can vary from approximately $60 to $200 per hour.

After you have checked out what kind of groups are available in your town, through the sources mentioned above, you can decide if any of the existing groups will meet your needs. If they do not, you may want to help structure your own group.

Finding a sponsor

Rather than starting a group meeting in your own home, think seriously about finding a sponsor for the group, for the following reasons:

♦ **The facility:** you don't have to clean it for meetings, it has restrooms, it has parking (you hope).
♦ **The facilitator:** She is responsible for preparations for each meeting. You may want to skip a meeting fromtime to time, but the facilitator will keep things going on schedule.
♦ **At some point, you may decide to drop out of the group** (this usually happens when a woman feels she has her feet on solid ground), and the sponsor will be responsible for maintaining the group for the benefit of other single mothers.

A sponsor provides stability and assumes all responsibility for meetings. All you have to do is attend.

To find a sponsor, you have to contact the resources listed above and talk with people until someone listens to you. You may locate a sponsor who is willing to do the organizing and publicizing and provide a facilitator for the group but who does not have an adequate meeting facility. Then someone will have to find a facility in which to meet. Or you may begin with the facility first, and then try to locate a sponsor.

The facility

You need a meeting room which will hold 10 to 20 women. You need access to a restroom. Nearby parking is ideal, especially if the group meets at night. And have a room for the children, if possible.

Child care

The Vanderbilt University Single Mothers Group was started by a woman with four children who came into the Women's Center and asked if the center knew of such a group in town. We said we would find out if one existed, and if not, we would start one of our own. This woman had four young children and worked at a part-time job. She didn't have the money to pay for a babysitter for four children in her home on a regular basis. So the Women's Center decided to arrange for on-site child care. For each two-hour meeting, the charges were

1 child:	$1.00
2 or more children:	$1.50

Such low fees allowed the women to bring their children with them to the meeting, knowing the children would receive care from a competent caregiver for a price they could afford. The children got to know each other and looked forward to going with their mothers. Every Tuesday, one four-year-old would ask her mother, "Is this club night?" The mothers and children felt that the support group event was one in which they *all* participated. Group members got to know each other's children, and the atmosphere of the group became one of family.

We held our meetings at the Vanderbilt Day Care Center, so that the children could use one of the classrooms. They met at one end of the building while the mothers met in a room at the other end.

The caregiver was a regular staff person at the Day Care Center during the day. She picked up some extra money with the Single Mothers Group, receiving $7 per hour for her work. If the mothers did not cover her $14 for the evening, the sponsor paid the difference.

There was a well-lit parking lot right outside the facility.

Cost

There was no charge for participating in the group. Women frequently commented that they could not easily afford to come if a fee was charged.

Meeting schedule

We met the first and third Tuesday of each month,
from 6:45 to 8:45 p.m.

Facilitator

We considered using a graduate student in psychology at the university, but in the end, a staff person from the Women's Center and a community volunteer with counseling experience co-facilitated the group. This probably worked out better than the graduate student, since the staff person and the community volunteer made a long-term commitment to the group, and consistency in the facilitator is important in building group cohesiveness.

The role of the facilitators was not to do all the talking, but to encourage the participants to talk, to explore their own issues, to ask their own questions and to problem solve with the support of the group and community resources. The facilitators opened the building at night, coordinated communication among participants with a group telephone directory and arranged for guest speakers.

Advertising and group size

Announcements of the first meeting of the group were posted in area day-care centers, mailed to appropriate family counseling services and published in a local newspaper. In response, single women called to find out more about the group. Later, the facilitators did radio and TV interviews to advertise the group and to discuss single mothers' issues.

The three women who showed up for the first meeting formed the core of the group. As other women joined, attendance averaged about 8 to 10 women per session. We felt that number, rather than 20 to 30 women sitting in a circle, enabled the group to maintain an intimate atmosphere where everyone felt comfortable talking. Due to scheduling conflicts, not everyone could attend each meeting, so the population was somewhat different each night, drawing from a total population of about 15 regular attendees.

Newsletter outreach

There were many women in the community who were unable to attend any meetings, though they wanted to. Work, child care or transportation problems, or exhaustion prevented them from doing so. When they called to find out more about the group, their names were put on a mailing list for the once-a-month newsletter.

This newsletter was a one- or two-page typed letter telling about group news (who got a job, whose mother was in town, etc.), dates of upcoming meetings and activities, news articles about single mothers or current research of interest. There was usually a cartoon or some other attempt at humor. Good ideas for children's activities which had originated from a recent group meeting were summarized.

Between meetings, the newsletter served as an important connecting link for group members, and it made the women who could not attend meetings feel they were not isolated or odd or abnormal but part of a group of women with whom they shared common concerns.

Group activities

There were two meetings per month. One meeting was a "dump session," in which we all sat in a circle and talked about what had been going on in our lives since the last meeting. Members talked about jobs, ex-partners, children, finances, dating—all the good news, and bad, in their lives. The facilitators participated in this process, including the one who was not a single mother. Much problem solving was done in these sessions as the group responded to the individual with ideas, options, resources and encouragement.

The second meeting in each month was a time for getting information. A professional might speak to the group, such as a lawyer specializing in family law. Or the group might bring in or discuss information on a certain subject, like the night we all sat around and developed the list of free and cheap fun for mothers and children (see pages 92-93).

After a while, mothers started bringing in snacks and juice to have at meetings. And we appreciated the opportunity to eat together. Then someone suggested we get together socially outside of the group, so once a month we decided on an outdoor activity that mothers and children would enjoy, such as going for a walk or playing in a park. We also enjoyed having a pot luck at someone's house, although we tried to keep social activities away from people's homes because we were all pressed for time, as single mothers, and it was such a chore to prepare for and clean up after this group. These social activities were optional, and we always had participation. Outdoor activities worked best. On one occasion, the group went to a nearby state park to camp out overnight. Some of the women had never been camping before, and we were all learning together how to set up borrowed tents and build a campfire. Many of the tents were mound-shaped, so we dubbed our compound "titty city." We went for hikes, went swimming, walked children back and forth to the restrooms, roasted marshmallows, sang songs around the campfire and drifted off to sleep.

This was a highly successful, very inexpensive trip which both mothers and children enjoyed—and will never forget.

The Big Hug—and beyond

We closed each group meeting with "The Big Hug." All the mothers stood in one large circle, with their arms around each other, and someone would call out, "Here we go: One, two, three!" And on "three," we all took one step toward the center of the circle. This caused a group squeeze which resulted in The Big Hug. Every member, and the children, enjoyed this tradition. It was a great way to end the meeting, feeling bonded to a group of sisters and empowered to face the world.

Appendix B

BusyMom

A Story About How Everything Turned Out Just Fine

Once upon a time there was a woman named Jane Wifeofman, but everyone called her Jane. She lived with her two children and a Husband. On the Saturday before Mother's Day, the Husband would go out and buy Jane a gift to show her what a good job she was doing with the children. Then on Sunday he would take the family out to dinner.

But all was not well with Jane and the Husband. They divorced. Jane got custody of the children and changed her name to BusyMom Notime-forherself, but everyone called her BusyMom. She washed clothes, packed lunches, worked in an office, made doctor appointments, wiped away tears, worked in the office, met with teachers, figured her own taxes, worked in the office, grabbed a movie when she could, cleaned the house when she could and sometimes collapsed at night when the last munchkin was tucked into bed.

Everyone worried about her after the divorce, marveled at how well she was coping, and then sort of dropped out of sight, except for family and a close friend or two.

And, of course, the children. They were always there—24 hours a day. Well, not in person, but *in her mind.* "They're at the day-care center now." "They're going to school now on the mini-van." "It's about lunch time for the kids." "Oh, my gosh, I've got to race to the day-care center to pick them up before 5:30!" On a separate freeway in her mind she was thinking, "The piles on my desk seem to grow larger . . . this was the day I was going to make some progress. I'm losing it . . . my supervisor told me I looked tired and should get some more rest. The Coke machine broke . . . no caffeine . . . I hope no one saw me dozing at 2:30. What a hell of a day I've had."

"Hi, Mommy!" said one of her kids one afternoon.

"Hi, sweetheart. How was your day?" said BusyMom. And those little arms reaching around her neck healed her for a moment.

Along came the second Sunday in May. Mother's Day. No Husband to say Happy Mother's Day. No gift. Just another day. BusyMom said to her two children who were passing through the kitchen, "It's Mother's Day." Three-year-old Stevie said, "Tie my shoe." Five-year-old Rhea said, "I'm hungry." And BusyMom thought to herself, "Yes, it certainly is Mother's Day."

This is the way things went for a few years. One day when Rhea was 11, she grinned and whispered in her mother's ear, "We have a surprise for you for Mother's Day. I hope you like it." It was the first time the children had planned something like this. Maybe it finally clicked with Rhea that this was an important day for them all, an opportunity to tell Mom just how much they appreciated her care and love through all the days stretching from before Rhea was born until this day, that there was something that they could do, resources that they had to initiate a happening. Thus, "We have a surprise for you for Mother's Day." What? A kiss? A hug? An offer to do the dishes? A plastic mirror from K mart? A drawing? It didn't matter. BusyMom knew this was a big step. After all these years, two important people were remembering her in a special way on Mother's Day: *her children*, on their own and because they really did love her.

BusyMom sat down and cried. Secretly she pondered. She couldn't decide whether she wanted hugs and kisses or the free dish washing! It was so nice to wait on her children, to trust in her children who had learned a new way to give.

Things to think about for Mother's Day:

❤ If you want to know if your children love you, ask them.

❤ If you want your young children to recognize you in a special way on this day, hope for help from the day-care center or their school teachers. Otherwise, wait a few years and the children will do it on their own. Formal recognition requries maturity; that doesn't mean they don't love you now.

❤ Let older children know that Mother's Day is coming and give them some choices, like, "I'd like you to make me a card, fix me breakfast in bed, bring me some flowers from the yard, paint my toenails or whatever you might want to do. Mostly I'd like a little recognition on my day." Discussing Mother's Day possibilites can be great fun.

❤ Think about another single mother you know who would appreciate being remembered on this occasion. Make her a card, call her on the phone or otherwise let her know you appreciate her contribution as a mother.

❤ If you want to go out to dinner on Mother's Day, do it. Take the kids and go—to a restaurant or on a picnic in a park. Enjoy!

RESOURCES

Divorce
Trafford, Abigail. *Crazy Times: Surviving Divorce.* New York: Bantam, 1984.

Health and Well-being
The Boston Women's Health Book Collective Staff. *Our Bodies, Ourselves.* 2nd ed. New York: Simon & Schuster, 1976.

Brody, Jane E. *Jane Brody's Good Food Book: Living the High-Carbohydrate Way.* New York: Norton, 1985. (Nutrition and recipes from *The New York Times* "Personal Health" columnist.)

Cushner, Harold. *When Bad Things Happen to Good People.* New York: Schocken Books, 1981.

Harris, Thomas A. *I'm OK, You're OK.* New York: Avon, 1976.

Maslow, Abraham. *Motivation and Personality.* (Not currently in print. Be sure to check in your library for this one.)

Phelps, Stanlee and Nancy Austin. *The Assertive Woman.* San Luis Obispo: Impact Publishers, 1975.

Viorst, Judith. *Necessary Losses: The Loves, Illusions, Dependencies and Impossible Expectations That All of us Have to Give Up in Order to Grow.* New York: Simon & Schuster, 1986.

Wurtman, Judith J. *Managing Your Mind and Mood Through Food.* Rawson Associates, 1986.

Parenting
Blume, Judy. *Letters to Judy: What Your Kids Wish They Could Tell You.* New York: Putnam, 1986.

Cohn, Anne H. and Thomas Gordon. *Tips on Parenting.* Chicago: National Committee for Prevention of Child Abuse, 1985. 31-page booklet. 332 S. Michigan Ave., Suite 1250, Chicago, IL 60604-4357.

Dinkmeyer, Don et al. *Systematic Training for Effective Parenting of Teens STEP-Teen: The Parent's Guide.* Circle Pines, Minn.: American Guidance Service, Inc., 1983.

Faber, Adele and Elaine Mazlish. *How to Talk So Kids Will Listen and So Kids Will Talk.* New York: Norton, 1982.

_____. *Siblings Without Rivalry: How to Help Your Children Live Together So You Can Live Too.* New York: Norton, 1987.

Roosevelt, Ruth and Jeannette Lofas. *Living in Step: A Remarriage Manual for Parents and Children.* New York: McGraw-Hill, 1977.

Simon, Sidney B., Leland W. Howe, and Howard Kirschenbaum. *Values Clarification: A Handbook of Practical Strategies for Teachers and Students.* New York: Hart Publishing, 1978. (A book full of questions, such as "How would you spend $5?"; "Do you think there are times when cheating is justified?" Intended for teachers, but parents can easily use it for family discussion. Ages 8 and up.)

Swan, Helen. L. and Victoria Houston. *Alone After School: A Self-Care Guide for Latch Key Children and Their Parents*. Englewood Cliffs, NJ: Prentice-Hall, 1985.

Takas, Marianne. *Child Custody: A Complete Guide for Concerned Mothers*. New York: Harper & Row, 1987.

Non-book parenting sources

National Foundation for the Prevention of Child Abuse. 3050 Central Ave., Toledo, OH 43606. (419) 535-3232. Free information on child abuse and prevention.

Parents Without Partners, Inc. 8807 Colesville Rd., Silver Spring, MD 20910. Has groups in all 50 states for single parents and their children as well as parenting materials. Toll-free 1-800-637-7974.

Relationships

Lerner, Harriet Goldhor. *The Dance of Anger: A Woman's Guide to Changing the Patterns of Intimate Relationships*. New York: Harper & Row, 1985.

McGill, Michael E. *The McGill Report on Male Intimacy*. New York: Holt, Rinehart & Winston, 1986. ("A landmark in the study of human behavior."—*Baltimore Sun*)

Norwood, Robin. *Women Who Love Too Much*. New York: Pocket Books, 1986.

Time Management

Bliss, Edwin C. *Getting Things Done: The ABCs of Time Management*. New York: Charles Scribner's Sons, 1976.

Working

Bolles, Richard Nelson. *What Color Is Your Parachute? A Practical Manual for Job Hunters and Career Changers*. Berkeley: Ten Speed Press, 1983. Updated1990.

Gray, Bonnie, Dorothy Loeffler and Robin King Cooper. *Every Woman Works: A Complete Manual for Women Re-entering the Job Market or Changing Jobs*. Belmont, CA: Lifetime Learning Publications, 1982.

Holland, John L. *The Self Directed Search: A Guide to Educational and Vocational Planning. Specimen Set*. Psychological Assessment Resources, Inc., Box 998, Odessa, FL 33556, or phone 1-800-331-TEST. (Excellent tool to match your abilities and interests with appropriate jobs. Costs under $10.)

Yate, Martin John. *Knock 'Em Dead with Great Answers to Tough Interview Questions*. Boston: Bob Adams, Inc., 1987. (Thoroughly prepares the reader for the psychology of the interview experience and offers offersother valuable information on nailing down a job.)

INDEX